"An untold story from those last days of Worl[d] [...] the unthinkable became real—when our all[...] when our POWs were left to die, and when a veteran pilot would receive a harrowing final mission—to fly against the might of the Soviet Union."

—Adam Makos, *New York Times* bestselling author of *A Higher Call*

"A little-known set of moving adventures, well-researched and presented." —*Kirkus Reviews*

"Vivid and engaging, *Beyond the Call* is partly a story of one officer's guile and bravery in the face of forces much larger and more powerful than himself. But it is also a moving and appalling tale of the full horror of World War II's last year on the eastern front."

—Randall Hansen, author of *Fire and Fury* and *Disobeying Hitler*

"Trimble's son has provided a riveting, tense, and ultimately satisfying account of his father's heroic effort." —*Booklist*

"This account delivers a different story from the norm . . . a remarkable (and virtually unknown) story of courage in the face of incredible danger."

—*Library Journal*

"*Beyond the Call* is the brilliantly told, fast-paced true story of a remarkable young man. Deceived by his superior officers, he found himself in a place where danger abounded and life was cheap, but, drawing on a courage he hadn't known he possessed, he began his assignment. Nerve-wracking, informative, yet profoundly moving, *Beyond the Call* is a truly inspiring book." —Susan Ottaway, author of *Sisters, Secrets, and Sacrifice*

BEYOND THE CALL

THE TRUE STORY OF ONE WORLD WAR II
PILOT'S COVERT MISSION TO RESCUE
POWs ON THE EASTERN FRONT

LEE TRIMBLE with JEREMY DRONFIELD

BERKLEY CALIBER, NEW YORK

An imprint of Penguin Random House LLC
375 Hudson Street, New York, New York 10014

ISBN: 978-0-425-27605-1

The Library of Congress has catalogued the Berkley Caliber hardcover edition as follows:

Trimble, Lee.
Beyond the call : the true story of one World War II pilot's covert mission to rescue POWs on
the Eastern Front / by Lee Trimble with Jeremy Dronfield. — First edition.
p. cm.
ISBN 978-0-425-27604-4 (hardback)
1. Trimble, Robert M., 1919–2009.   2. Prisoners of war—Poland—
History—20th century.   3. Rescues—Poland—History—20th century.
4. Subversive activities—Poland—History—20th century.
5. World War, 1939–1945—Underground movements—Poland.
6. Air bases—Ukraine—Poltava—History—20th century.
7. Bomber pilots—United States—Biography.   8. Heroes—United States—
Biography.   9. United States. Army Air Forces. Air Force, 8th—Biography.
10. United States. Office of Strategic Services—History.
I. Dronfield, Jeremy.   II. Title.
D805.P7T75 2015
940.54'72438—dc23
2014044108

PUBLISHING HISTORY
Berkley Caliber hardcover edition / February 2015
Berkley Caliber trade paperback edition / February 2016

PRINTED IN THE UNITED STATES OF AMERICA

10   9   8   7

Cover photo of train tracks by Jeremy Woodhouse / Getty Images; airplane by
Macl / Shutterstock; concentration camp by Patryk Kosmider / Shutterstock
Book design by Laura K. Corless
Interior maps by Jeremy Dronfield

Penguin
Random
House

In memory of Robert M. Trimble,

who went to war,

and Eleanor Trimble,

who brought him home again.

This story is based on the recollections of Robert M. Trimble, as recorded by his son, Lee Trimble. Every effort has been made to verify all aspects of the story, and at most key points it has been corroborated by independent evidence. However, for some episodes there are no traceable surviving eyewitnesses, and because of the hastily improvised, top-secret, and politically sensitive nature of Captain Trimble's mission, there is no direct official record. Those parts of his recollections must be taken on trust. Where corroborating evidence exists, it is cited in the book's endnotes.

CONTENTS

ACKNOWLEDGMENTS

From the first inception to the final proof, this book and its authors have been helped along their way by a host of kind and gifted people.

Michael and John Kaluta assisted with the early research, and gave access to the rich resource of photos, film, and documents belonging to their father, Lieutenant William R. Kaluta, who was at Poltava throughout the duration of Eastern Command and became its official historian. William MacLeod kindly passed on to us the recollections of his father, Sergeant Don MacLeod, and helped with the sourcing and identification of photographs of the Lieutenant Tillman crew during their time in Poland and Ukraine. Don Nicholson (former major, USAAF) kindly gave his recollections of Poltava and Lwów, and of his work on aircrew rescue for Eastern Command, along with copies of documents and help with photo identification. The Vergolina family generously allowed us to read the POW memoir and press clippings of Sergeant Rudy Vergolina; his son Al and grandson Joseph helped with discussion of Rudy's experiences in Normandy and Poland.

David Schmitt of the 493rd Bombardment Group (H) Memorial Association provided a wealth of information about the group's missions, including copies and transcripts of original mission documents. Lisa Sharik of the Texas Military Forces Museum, Austin, was very helpful in providing information and photos from the Lieutenant Tillman Collection.

The tracing of the record of the Croix de Guerre awarded to Robert Trimble was assisted by Gérome Villain, along with Lieutenant Colonel Michèle Szmytka of the Ministère de la Défense et des Anciens Combattants.

Mike Allard helped with the early research, and brought to light the short snorter signed by Robert Trimble and the Tillman crew. Mike Mucha of the Aircraft MIA Project, Poland, and Geoff Ward of the 96th Bomb Group Association (UK) gave valuable information on the adventures of the crew. Doug Sheley's online albums were helpful in sourcing photos from the USAF archive. Irena Kotlobulatova kindly gave permission to use a photo of the George Hotel in Lviv, Ukraine (formerly the Hotel George, Lwów, Poland).

The staff at the National Archives and Records Administration in Washington, DC, and the Cambridge University Library were invaluable in easing the path of documentary research.

Thank you to Natalee Rosenstein, Robin E. Barletta, and everyone at Penguin/Berkley for having faith in the book. Special thanks to our agent Andrew Lownie for seeing the potential in the story of Captain Robert Trimble and bringing the two of us together to tell it.

Finally, heartfelt gratitude goes to Carol Trimble Minnich and Robert Howard Trimble, Lee's sister and brother, for their help and support in bringing their father's war stories to light, and to Lee's beloved wife, Robin, and children, Rachael and Aaron, for their tireless re-reading, opinions, and encouragement.

ABBREVIATIONS

AAF	(United States) Army Air Forces
AC	Air Corps
ATC	Air Transport Command
Eascom	Eastern Command
NKVD	People's Commissariat for Internal Affairs (*Narodnyy Komissariat Vnutrennikh Del*); Soviet police/intelligence force
oflag	German prisoner of war camp for officers (*Offizierslager*, "officers' camp")
OSS	Office of Strategic Services
POW	prisoner of war
RAF	Royal Air Force
RCAF	Royal Canadian Air Force
SHAEF	Supreme Headquarters Allied Expeditionary Force (Europe)
SMERSH	Special Methods of Spy Detection (*Spetsyalnye Metody Razoblacheniya Shpyonov*); Red Army counterintelligence arm
SOE	special operations executive
stalag	German prisoner of war camp for enlisted men (*Stammlager*, "main camp")
TD	temporary duty
USAAF	United States Army Air Forces
USSTAF	United States Strategic and Tactical Air Forces in Europe

Captain Robert M. Trimble's route from the UK to Ukraine, January–February 1945.

Map by J. Dronfield

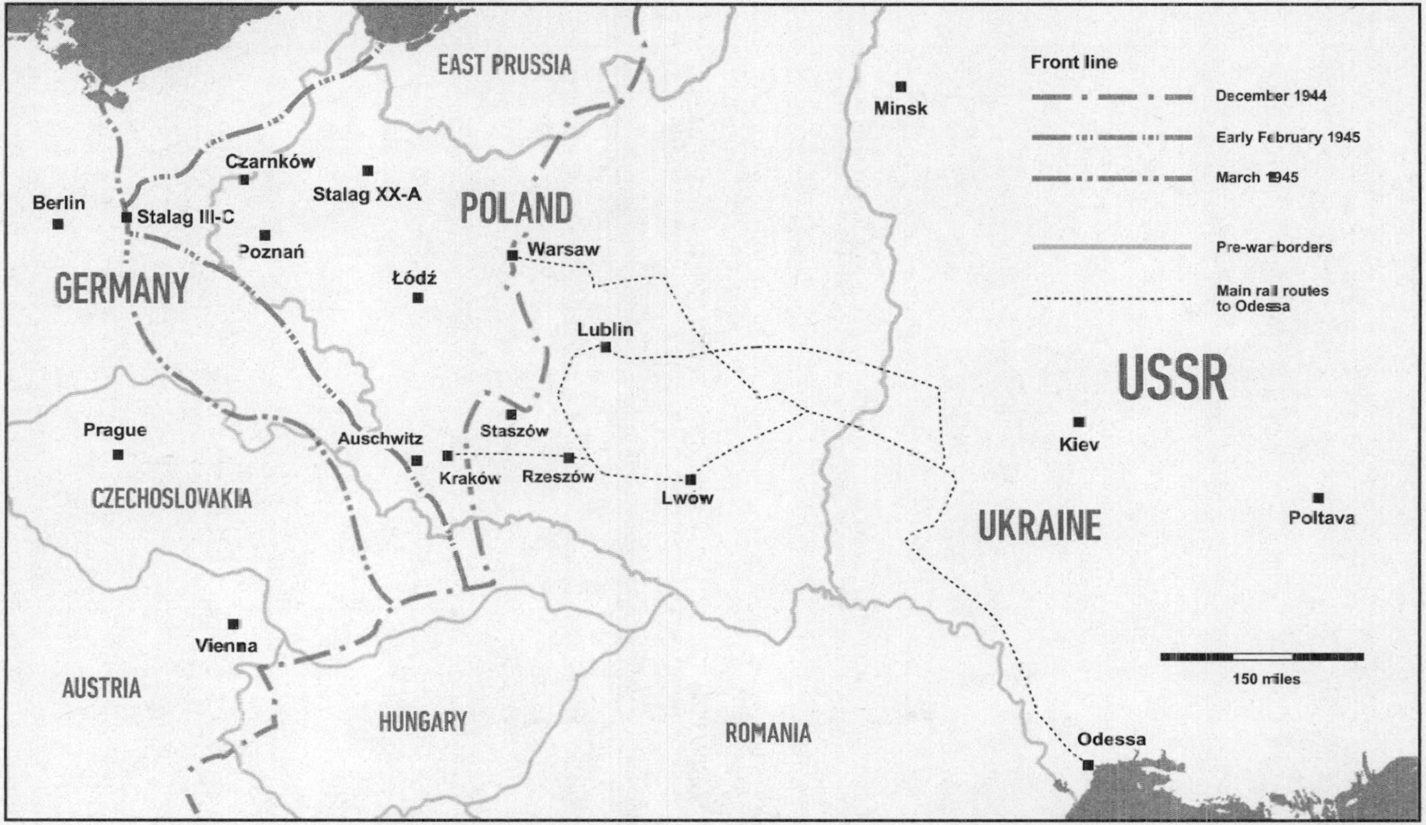

Front line

December 1944
Early February 1945
March 1945
Pre-war borders
Main rail routes to Odessa

USSR

Minsk

Kiev

UKRAINE

Odessa

Poltava

150 miles

ROMANIA

EAST PRUSSIA

POLAND

Warsaw

Lublin

Lwów

Łódź

Staszów

Rzeszów

Kraków

Auschwitz

Czarnków

Stalag XX-A

Poznań

Stalag III-C

Berlin

GERMANY

Prague

CZECHOSLOVAKIA

HUNGARY

Vienna

AUSTRIA

Map by J. Dronfield

Eastern Europe, early 1945. Captain Trimble's area of operations

PREFACE

By the fall of 1944, the mighty forces of the Red Army, at a bitter cost in lives, had pushed the Nazi invaders out of Russia. As the front line rolled steadily across the Ukraine and Poland, the grim prison camps of the Third Reich were discovered and liberated: concentration camps, death camps, slave labor and POW camps. In their thousands, the suffering inmates were set loose.

The Soviets' attitude to the freed prisoners of war was not charitable. Setting the moral mood for the "Great Patriotic War" against Nazi Germany, Stalin had decreed in 1941 that there were no prisoners of war, only traitors and cowards. His declaration, coupled with the culture of savage violence on the Eastern Front, led to cruel treatment and even atrocities against former Russian soldiers who were liberated from POW camps.

It also affected the treatment of Allied ex-prisoners. They were left to wander, starving, sick, and dying. Some were fired upon indiscriminately by Russian troops; some were robbed; many more were marched to the rear and abandoned. Even worse, hundreds were rounded up into camps where they were treated as potential spies or anti-Soviet partisans and kept in squalid conditions. Those who were able to went into hiding in the forests and abandoned farms, where they mingled with freed slave laborers and escapees from the Nazi death marches. The fortunate ones were given shelter by Polish citizens. Many lost hope of ever seeing their homes again.

Britain and the United States pleaded urgently with the Soviet government to honor their obligations to Allied prisoners of war. The United States offered to bring in planes, supplies, and contact teams to round up the liberated POWs and evacuate them. Stalin refused. He didn't want foreigners wandering around in his territory, seeing things he didn't want them to see. A tense, increasingly angry exchange of letters between President Roosevelt and Marshal Stalin failed to resolve the situation.

The ex-POWs were caught between callousness and politics.

Stalin began using the POWs as leverage to force Britain and America to repatriate Russians who had been liberated from POW camps or captured fighting for the Germans. *Give me mine, and I'll give you yours* seemed to be the attitude. Roosevelt and Churchill rightly mistrusted Stalin's motives, and feared for the lives of any Russians repatriated to the USSR.

Stalemate.

President Roosevelt, his diplomats, and the United States military high command were left with no option: Relations with the USSR were tense and deteriorating, but had to be preserved. If they were going to save their missing men—not to mention the other Allied ex-prisoners—from starvation, imprisonment, and death, they would have to go undercover.

The Office of Strategic Services, forerunner of the CIA, provided the means. The options were limited. The OSS European branch, based in London, had no established presence in the regions where the POW camps were. However, the United States did have just one small foothold in Soviet-occupied territory: the air base at Poltava in the Ukraine. Earlier in the war, the Russians had allowed an American unit to be set up there to service long-distance "shuttle" bombing operations from England and Italy. The shuttle missions had ended by late 1944, and Eastern Command had been scaled down to a tiny winter detachment with few duties, almost forgotten, just waiting for the war to end.

Poltava, a tiny dot of freedom in a sea of Communist red, would be the base for the covert rescue mission.

They had the location; they had the mission. All they needed was a man to undertake it. . . .

My father was a regular guy. Not quite what you'd call ordinary, but not noticeably exceptional either. Not a bad father, for someone whose own dad had deserted his wife and children. Dad was faithful and did his best, despite the lack of a role model. As a citizen, he did his duty in the war, and survived, then came home and raised a family. I couldn't have told you anything extraordinary about him, had it not been for an astonishing confession when he was eighty-six years old, which revealed a whole period in his life that I knew nothing about.

The events that led to his confession began on a hot summer day in 2005, when Dad was working alone in the communal garden of his retirement community. After a couple of hours under the sun, he began to feel dizzy. He'd forgotten to bring his medicine and water. Rising from his work, he felt faint. He was unconscious before he hit the ground. He lay there for hours before he was found, sunburned and close to death. But Robert Trimble had always been a survivor.

Around noon of his second day in the Willow Valley Manor infirmary, he was done lying in bed. Without permission, he got up and dressed himself in the dirty, sweaty gardening clothes he'd been brought in wearing. Having paid a visit down the hall to his dear wife Eleanor (her dementia had confined her permanently to the infirmary), he was back in his own apartment. He got some homemade bean soup out of the refrigerator, then turned on the ball game. After dinner he put on his cap, the one with his WWII squadron insignia, and headed back to the garden.

Dad's fall made me realize that the time I had left with him and Mom was limited. And so, in the winter of 2006, I began the first of several long drives up from Virginia to Pennsylvania.

I needed Dad to help me get reacquainted with my heritage. I knew he'd been a bomber pilot in the war, and I wanted to hear those stories again in detail and learn more about his earlier life. He had been a mystery throughout my life. He was a sociable, friendly kind of guy, yet he wasn't someone we children could share our troubles with intimately. He had even greater difficulty sharing his own feelings. He was kind and caring, but none of us had a close personal relationship with him in our younger days. He was a disciplinarian, so I tended to steer clear of him when I was in trouble, which meant most of the time.

On that winter day, when I knocked on the door of his apartment he answered with a happy greeting. But when I announced casually that I wanted to spend some time talking about his early life and his experiences in the war—and that I'd brought a recorder with me to preserve his memories—he frowned and said, "All right, if that's really what you want to do." He suggested we go and shoot some pool in the rec room.

"Okay fine, Dad," I said, chuckling inside that he was still deflecting after all these years. I was determined to get him to open up. I asked him about his experiences as a pilot. I knew this would hook him. Although he didn't like to talk about the past, he did love to talk about flying. Our conversation lasted until dinnertime. He was relaxed and forgot that he was being recorded.

We kids always admired him for his WWII heroics—my brother Robert (who was named for him), my sister Carol (who was born in the midst of it all), and I. He didn't talk about the war very often, but when you got him started, he always spoke vividly, reliving the memories as he spoke—right down to the remembered conversations and the emotions.

On that day in 2006, I finally realized my lifelong wish of recording his story, the tales of adventure in the hostile skies above Europe. At the controls of a heavy bomber (B-24 Liberators at first, later B-17 Flying Fortresses), he ran the gauntlet of thirty-five harrowing raids over Germany and France during the last six months of 1944. He withstood the horror of seeing his friends blown to bits by German flak. He fought courageously to return to base with engines in flames or, worse, blown completely off of the wing, leaving a hole ten men could stand in. Hearing the stories in our youth, we hadn't realized, of course, how lucky he was to have survived to tell them to us.

As long as he was talking war stories that weekend, his conversation was self-sustaining. When asked about his personal feelings, though, he would deflect by commenting on the ball game that was usually running on TV in the background. But I was feeling content that I had thoroughly documented all Dad's wartime testimony. Above all, I felt I was beginning to know him, to bond with him again.

Before leaving that Sunday afternoon, I asked Dad about his father. He fell silent. When he finally spoke, his voice quivered with anger. I felt the urge not to press him, as he was old and frail, but I had to know. It seemed like I had touched a hidden trigger, and at last Dad's feelings started to come out.

"Lee," he said, "I don't know how to start. When my dad left, it devastated all of us. I hated him. My mom despised him. I was always happy up until that day, then not for a long time after. Life got hard; all I felt was emptiness and anger. Then I met your mom, and boy, she saved my life. She saved my life more than once."

I was mystified. Suddenly he'd opened up a seam of memory I knew nothing about. "What do you mean?"

"Don't interrupt me," he growled. Having finally allowed his feelings out into the open, he was going to do it his way. "I met Eleanor and I was happy again." He looked at me. "There's so much I need to tell you that you and your brother and sister never knew."

"What are you talking about, Dad?"

"In some ways going off to war helped me escape my past for a while; I was so excited. But while I was in Europe something happened to me that changed how I looked at life. It was terrible. I came home from Russia depressed, not caring about my relationship with Eleanor, the military, or anything. I was a mess."

I could see that the question about his father had awakened a world of pain. I decided not to push the discussion. Later, as I was leaving to drive back to Virginia, while embracing Dad (the warmest I remember), one of the words he'd used suddenly jumped to the front of my mind.

"Russia?" I said.

"What, Lee?"

"Russia. You said you returned from Russia after the war. You never said anything about Russia in your stories."

He shook his head. "We'll talk about it next time, Lee. I purposely never mentioned it to any of you. In fact I was ordered not to. No one knew about it, except your mom. It was painful then and it's taken a lifetime for me to recover. It was a dark, evil time." He stuffed a ten-dollar bill in my shirt pocket. "Here, drive safely."

I drove home to Virginia through a snowstorm, which matched my state of mind. *Russia?* What would an American bomber pilot be doing in Russia? I'd always thought Dad had returned home after serving his tour of duty in England. And why would he have been ordered not to talk about it? *It was a dark, evil time . . .*

The snow flew thick and fast out of the darkness, danced in the headlights, and spattered against the windshield. I didn't know it at the time, but my drive home was a strange echo of one of Dad's untold tales—with instead of a heated, comfortable car, a thundering, half-repaired bomber that he had defended at gunpoint from a furious Soviet officer and flown off from a field, limping along at zero feet through a wild Polish snowstorm . . . and the small group of freed prisoners he took with him, and the trouble it caused when Moscow found out. . . . It was just one of the experiences that had harrowed him in the hidden period between the completion of his combat tour and his return to America.

I realized there and then that I was being compelled toward a new mission: discovering my father's secret past.

I was full of anticipation when I arrived at Dad's place two weeks later. We shot pool for a while; he loved to play, in spite of his frailty. I was more aware than ever of his deteriorating body. Once a tall man, he was now hunched over, and used a cane. But he was a proud man and wouldn't accept help. He drove himself everywhere, and always volunteered to drive other residents in the community to their appointments. Dad had a strong sense of giving. He loved to help people, and still gave blood when he could. But that was nothing compared to what he had given of himself during World War II.

"Two weeks ago as I was leaving, you dropped an incendiary on me about spending time in Russia."

"I did?" he said dryly.

"Yes, Dad. We all thought you came right home after your tour. What happened in Russia?"

He was silent for a while. "It was a horrific time in my life. I don't know if I can talk about it even now. I saw atrocities. I saw the worst in people. I was deceived into going there—misled and lied to by my own people."

Slowly, piece by piece, the story began to come out. A story bottled up for decades must be hard to tell and keep straight. He skipped over whole episodes, left out details and had to backtrack; some things he struggled to recall, but most were as vivid in his mind as the day they happened. And so were the emotions.

It was an incredible story—literally incredible. A story of a mission in Soviet territory, a mission so secret that even the OSS had to keep a distance from it because of the diplomatic furor that would blow up if the Soviets knew about it. As a cover, they had picked an innocent bomber pilot and sent him out to a US base in the Ukraine. From there he was sent into Poland. His task: to rescue Allied prisoners of war set loose by the Soviets. He had to help them survive and get them to freedom. He was sent beyond the protection of his own side, beyond the call of duty. He helped not just American POWs but slave laborers and concentration camp survivors; all the lost souls of Poland learned to seek out the American captain.

Anyone else hearing Dad's story might have thought the old man was delusional. But he was my father, and I'd known him to be a straight shooter all his life. Although even I had doubts. After all, he'd taken quite a blow to the head from his fall. I knew he wouldn't invent a story like this, but could he have dreamed it, and convinced himself it was true?

Dad brought out his cigar box of remaining war memorabilia. I was surprised at what we found in that box. Aside from his pilot insignia, it contained his Air Medal, Bronze Star, and Distinguished Flying Cross, his discharge papers and War Department ID card. Farther down was an astonishing item—a passport issued by the United States Embassy in London in January 1945, for travel to the USSR, via Cairo and Tehran, on "Official Business." Inside I saw Dad's youthful face, looking stern and kind of wary (like he guessed something strange was going on but didn't know what), stamped over with "American Consular Service." There were also two medals I had never seen before—a French Croix de Guerre and, at the very bottom of the box, a letter from the Russian government, dated 1996, with a commemorative medal awarded for participation in the "Great Patriotic War."

I was stunned. Aside from the first few items, these were hardly the typical belongings of a bomber pilot stationed in England. *I'll be damned*, I thought. *The old man had a big secret.* He had lived in fear (real or imagined) for sixty years, that if he talked he might get in trouble with the government, or even suffer some sort of retribution from the Russians. He told me he had declined an invitation to an award ceremony for the Russian medal because of that mistrust. According to Dad the letter and medal would have been round-filed had it not been for Mom's insistence that he keep them. His bitterness about the Soviets ran deep, and the more I heard of his story, the better I understood why.

There existed a set of stories within his story, each more intriguing than the last. The rescue of freed POWs was just a part of it—there were seat-of-pants flying adventures, plus encounters with desperate Frenchwomen, seductive Russian spies, Soviet agents, and more. My father was suddenly more of a mystery to me than ever.

Dad died in 2009, in his ninetieth year. I continued researching his story. There was still a lingering doubt in my mind—could such an incredible story really be true? I wrote to military historians, consulted official histories, and acquired documents from government archives. The more I searched, the more evidence I found that corroborated my father's story. I found a report he had written, describing an aircraft salvage operation which turned into an impromptu POW rescue and almost led to a diplomatic incident. I found a letter from the commander of the American Military Mission in Moscow, alluding to the "exceptional nature" of Captain Robert M. Trimble's duties and his outstanding performance. I learned about the indignant letters sent to Stalin by President Roosevelt and Ambassador Harriman, protesting the treatment of freed Allied POWs, and about how Stalin stonewalled his supposed ally.

Inevitably there were gaps. My father's mission in Soviet territory was hastily improvised, beyond top secret, and of such a diplomatic sensitivity that even the OSS could only be involved off the record. But wherever you would expect to find documentation, I found it, and it matched Dad's story. Even in situations where he didn't understand what was happening, the historical record made sense of the facts that confused him—such as the misunderstanding which, unknown to him, nearly caused a breach of OSS security in the US Embassy in London.

Robert M. Trimble was such a meticulously truthful man, and his story so fully corroborated wherever it could be, that I believe we can take his word that his undocumented activities—the long-distance, ad-hoc missions out in the lonely snows of Poland—occurred just as he described them, reliving them as he talked, feeling again the anger, the fear, and occasionally the humor.

I am proud of my father. America—the land that gave birth to him and shaped him—can be proud of him too. An ordinary American who undertook a most extraordinary mission. This is his story.

PROLOGUE

March 1945: Poland

Freedom held its breath . . .

Ten miles east of the Polish city of Lwów, the main rail line, snaking its way through the snow-covered farmlands, passed through a mile-long stretch of forest. On this day, hidden among the pines on a slope overlooking the tracks, shivering in the bitter cold, was a young woman. Her name was Isabelle, and she had been hiding here, keeping an anxious vigil, all through the freezing night. She was waiting for a train. Not just any train: the train to freedom.

Isabelle was a long way from home, a fugitive in an alien land. Two years ago she had been taken from her hometown in France by the German authorities, herded together with other young women and men, and taken away to the Reich. There the captives—the so-called *Zwangs-arbeiter* or forced workers—were incarcerated in camps and put to work: some in the factories, some in the mines, others on the farms of Germany and occupied Poland.[1] Isabelle and her compatriots had endured years of captivity, forced labor, hunger, and in some cases, rape.

The approach of the Russians caused the camps to be evacuated. The Nazis drove the foreign laborers in Poland westward toward Germany, murdering those who resisted. Many escaped the forced marches. But although they were at liberty, they were still far from freedom. Like countless other escapees—laborers, prisoners of war, and even some concentration-camp survivors—Isabelle and her friends took to a fugitive life. Grouping together for safety, some of the Frenchwomen made their way eastward, away from the battlefront. From various camps they came—*Zwangsarbeiter* camps, concentration camps; a few had escaped the death march from Auschwitz. Hundreds of them, all French, gathered in the countryside around Lwów, some hiding out in farms that had been destroyed when the battlefront passed over the region, others sheltered by sympathetic Polish farmers and villagers. Many, including Isabelle and her friends, hid among the very farms where they had labored; they knew the region, knew the safe places and the local people. The women lived in daily fear of being taken by the Russians, who would treat them as illegal aliens—potential spies and anti-Soviet insurgents—and incarcerate them in their own hellish camps. Sometimes these camps were the very ones the refugees had been liberated from in the first place.[2]

Now at last there was hope. Word had reached the groups scattered around Lwów, passed along through the word-of-mouth network that had sprung up among the fugitives: freedom was at hand. Isabelle had dared to go into the city, and there she had found the man who could arrange to get them home to France. He was neither a Pole nor a Russian—he was an American officer. He could arrange for a train to take them to the coast city of Odessa, where they could board a ship bound for home. In small groups the women cautiously made their way to the forest rendezvous in the twilight gloom: there they concealed themselves and waited through the cold night hours.

The forest wasn't a regular rail stop. The rendezvous had been arranged by the American officer. He had come to this country to rescue his fellow Americans, he said: helping Isabelle was a side issue, a matter of humanity. He had become a magnet for the lost souls of foreign nations washed up by the tide of war in Poland; he was a conduit to home and liberty, and all who could found their way to him.

Isabelle believed in the American. She knew the train would come.

Morning had dawned and slowly worn away; midday had passed, and the train was hours late. If it didn't come, or if it was filled with Russians, or if any one of a hundred mishaps occurred, all the women could look forward to was more incarceration, more suffering, quite possibly death. Isabelle, her heart sinking, dug into the dwindling reserves of hope that had kept her going through the past two years. The train *had* to come; it must.

At this very moment, she knew, the American would be using every trick he could think of to avoid, stall, and sidetrack the Soviet secret police and prevent them discovering and foiling the escape plan. He was a good man, Isabelle believed; perhaps even a hero. But in this world, there were limits to what good men could do. Her faith was wavering, hope slipping from her fingers, when she heard the faint whistle in the distance. She tensed. There was no mistaking it: the sound of an approaching train.

Would it be the right one? Would there be Russian soldiers on board—or, worse, agents of the secret police? Those creatures were everywhere. This moment would show whether the American was a hero after all. Isabelle's heart beat faster. As soon as she saw the steam above the trees in the distance, she rose from her hiding place and ran down the slope. Stumbling over the stones, slipping on the ice, she clambered onto the rail bed and stood up in the center of the tracks. She raised the hopeful sign she had made: a sheet of board bearing a single word scratched in charcoal: "France."

The locomotive thundered toward her, shaking the ground under her feet. Holding her sign in the air, Isabelle waited for freedom . . . or death.

Three months earlier . . .

TELEGRAM M-22121

December 22, 1944

To: General Carl A. Spaatz
    US Strategic and Tactical Air Forces in Europe

Request for Personnel

Due to existing conditions at Poltava, it is
requested that you send two Counter-Intelligence
personnel to that base for duty.

New subject: At the present time there are only
two rated pilots in Poltava. Due to the increasing
number of flights from Poltava to areas behind the
front lines for purpose of picking up crews and
bringing parts to damaged bombers, an additional
pilot is needed. This pilot should have both
four-engine and twin-engine experience.

                              Major General Edmund W. Hill
                              U.S. Military Mission, Moscow

1.

ONE LUCKY BASTARD

December 30, 1944: Debach, England
Base of 493rd Bomb Group, US Eighth Air Force

The wintry afternoon light was beginning to fade to dusk as the
formation of B-17 Flying Fortresses streamed in over the Suffolk
coast. The individual bombers began peeling off from the formation,
joining the airfield circuit and lining up to land. Some, shot with holes,
were limping as they covered the last leg of their journey home. One
Fortress was absent, its crew having bailed out over the sea.[1] The 493rd
Bomb Group, along with the other groups in its division, had been to
bomb the marshaling yards at Kassel, Germany, and they hadn't been
welcome.

Landing lights glittering on their wings, the heavy bombers touched
concrete with a rubbery squawk and rolled on down the runway, swung
onto the taxiways, and headed, engines rumbling, toward their dispersal
areas around the airfield. Some jolted, wings tipping awkwardly, as they
taxied over the pits and breaks in the concrete. Debach (pronounced
Debbidge by locals, to the bewilderment of some American personnel)
was the last of the heavy bomber airfields built for the Eighth Air Force.
The construction was poor, and the runways had already deteriorated to
the point where the 493rd might soon have to move elsewhere.[2]

Avoiding the worst pitfalls, B-17 *Big Buster* eased to a halt on its hard-standing. In the cockpit, Captain Robert M. Trimble and his copilot, Lieutenant Warren Johnson, went through the elaborate ritual of shutting down the shuddering aircraft, flicking switches and sliding levers. One by one the four huge propellers chopped and swished to a halt, and a hush punctuated by the ticking of cooling metal settled on the cockpit.

"Home she comes!" said a voice on the interphone.

Trimble and Johnson smiled at each other as the last switch was flicked and the dials dropped to zero. *Home*—now there was a thought to heal a weary heart. Captain Trimble and his crew had been in England for nearly six months, and flown their fill of missions: today had been the thirty-fifth, and their tour of duty was complete.[3] Robert Trimble had beaten the odds, and it was time to go home. Home, where his wife, Eleanor, and the baby daughter he hadn't yet seen were waiting for him. Little Carol Ann had been born exactly two months ago, while her father was flying into Germany on his twenty-fifth combat mission, heading for the fearsome target of Merseberg. As if fate was working in his favor that day, the bombers were recalled due to low cloud over the target, and they flew back to England unharmed.[4] That had been a lucky day, and this was another.

One by one the crewmen dropped through the escape hatch onto the concrete. Some stretched their stiff backs; a few went to the edge of the concrete, unfastened the layers of coveralls, heated suit, pants, and underwear, and watered the frosty grass, sighing with relief. Tired but jubilant, the nine men tossed their gear on the waiting jeeps and climbed aboard, joking and taunting one another, free of the silent gloom that often came over them as the adrenaline drained away at mission's end. Captain Trimble dropped into the jeep's passenger seat.

"The CO wants to see you, sir," said the sergeant driver as he put the jeep in gear.

"Me?" said Trimble, startled. "Now?"

"At your convenience, sir." The sergeant crunched the gears; the jeep revved and swerved away.

Captain Trimble gripped the edge of the windshield as the overloaded vehicle sped across the field toward the complex of buildings in the far distance. He couldn't imagine why the CO would want to see him, but he didn't give it too much thought. Dog-tired after seven hours of piloting the Fortress through flak, fighters, and ungodly cold, he rode back to the airfield HQ with happy thoughts of home swimming in his head, violently jolted though they were by the jeep's bouncing progress. By the time the crew was dropped off at the debriefing room, he had forgotten all about the summons.

It was shaping up to be a good weekend. The Trimble crew were not the only men whose tours were done—their squadron-mates under Lieutenant Jean Lobb had also completed today. As wingman to the group leader, Lobb had been on Trimble's starboard nose all the way to Germany, but had to drop out of formation with supercharger failure before reaching the target (leading to a tense moment of urgent re-forming as Lieutenant Parker crawled up from the rear to take his place). Luckily for Lobb, he was credited with a sortie, despite bringing his bombs home with him.[5]

With end-of-tour celebrations, and New Year's Eve tomorrow, it was all good cheer for the homeward-bound boys.

Despite the carousing that went on in the mess that evening, Robert Trimble had the best night's sleep he'd had in months: no mission in the morning, no fear of a mission alert during the day; just a beautiful future to look forward to, a future with Eleanor and baby Carol Ann. He wondered if Camp Hill, Pennsylvania, had changed at all in the months he'd been away. One thing was for sure, he reflected happily: it had changed by the addition of a brand-new baby girl. . . .

Rested and groomed, Robert put on his dress uniform—olive-drab jacket with tan pants and shirt, the sharp combination known as "pinks & greens"—and set off for his appointment at group headquarters. Unlike the permanent airfields in the States, Debach sprawled over a tract of otherwise untouched Suffolk countryside, and the routes between the technical and domestic sites, the airfield and the munitions stores were winding country lanes lined with hedgerows. In no hurry, Robert strolled along under the winter-bare sycamores. It was quiet, with the group out on a mission.

Headquarters occupied what had been a farm field this time last year, beside a lane connecting the main airfield with the little hamlet of Clopton (the equally tiny settlement of Debach was straddled by a couple of aircraft hardstandings on the far side of the base). Robert presented himself and was admitted to the commanding officer's inner sanctum—a modest set of offices in a Quonset hut.

Colonel Elbert Helton, CO of the 493rd, was an undistinguished-looking man. Placid and serious, with large ears and a touch of humor in his eyes, he looked more like a friendly small-town doctor than what he actually was—a seasoned bomber pilot with a long string of combat missions in the Pacific and Europe under his belt. The young Texan had been propelled up the ranks by the pressure of war, and he now commanded the four squadrons that made up the 493rd Bomb Group and the sprawling military base that housed them. He had only just turned twenty-nine years old.[6]

He waved Captain Trimble to a chair. "I just got done signing these," he said, taking a paper from a small pile. "You might as well have yours now." Robert took it and smiled. It was the customary document, signed by Helton and the other senior officers of the 493rd.

On This 30th Day of December Nineteen Hundred and Forty Four
The Fickle Finger of Fate Has Traced on the Rolls of the

"Lucky Bastard Club"

the name of

Capt. Robert M. Trimble 0-1289835
493rd Bombardment Group (H)

Having successfully completed a tour of operations
in this European theater with "Butch" Helton's hard hitting hagglers
he is hereby graduated as an Honor Student
from Debach's College of Tactical Knowledge . . .

. . . Therefore it is fitting that he should be presented
with this Certificate that all may know that he is truly
a "Lucky Bastard."

"Congratulations, Bob," said Helton. "You made it. You're on your way home."

"Yes, sir," said Robert. He knew Colonel Helton well, and something in his tone of voice made him feel uneasy. Helton paused, then stuck a pin in the blissful bubble that Robert had been walking around in since yesterday.

"You know you'll be called back, don't you? For another tour."

This was exactly what Robert didn't need to hear right now. He knew it was a possibility, but Helton said it like it was a stone-cold certainty.

"You're going home for now—you're entitled to twenty-one days' leave stateside—but at the end of it you'll be recalled. Maybe here, or maybe to the Pacific. The Army's got plenty of pilots, but not so many good ones, let alone experienced."

That was true. Earlier that year, the length of a tour for bomber crews had been raised from twenty-five missions to thirty. In September, halfway through Robert's tour, they raised it to thirty-five. Who could tell when they might raise it again? Sending experienced pilots back into combat seemed all too likely.

"I know your wife just had a baby," the colonel said, "and I know you'd like to go home. But you go on and go home now, you're only going to be there for twenty-one days, and more than likely they'll send you right back."

"I see, sir." Robert was wondering if there was a point to all this, besides wrecking his moment of happiness.

Helton stood up and took out a bottle of scotch and two glasses. "The last of the November special mission supply," he said, pouring it out.

Robert smiled and took his glass. Part of his unofficial duties in the 493rd was as the commanding officer's whiskey courier. Once a month he piloted the squadron hack up to Edinburgh and snagged a few bottles.

"I have an offer for you," Helton went on. "Maybe you'd like to take advantage of it."

"What kind of offer?"

Helton took a sip of whiskey. "The brass want you, Bob," he said. "They've asked me for a good man, and I'm giving them you."

The whiskey turned to battery acid in Robert's mouth. It wasn't healthy to get noticed by the brass.

"That is, if you want to take advantage of it. They're looking for an experienced multi-engine pilot—someone rated on both the B-24 and B-17. You're the only one I know who'd like a job like this. They want to send you to Russia." Robert's brain did a backflip. *Russia?* "You know we've got bases there?" Helton went on. "No, well neither did I, much. They were set up for shuttle mission support."

Colonel Helton sketched in what he knew about the background. A shuttle mission was one in which a bombing force took off from its base, hit a target, then flew on to another base in another country; it was a solution to the problem of targets that were too far away for bombers to reach them and make it back to their home bases. The 493rd had never been involved in Operation Frantic (as the shuttle program was codenamed), so Helton couldn't tell Robert very much. He would be sent to the Eastern Command base at a place called Poltava in the Ukraine. Now that Frantic was on ice, the US detachment there had changed roles, and Poltava had become a base for salvaging US aircraft that had been damaged in combat and made forced landings in Soviet-occupied territory. Robert's job, as Helton described it, would be to collect salvaged bombers from Poltava and fly them out—either back to England or down to Italy.

"The Soviets are itching to get their hands on our planes," Helton said. "Given half a chance, they'll haul 'em off and tear 'em down to find out how they're made. Our guys are getting them patched up and the hell out of there before those Reds get the chance. You have experience of emergency soft-field takeoffs, don't you?"

Robert nodded. Back in the summer he'd been forced to land his B-24 at a Luftwaffe fighter airfield in northern France. Anticipating either a firefight or captivity, he and his crew were relieved to be greeted by American infantrymen who'd captured the field a few days earlier. After refueling and repairs, Robert had learned the hard way about the challenges of taking off a laden four-engine bomber from a short grass strip intended for single-engine fighters.

"I thought so," said Helton. "So, what d'you say?"

"You mean I have a choice?"

"Of course." Helton paused. "There's a catch. They want you right now. You wouldn't get the chance to go home."

"Then I'd rather not, sir."

The colonel glowered. "Listen, Bob, if you take this job, you'll be out of the combat zone—just flying back and forth, absolutely safe. It'll take you maybe a few months to ferry those planes. After you get that done, you could tell them you're going home. Then, after your twenty-one days are up, maybe the war will be over."

Robert was silent. Colonel Helton was trying to help him out, and the colonel was right—if he went home now, the system would scoop him right up and send him back to the fight. Another tour—another thirty-five missions. He'd beaten the lottery once—could he count on being a Lucky Bastard twice?

"You know the score as well as I do," Helton went on. "Yesterday was almost a milk run by all accounts.[7] Right this minute the group is on the way to hit the refinery at Misburg, and I'm not expecting to see them all back tonight. How would you reckon your chances if there were another Magdeburg? Nine ships out of thirty-six went down that day."

Robert felt a chill at the mention of the Magdeburg mission—a name invested with dread. It had been mid-September, and the 493rd had only just completed the transition from B-24 to B-17 bombers. Poor formation flying over the target (oil industry facilities at Magdeburg/ Rothensee) opened the door to attacks by two squadrons of German Fw 190 fighters. They came from front and rear, raking the straggling Fortresses. The 493rd lost nine bombers that day—four exploding in flames before their crews could get out. Only half a dozen parachutes were spotted from all the stricken planes.[8]

Captain Robert Trimble had not taken part in the Magdeburg mission; it had been his squadron's turn to stand down.[9] He figured it just wasn't his day to die. That day could come anytime, though, and Colonel Helton's offer showed a way to put it off.

But Robert wasn't the kind of man who could be stampeded so easily. He looked his commanding officer in the eye. "What if I turn it down?"

Helton shrugged. "I pass it on to the next fellow on my list. But I was asked for the best, and you're the best I've got available." The colonel finished his whiskey and stood up. "Listen, go call your wife. Talk it over with her. When you're done thinking, come back and talk to me again."

Robert walked across to the communication building, turning the proposal over in his mind. It was a big thing to take in. He didn't want to go to Russia (or the Ukraine or wherever the hell it was), but maybe it would be for the best. He and Eleanor had been apart for much of their two-and-a-half years of married life. She had followed him dutifully from state to state as he progressed through his pilot training, and then bravely said goodbye to him when he went overseas. That was nine months ago now. Would she be willing to wait another who-knew-how-long, when she'd been hoping to see him any day now? But how could he expect her to wave him off to war again, after only a brief respite? He just didn't know what to think.

Harrisburg, Pennsylvania

Eleanor Trimble was hard at work, enveloped in steam and sweltering heat. It leaked through even into the side office where she worked at the company accounts. Tonight was New Year's Eve, and the whole world wanted their dry cleaning this minute. She'd been back at work in the laundry for several weeks now, even though it was only two months since the baby's birth. She needed the wages. Even sharing a rented house with Robert's mother, Ruth, money was tight. Ruth and the landlady took turns looking after little Carol Ann, while Eleanor caught the bus each day from Lemoyne to Harrisburg to bring home her meager $12 a week.

It was hard enough living without her husband; harder still to know what a dangerous calling he'd followed. (It was as well, perhaps, that Eleanor didn't know just how dangerous it was: that flying bombers was the most fatal military occupation in Europe.[10]) She carried the worry day after day, the fear that one morning a War Department telegram might arrive and explode its payload of grief in her home. Eleanor had already lost her brother to the war; she couldn't bear the thought of losing her husband too, or that Carol Ann might never know her father.

The days passed in a forgettable blur of routine. Apart from the seasonal rush, this morning was no different than usual. As Eleanor worked, her mind was far away, oblivious to the distant ringing of the phone in the next-door office. She was startled out of her daydream by the office door slamming open and her boss leaning out. "Eleanor! Call for you—it's your old man!"

Eleanor froze. Every repressed fear instantly loomed up in her mind. Her heart thumped and her skin prickled as she hurried across to the office. She was out of breath by the time she picked up the phone. "Hello?"

"Eleanor—"

"Robert! Is that you?"

The voice that came down the line sounded thin, crackly, and unbearably distant. "It's me, I—"

"Robert! Are you okay? Are you hurt? They scared me when they said it was you. I thought something had happened. When are you coming home?" She had known that the time was drawing near when he would finish his tour, and it had heightened her anxiety as well as her hopes.

"Eleanor, that's why I'm calling. Colonel Helton made me an offer . . ."

"Robert, first tell me you're not hurt. When are you coming home?"

"I'm okay, Eleanor, I'm fine. Now listen . . ." Robert's voice took on a serious tone that Eleanor didn't like at all: even across thousands of miles of ocean it echoed with foreboding. "Colonel Helton has given me a tough decision to make, and you and I have to decide what we want to do. And we have to decide right now."

"I don't like the sound of this . . ."

"I'll get right to it. I've finished my last mission. My tour is over and I can come home." Eleanor's heart lifted, although she suspected it shouldn't. "I'll get twenty-one days and then I'll likely be called back to do it all over again—another thirty-five combat missions. Or I can accept the colonel's offer and go on a mission—"

"Mission? What are you talking about? Robert, I want you home!"

"I can't talk about it. Listen, it's overseas, but it's outside the combat area. Just flying and light duty. The colonel singled me out for this. I'd be safe until the end of the war." He paused. "What do you say?"

There was a deathly hush on the line, filled with crackles and the ghostly echo of aching distance.

"Eleanor?"

She found her voice, and it shook with emotion. "No, Robert. No. I need you home with me. I need you now; I can't take this anymore."

A gusty sigh came down the line. "All right then," said Robert. "I'm coming home."

His tone was so heavy, so resigned, that Eleanor wished she could unsay what she had just said. "Robert, no. I've changed my mind. You have to do the right thing. I'm being selfish. I'm hurting, but I know you are too." She lacerated herself with every word. "I think I can stand life like it is for just a while longer"—even though she couldn't—"if it means you being safe. But I know I couldn't stand to think of you going back into danger."

"Eleanor, are you—"

"Stay; do what you have to do. Then come home to me alive, and never leave me again. Do you hear me?"

"Are you sure?"

"You heard me, soldier." Eleanor's eyes were prickling with tears. "I love you."

"I love you too. How's Carol Ann?"

The tears overflowed, and a little sob escaped Eleanor's throat. "She's fine! She's fine . . ." Eleanor could feel the knot tightening in her chest now, threatening to choke her. "Robert, I have to go now. I love you. Goodbye."

"Goodbye."

Eleanor put the phone down, fumbling to set it on its cradle as the weeping flooded out of her and her vision dissolved in a blur.

Half a world away, in a freezing, concrete-paved field in Suffolk, Captain Robert Trimble stood under the lowering, slate-gray East Anglian sky—one of the biggest skies in the world, and at this moment the gloomiest. It matched his mood. Oh well, there it was. Eleanor had decided for him. He would be going to Russia.

Later that day, he walked across to the control tower to report his decision to Colonel Helton, and to watch the squadrons fly in from their mission.

Helton had been right—they were pretty beat up, and not all of them had come back. One ship had been lost somewhere over Germany. Altogether, more than five hundred bombers from the 3rd Air Division had gone to bomb Misburg; twenty-seven had been lost, ten times that number damaged, and more than two hundred and fifty men would not be coming back to their bunks that night.[11] Robert could picture the whole thing vividly: the puffs of black flak, the shreds of torn metal falling from hit planes, the blossoming parachutes, the big silver bird turning helplessly over and sinking down to death. And one of the worst sights of all: a chute blooming prematurely, snagging on the falling bomber, and the entangled dot of a man being dragged down toward the distant earth.

Maybe he really had made the right decision; better to postpone his homecoming than go through all that again. Assuredly the right decision. Robert felt better—resigned to his future, resigned to temporary unhappiness and permanent safety. As he watched the lumbering planes taxiing to their dispersals, he reflected that he was indeed a Lucky Bastard.[12]

It was to be a while—more than a month, in fact—before Robert discovered the full extent to which both he and Colonel Helton had been lied to.

Had he been able to see into the future, Robert might have gone to headquarters that minute and willingly signed up for a second combat tour. But even if he'd been granted a sight of what was to come, he might not have believed it. The creaking footfalls in the snow under the winter pines . . . the wild, demonic shapes of Cossacks cavorting around a flickering fire . . . the terrified, hate-filled eyes of the Russian colonel over the leveled barrel of the Colt . . . frozen corpses laid in rows along the lonely railroad tracks . . . the controls of the patched-up bomber shuddering in his grip as the blizzard battered her . . . the mystery of a freshly filled grave in the woods . . . and those lustrous Slavic eyes smiling into his amid a haze of perfume: *Captain, you are so handsome . . .* yes, there would be good memories in there, too, but he would pay for them with the nightmares.

Robert knew none of this as he watched the last of the Fortresses touch down on the runway. He patted his breast pocket, where he'd placed the neatly folded Lucky Bastard certificate, then turned, went down the tower steps, and walked away into the gathering English dusk.

2.

AN AMERICAN IN LONDON

January 1945: London

They called it "Little America." Grosvenor Square, in the heart of London's Mayfair district, with its palatial Georgian town houses surrounding the huge public garden, was older than the United States itself and had deep ties with the former colonies. John Adams had begun the first American mission in the square right after Independence, and now it was home to the United States Embassy, which loomed over one corner.[1] Near the opposite corner, an elegant red-brick mansion had been commandeered for General Eisenhower's headquarters ("Eisenhower Platz," some people called it). Next-door to that was the HQ of the American Red Cross. Less conspicuously, the London headquarters of the secretive Office of Strategic Services, nest of spies, saboteurs, and secret agents, was a short walk away in Grosvenor Street.

Ike and his staff had moved to Paris a few weeks ago, but the square still teemed with American military and diplomatic activity. The former residences and gardens of the cream of Britain's ruling classes now buzzed with the accents of Texas and Virginia, West Point and Annapolis, and every state, city, and homestead.

On this cold January evening, the gardens were dusted with a fresh fall of snow, which glowed in the starlight—the only illumination in the

blacked-out city. A car drew up in front of the embassy, and a young officer stepped out; he glanced up at the forbidding façade, and shivered.
Captain Robert M. Trimble was already wondering what in the world
he'd got himself into. In the past eight hours he'd had one strange experience after another. And if not strange, at least somewhat embarrassing . . .

Robert had caught the early afternoon train from Woodbridge, the
nearest station to Debach, and settled down to enjoy the ride, still
feeling the inner glow of a man who knew he was safely but honorably
out of combat for the rest of the war.

Sharing the compartment were two English girls, wearing the blue
uniform of the Women's Auxiliary Air Force. Born with a susceptibility
to feminine charm, and feeling pleased with himself, Robert struck up a
conversation. He liked the girls; they had an attitude that was common
among the British—the phlegmatic determination to carry on serenely
in spite of the pounding they'd taken from Hitler. They were cheerful
and talkative. Not overly concerned about the danger of loose lips sinking
ships, they chatted freely about life in the WAAF. They were stationed in
London, assigned to RAF Balloon Command, where they helped crew
one of the city's hundreds of barrage balloon wagons.

Talking blithely, they didn't notice that the American had fallen
silent. At the mention of barrage balloons, Robert felt suddenly very
uncomfortable, recalling an incident just over a month ago which he
hoped they hadn't heard about—or, worse, witnessed firsthand.

It had happened on his last visit to London—an unorthodox and
entirely unscheduled visit from the air. The 493rd were returning from a
mission to Germany near the end of November. Debach was socked in by
freezing rain. Fortresses were skidding off the runway, and the squadrons
still airborne were diverted to another airfield, hundreds of miles away in
Cornwall. The next afternoon, with the weather improved, they set off on
the return flight, on a route that took them near London. Robert, in a
rush of high spirits, figured they were technically on a three-day pass

after yesterday's mission, so maybe they ought to divert and take a flyby to look at the sights of the capital.

He ought to have known better. Even his copilot, Lieutenant Warren Johnson, said it was a bad idea. Warren was a fun-loving guy; a singer and jazz trumpeter, he always brought his horn on missions, stowed beside his seat, and liked to entertain the boys with swing tunes over the interphone during the long, tedious mission flights. He kept the mouthpiece on a chain tucked inside his suit to keep it warm, and smeared it with Vaseline to prevent it freezing to his lips. Warren had nerve; on one memorable occasion, on the approach to a bomb run, with the Fortress shaking and battered by a storm of flak, losing altitude with a gaping hole in her wing, he boosted the men's spirits with a verse of "Amazing Grace." But even Warren balked at the idea of a pleasure flight over London. There were rules—very strict rules.

But Robert had a reckless streak in him, and it was in control right now. He had a gift for persuasion, and it helped that he was also the airplane commander. "We can spot where we want to go at the weekend," he said. "Tell you what, we'll fly over St. Paul's Cathedral. Eleanor always wanted to see it; she'll be excited to hear what it looks like."

With this unwise idea in mind, he turned the bomber off the planned route and headed toward the capital, easing down to low altitude for the best view. The gray river Thames snaking through London's urban sprawl was their guide. For a major city, London had hardly any tall buildings, and the landmarks were easy to spot—Big Ben, Tower Bridge, and then, rising immaculately among the bombed-out buildings of the City district, the great dome of St. Paul's. Dotted here and there, mostly over toward the docklands in the east, were the silver blobs of barrage balloons.

"Not bad," Warren admitted. "We'll have to see her on foot when we get the chance. Now can we get the hell outta here?"

Robert wanted a better view right now. He turned the plane's nose toward the dome, about half a mile away, and eased the control column forward, intending to drop down to about three hundred feet. He looked down at the instrument panel, then back up—and swore. Directly ahead, rising rapidly into the previously empty sky, was the fat, gleaming bulk of a barrage balloon. And there was another, off to one side, and another, and another . . . all trailing the steel guy wires that were designed to snarl the wings of bombers. The only way to go was up, but the balloon ahead was a hundred feet higher than the B-17 already, still ascending, and getting closer by the second. Robert pushed the throttles to full emergency power and hauled back on the control column. The bomber lifted, and the men inside prayed. The silvery mass of the balloon flashed beneath the plane's nose, and there was a gentle bump and scrape as it dragged along the fuselage.

They weren't clear yet. As the balloon passed beneath, Robert was conscious of a sporadic pinging noise—the familiar sound of bullets hitting the plane. Robert's assumption—that London's defense forces would recognize the B-17 as an American aircraft—had been wrong, just like his assumption that the barrage balloons parked permanently in the sky over the city were the only ones available. Balloon Command had quick-response wagons too.[2] To the defenders on the ground, any bomber was the enemy; they didn't have time to distinguish friend from foe. Even if they had, rumors abounded of captured bombers flown by devious Luftwaffe crews; no chances were taken, and the tendency was to shoot first and think later. As Robert and his crew climbed and steered away from the city, they were lucky not to be fired on by the anti-aircraft batteries that were everywhere.

Somebody—probably an RAF plane on patrol—must have identified the aircraft, and got a clear enough view to note the group ID and call sign; a report was passed immediately to VIII Bomber Command, and then down to 493rd headquarters. As the Fortress flew on toward its proper destination, the tourist atmosphere having long dissolved into grim silence, an irritated voice came over the radio from the Debach control tower.

"This is Whitewash to Pillar 366.[3] You are reported off course and in London airspace. Explain yourself."

"Compass malfunction," said Robert. "Lost bearing and descended below cloud base for visual navigation." It wasn't a bad attempt under the circumstances, but the tower wasn't buying it.

"Not good enough. Report to HQ immediately on landing." The voice added peevishly: "And no more sightseeing—that's an order."

There was an official inquiry. The crew backed Robert up (even though they were furious with him), and Colonel Helton decided to accept the "compass malfunction" story. If Robert hadn't been such a favorite of the CO, things might have turned out differently. He'd have been grounded at best, maybe even busted down a rank. When he wrote his next letter to Eleanor, he judged it best not to mention his visit to St Paul's. She would have seen it as disrespectful to the church, and maybe regarded his narrow scrape as a just warning from God. Colonel Helton might have forgiven him, but Eleanor and the Almighty were another matter.

Listening to the two young WAAFs chatting gaily about the life of a balloon wagon crew, Robert felt the heat of shame rise up his neck, turning his cheeks red. He had the absurd thought that they might have heard of him, or even recognize him. But if they knew about the incident, they made no mention of it.

Evening was coming on as the train pulled into Liverpool Street Station (just a short walk from St. Paul's, had Robert had time to revisit the scene of his shame). In his pocket was a slip of paper with an address written on it. His orders were to report there immediately on arrival. He managed to hail one of the small number of black cabs that still plied the wartime streets. Gasoline was rationed, and many of the drivers had been drafted. The few that remained scraped a living mostly from US military personnel.

Like many American tourists before and after, Robert discovered the marvelous ability of London cabdrivers to know their way, without hesitation, to any address in the metropolis, no matter how obscure. Even in the blacked-out city, with only hooded headlights to guide him, the cabbie found the street requested, and drove without hesitation right up to the door.

As the taxi rumbled off into the night, Robert looked in bewilderment at the building in front of him. He thought he must have come to the wrong place. He'd been expecting some kind of military facility or other official building. What he was looking at, as far as he could tell in the darkness, was a modest row house in a residential street. But the number checked out. There must have been an error somewhere. He'd been given a wrong address, or the cabbie had deposited him in the wrong street. There was nobody about. He figured he might as well knock on the door; maybe they'd have a phone he could use to call for instructions.

He knocked. There was a pause, and then a muffled voice called out, "Who's there?" A female voice with an English accent, which rather confirmed that he'd come to the wrong place.

"I'm an American officer, ma'am. I'm lost, and hoping to use your telephone if you have one."

There was a click of a latch, and the door opened. Against the darkness of the blacked-out hallway, Robert could make out the dim shape of a woman. Before he could apologize for disturbing her, she spoke: "Are you Captain Trimble?"

He was stunned. "... Why yes, yes I am."

"Do come in," she said warmly. "I've been expecting you."

Mystified, Robert stepped inside. The door closed, and the hall light was switched on. Smiling pleasantly at him was a tall, middle-aged lady.

"Come in and sit down," she said, leading him into the front room. She guided him to a chair by the unlit gas fire. The house was even more modest inside than outside, with bare walls and hardly any furniture. The lady's cut-glass accent seemed bizarrely out of place in this shabby setting. She fed a shilling into the gas meter and lit the fire. "There. Now I need to make a telephone call. Cup of tea?" Robert nodded mutely.

The mysterious woman was gone for a few minutes and came back with a tray on which were cups and a teapot, and a plate of ham sandwiches. "You must be hungry after your journey," she said. "Do take a sandwich."

"Yes ma'am. Thank you."

She turned away to pour tea. "I suppose you must be wondering what this is all about," she said sympathetically.

"Well, ma'am, I was told I was going to Russia to fly airplanes." He looked curiously at her, wondering if she was about to offer him an explanation. She wasn't.

"Honestly, I don't know what plans they have for you. I'm just an intermediary. It's better that you don't ask me any questions. The embassy is sending a car for you. In the meantime, do help yourself to sandwiches."

The embassy? Don't ask any questions? What was going on here?

Despite his confusion, he managed to concentrate some of his attention on the sandwiches. They were another feature that marked this out as no ordinary house; with meat rationed, there wouldn't be anyone else in this street eating ham sandwiches right now. Robert had eaten two and was reaching for a third (it had been a long day) when they heard the sound of a car pulling up outside. There was a knock on the door, and a suited civilian was admitted. He looked Robert up and down and spoke without ceremony: "Come on, it's late." He had an American accent and an irritable tone; he looked like someone who didn't get too much sleep. Robert followed him out to the car.

It seemed like an awfully big charade for a ferry pilot. As they drove through the city, Robert decided to chance an inquiry. "So," he said, "what's all this special treatment about?"

"I don't know," the man said. "And I wouldn't tell you if I could. To you I'm just your driver."

Robert let it be, and lapsed back into silence.

Even in the dark, he could see that the streets were getting wider and the houses larger as the car headed west. Finally they turned a corner and pulled up in front of a large, looming building. It didn't look like much in the dark, with its pillared façade in shadow, and its dozens of elegant windows blacked out, but this was 1 Grosvenor Square, Mayfair—the United States Embassy and heart of Little America.

Inside, Robert was left waiting in the large, cold foyer. It was 9:30 P.M. when at last an attaché came to collect him. Once again there was no introduction, no explanation. He was merely asked to confirm his identity, told that he would be called for in the morning, then handed over to an attendant, who escorted him to one of the embassy's guest rooms.

Too dog-tired to think, Robert undressed and sank into bed—a bed that he would later recall as the best and most comfortable he had ever slept in in his life.

Next morning, an attendant woke him at seven and warned him to be down for breakfast in thirty minutes. After a shower in lukewarm water, he ventured downstairs. Following his well-trained soldier's nose, he found his way to the staff dining hall. That breakfast was some of the best food he'd had since arriving in England. These diplomats sure knew how to live the civilized life, even in a city on the front line of a war.

Afterward, he was taken in hand again and brought to an office where he was met by a senior-looking attaché. Yet again there was no introduction, no pleasantries, but this time there was at least some information. However, it was not the kind of information calculated to settle Robert's qualms about this whole business.

The attaché looked quizzically at Robert's uniform, then spoke briskly: "The first thing to do is have you fitted out with a suit. That will be done this morning." He wrote on a piece of paper and handed it to Robert. "Go to this address. You're to be supplied with two suits. They'll be ready by this evening. Then you'll be transported to pick up your flight to Stockholm. You—"

Robert interrupted. "Suits? What do I need suits for? I have my uniform."

The attaché peered at him. "You need civilian clothing. You will be provided with two suits. It will be taken care of today, in time to make tonight's flight to Stockholm."

"Whoa, whoa!" Robert put up his hands. "You're gonna put me in a *civilian suit*, and then send me in a plane over *Europe*?"

"Oh, you don't have to worry," the attaché said. "That plane goes over every night. You'll be perfectly fine."

"You don't understand. I'm wearing a dog tag. If that plane has to make an emergency landing in enemy territory, and I'm caught in a civilian suit with a dog tag, I'll be shot." The attaché stared while Robert went on objecting. "I just put in thirty-five missions; I don't want to stick my neck out now. And what's this about Stockholm?" he demanded. "I'm supposed to be going to Russia, not Sweden."

"Russia? I assume there's been a change of orders," said the attaché.

"No, no, I never signed up to go to Stockholm in a civilian suit. I'm supposed to be going to Russia to fly airplanes!"

The attaché hesitated. Throughout the short interview, he had become less and less sure of himself. "Captain," he said at last, "step outside and wait."

Simmering, Robert did as he was told. Out in the hallway, he sat and waited . . . and then paced up and down and waited . . . and then waited some more. All the while, his mind rehearsed the indignant speeches he would make if they tried to discipline him over this. Stockholm! In a civilian suit! Were they trying to use him as a spy? He'd be safer flying another combat tour. He wasn't cut out to be a spy—or trained, for that matter. No, he'd be damned first. His reckless side was back in control again, and he was perfectly prepared to face the stockade and a court-martial rather than go along with this insane, half-cocked plan. Had Colonel Helton known anything about this? Surely not.

After about an hour of waiting, Robert had had enough. He made his way back to the dining hall. By now it was long past breakfast. A cook offered him a turkey sandwich, which he accepted gratefully. His indignation hadn't affected his appetite. If he was going to be incarcerated, he figured it might as well be on a full stomach.

After a while, an attendant came looking for him and told him to come at once. Robert stood up and went to face his doom. To his surprise, he was taken to a different office, where he was met by an entirely different embassy official—a tall fellow who greeted Robert with a smile. Again no name was given, but at least this time he got a warm welcome.

"Captain Trimble, come in and sit down. Colonel Helton gave you a strong recommendation."

Robert felt a surge of relief at the mention of Helton's name. "Sir," he said, "I came here as an officer of the Army Air Forces, and I intend to go home the same way. I don't know what all that business about civilian suits and flying to Sweden is all about, but I'm a pilot. I can't change my skin, if you know what I mean."

"I understand, Captain. We've changed our minds; we can go back to the original arrangement. You'll be going to the Soviet Union."

"And I'll be ferrying planes back to England, like Colonel Helton said?"

"Yes . . . and other functions as deemed necessary. You wouldn't want to be bored, right, Captain?"

"No, sir. What would the other functions be?"

Somehow he never got told about the other functions. Suddenly the official became very busy, and Robert was escorted away by an attendant.

Like an aero engine on a cold morning, the bureaucratic machine had got off to a halting, juddering start. But now that it had been set in motion, it turned with a will, and Robert was swept along in the prop wash. In short order, he was equipped with travel warrants and other requisites for the long and roundabout journey to the USSR. He was also photographed and fingerprinted for ID documents. Unlike the plain, regular War Department AGO card he and every other officer carried, this was a real embassy-issue passport. Still unsure what intentions the military machine had for him, and whether they would be for good or ill, Robert lost the cheerful countenance he usually wore when a camera was pointed at him, and stared with deep suspicion into the lens.

The photo was printed, and he signed it; then it was fixed into the passport, and "American Consular Service" was stamped across it.

He was now officially part of the machine. Unofficially, and though he didn't yet know it, he had passed beyond the bounds of the Army, and was now in the orbit of the Office of Strategic Services.

To the end of his life, Robert never understood what had gone on in the embassy, even in the light of what came later. It was almost certainly a bureaucratic screwup: a case of mistaken identity. In 1944, the OSS, in cooperation with the British Special Operations Executive, had established a base in Sweden—the Westfield Mission.[4] In early 1945, Westfield was being used as a way station for field agents (known as "Joes") being infiltrated into Germany and German-occupied Poland.[5] They did indeed have flights going to and from Sweden virtually every night, taking supplies and ferrying Joes. When Robert showed up at the embassy, having been passed along from the OSS/SOE handler, the embassy attaché (probably an OSS officer from the headquarters round the corner in Grosvenor Street) believed he was a Joe, and treated him accordingly. The "change of plans" was presumably the result of the realization that Captain Trimble was actually the pilot for the Ukraine mission.

It was all too easy for such a mix-up to occur. A lot of Joes were being processed for infiltration missions. Whole networks of them were built up behind German lines. Joes were trained at the OSS's British bases, either in London or one of the secret "areas" in the countryside, and then passed along to Area T (Harrington in Northamptonshire) for air transportation. Typically they would liaise with their mission handlers at a safe house, which would be a shabby, partly furnished place, often in a London backstreet, exactly like the one Robert was sent to.[6] For all OSS personnel other than the handlers and mission briefers, there was a strict culture of silence surrounding Joes. For everyone, from the administrators who processed them to the specialist aircrews who transported them, there was a code of conduct: *You do not ask a Joe any questions about himself, and you do not tell a Joe anything that he doesn't need to know.*[7]

The OSS attaché at the embassy might have been a little puzzled by Robert's uniform on an agent, but it was common for OSS personnel in England to wear AAF uniforms in order to blend in with the people they had to mix with at the training and operational bases.[8] The fitting for a civilian suit was also part of standard procedure; the OSS clothing depot was nearby, in Brook Street, Mayfair, and the tailors there could create any kind of clothing, from authentic European work overalls to civilian suits and even enemy uniforms, all with the correct stitching styles and labels.[9]

Having realized their error, the anonymous officials at the embassy put Captain Trimble back on his proper intended course and sent him on his way, shaken and puzzled by the experience but completely innocent of what was in store for him.

3.

THE LONG WAY ROUND

January 29, 1945: Between Paris and Marignane, France

A heavy, relentless droning filled the passenger compartment of the C-47 Skytrain—so loud and so constant, it was physically oppressive. It was different from the sound Robert was accustomed to. The two Pratt & Whitney Twin Wasp engines that powered the C-47 made less noise than the four Wright Cyclones that propelled the huge weight of a B-17 into the sky; but it wasn't just the tone and volume of the engine noise that sounded different in Robert's ears—it was the way it resonated through the airframe. He was accustomed to the sound thrumming into the cockpit, not vibrating around the hollow tube of a passenger cabin.

That was another thing—he wasn't used to being a passenger. It didn't seem right to be sitting out back when he should be up front, with the half wheel of the control column in his hand and eight men on the other end of the interphone, ready to follow his orders.[1]

He shifted uncomfortably in the steel dish that passed for a seat. Some C-47s were fitted out for carrying cargo; a few were set up for VIPs and had real seats. Most were like this one: troop carriers designed for airborne infantry. The seating comprised two long benches, one down each side of the fuselage, with shallow steel hollows designed to receive steel butts; if you were unlucky and had the regular fleshy kind, you were in for a hell of a ride. Robert glanced around at the other passengers—miscellaneous servicemen on their way to who knew where. They didn't seem to be enjoying it any more than he was. A few were trying to carry on conversations over the noise, some were staring into space, and a few were reading letters.

Robert looked through his jacket pockets and extracted a rumpled piece of paper. He looked at it a moment, puzzled, then recognized his Lucky Bastard certificate. Still where he'd put it that evening back in Debach, when the world was a more dangerous but slightly less confusing place.

In another pocket he found his brand-new passport. He flipped it open and looked idly through it. It had his planned route written in it, in the form of a list of countries it was valid for: "British Isles, Union of Soviet Socialist Republics and necessary countries en route via Casablanca . . ."[2]

. . . Casablanca. What he'd have given to go to Casablanca again! His itinerary had been changed at the last minute, rerouted via Paris. As always happened in this war, days of waiting around had turned suddenly into desperate urgency, and he had to make do with whatever flights were available. Right now he was somewhere over the middle of France, having taken off a couple of hours ago from Paris. The plane was due to land soon at Marignane on the Mediterranean coast, where he had to pick up a connection to Italy, or wherever a ride happened to be going. It was a long, roundabout journey from England to the Ukraine, avoiding the huge, lethal but ever-shrinking blot on the map known as the Third Reich.

But Casablanca was out. Robert sighed and put the passport back in his breast pocket.

His first and only visit to Casablanca had been a momentary idyll on the way to combat. It was the tail end of May 1944, and Lieutenant Robert M. Trimble was running late for the war.

He and his crew, having been put together at March Field Army Air Base in California, hadn't yet been assigned to any unit. They were caught up in the general rush to get men and equipment to Europe in time for the D-Day invasion. They had one another and they had a brand-new Consolidated B-24 Liberator, which they were tasked with ferrying to England. They would be posted to a bomb group on arrival. While most crews flew the northern route, with stops at Labrador, Iceland, and Northern Ireland, Robert's was sent via the southern route, from California via Arizona, Florida, Trinidad, Brazil, and North Africa.[3] And even that, it seemed, was too straightforward for Robert M. Trimble. Flying into Fortaleza, Brazil, he was taken sick.

He'd had surgery on a wisdom tooth just before departure, and an infection set in. His jaw was on fire, his throat swelling, and he could hardly breathe. After landing at Fortaleza, he was taken directly from the plane to a hospital. The rest of the crew spent a week waiting for Robert to improve.[4] They found diversion with the local women and in the challenge of keeping their belongings dry in the daily torrential thunderstorms. Finally their command decided that the war couldn't wait; they were ordered to get going, healthy or not, on the next leg of their journey.

It was an overnight flight of some twelve hours over 1,946 miles of open ocean to Dakar, on the very western tip of Africa. They flew through almost continual electrical storms that played havoc with the radio. Lieutenant Walter Hvischuk, the navigator, did a superb job, bringing the ship in right over the Dakar runway at noon the next day, May 5, 1944. Copilot Warren Johnson had sole charge of the controls, while Robert formed an intimate bond with the cockpit floor, curled up in a ball in the small space behind the seats. When they landed in Dakar, he was again carried off to a hospital. This could become a way of life. His temperature was around 106 degrees, so they packed him in ice and gave him sulfa drugs (the first antibacterial drugs he'd had since the wisdom tooth operation).[5] He was so sick, his swollen throat had to be intubated.

The crew hung around in Dakar for ten days, watching movies, or swimming at the beach, or lying in their cots in the hot, dirty camp where everything was covered in a layer of red dust. Eventually they were sent on to Marrakech, Morocco, with a temporary substitute pilot, a Captain Van Eden, taking the controls. Robert was left behind, too sick to be moved. It was looking like they might lose their commander—Robert was likely to end up being reassigned to a different crew. He might even be facing a discharge on medical grounds.

After the boys had gone, Robert stayed in the hospital another ten days. Eventually he was well enough to lift his head from the pillow. What he saw of his surroundings wasn't reassuring—heat and red dust, and camel dung. The dust and dung got everywhere, even into the hospital, spreading a stench into the wards.

The doctors wanted to send him back stateside to convalesce. Robert wasn't having that, and he rebelled. He couldn't stand the thought of losing his ship, his crew, and maybe even his chance to fight in the war. He'd trained long and hard to fly combat, and doctors' orders weren't going to hold him back. Still weak but running on a mixture of adrenaline and inborn stubbornness, he got himself discharged, hitched a ride on a B-25 Mitchell bound for Marrakech, and set off in pursuit of his crew.

For a brief moment, as the B-25 came in to land, he thought he'd succeeded; he recognized his Liberator parked near the runway at Marrakech. It was definitely his ship—the markings were clear. After landing, he walked over to take a look. It was his all right, but it had a sad, dilapidated look, its silvery surfaces glaring dully under a layer of dust in the blazing Moroccan sun. As Robert walked around it, he noticed that two engines were gone, cannibalized by ground crews. Nobody was going to be flying this crate anywhere. Where was his crew? And what in the world had happened to the ship? (He discovered later that the substitute pilot, Captain Van Eden, had vanished immediately after landing, and Marrakech's ground crews began cannibalizing the plane for spare parts.)

Unable to find his friends, Robert boarded his ride again, and flew on to the next destination—the coastal city of Casablanca. On the approach to the airfield, the pilot, who obviously had a reckless streak similar to Robert's, decided to buzz a camel caravan; a memorable experience. A B-25 Mitchell is an unusually noisy aircraft—much louder than a Fortress or a Liberator, despite having only half as many engines[6]—and to have one come over at high speed at an altitude of fifty feet would be a pretty alarming experience. As the green monster blasted overhead, Arabs and camels scattered across the desert in a cloud of dust and panic. Robert decided that buzzing caravans in Africa was much more diverting than chasing coyotes over New Mexico.[7]

In Casablanca Robert finally caught up with Warren, Walter, and the rest of the boys. They had taken up residence in the colonial splendor of the old Italian Consulate building. Abandoned after the defeat of the Axis in Morocco, the building had been used by the US Army as an evacuation hospital during the Tunisian campaign;[8] now that the war had moved to Italy, it had become a hostel for American airmen.[9] The men had good beds, real bathrooms, and excellent food cooked by the consulate's Italian chefs, who remained in residence despite the radical change in occupancy. For most of the men who passed through, it was the greatest comfort they had experienced since leaving their own homes. For Lieutenant Robert Trimble, after the dust and dung of the Dakar hospital, it was paradise.

Casablanca itself was a marvel, full to the brim with sunlight, gleaming on the Moorish colonnades and the white stucco of the old French colonial buildings. Ingrid Bergman was nowhere to be seen, but there were plenty of high-class young French ladies with whom to while away the drowsy hours. Summer was rising, and the Moroccan coast was a hot haven of turquoise sea and white sand, where both home and the war seemed far away. The men swam and bronzed their young limbs on the beach, and drank cold beer in the long evenings.

It was a good place to pause on the way to war. With the prospect of a premature, violent death hull-up on the horizon, it was also a good place to reflect, if you were that way inclined. Most of the men were young, and full of the youthful certainty that life was theirs for the keeping. They didn't believe they were going to die. Robert was young too—a few months shy of his twenty-fifth birthday—but he saw further than most, and felt the oppressive menace that was in the world. Unlike many of his peers, he understood that he might die in the inferno they were heading toward. The knowledge didn't shake his resolve or his excitement, but it did give him pause for thought. Foremost in his thoughts now was Eleanor—and fatherhood.

His last sight of her as the train pulled away—she was on board, he was on the platform, a reversal of the usual wartime farewell—was still clear in his mind, as were the words she said to him.

For some time the tension had been building. At March Field Robert's training had reached its final stages: he had completed the transition to the B-24, been assigned a crew, and trained with them in the intricate skills of managing a heavy bomber in tight formation, dropping dummy bombs by day and night onto imaginary targets in the Mojave Desert.

He and Eleanor could both feel the war coming closer to them. She had followed him loyally from town to town as he went, through his training, but now he would have to move on where she could no longer follow: overseas to the front line. He had received orders to fly up to Hamilton Army Air Base, near San Francisco, and pick up their brand-new B-24 (the very one that finished up being cannibalized in Marrakech).[10]

Eleanor was only twenty-one years old, and she dreaded being left behind. She had nobody in the world. Just a few weeks earlier, she had received the news that her father had died (her mother had already passed on some years earlier), and within days the terrible blow that her beloved brother Howard, who had joined the Army right after Pearl Harbor, had been killed. After serving through the North African campaign, he had been badly wounded in Italy, and died shortly after. They had been intensely close, just a year apart in age, both keen basketball enthusiasts. Eleanor was knocked flat by the news. Robert was all she had now, and her only home was wherever he was.

Her forebodings had been growing ever since he was in advanced training and the war began to feel like a real, threatening presence that would soon come between them and force them apart, maybe forever. In November 1943 she had written to her best friend, Esther Burk, who was still living back in Lemoyne, Pennsylvania:

I am so afraid for Robert and for us. . . . I know the time will come too
soon when he's off to the war. I am so afraid I'll never see him again. I
want to keep a part of him with me, you know, have a baby. He doesn't
want us to have a child yet though. He says the war will be tough. No
saying what could happen. He doesn't want to have a child if it can't
know its father. I never realized how important this was to him. He
won't say, but I think his father's running out on the family has a lot to
do with it. I think it's important to him to be there for our kids. His talk
doesn't make me feel good about what's coming.

The feeling grew heavier and harder to bear. When the time came, Robert went with her to the train station at Riverside. She should have been waving him off, but instead she was the one leaving. There was no home for her in California now, and she was traveling back to Pennsylvania. Robert's mother would be her companion through the rest of the war, and her life would be dominated by the routine of a drudge job.

Robert looked uneasily at the trunk and two huge suitcases that were being loaded aboard the AT&SF *Super Chief* that would carry Eleanor as far as Chicago, and he wondered how she would manage it all. In a few short years of itinerant married life, they seemed to have accumulated an awful lot.

The huge red-and-silver diesel locomotive stood hissing patiently on the track. Eleanor sobbed and clung to him, staring up into his face, preserving this last sight of him in her memory. Caught up in the excitement of the adventure that was ahead of him, Robert didn't quite understand how much this moment meant to her. But he could see the tears, and the few words they exchanged stayed etched in his memory forever.

"Are you going to be okay?" he asked, seriously concerned about the long journey she had ahead of her, and the delicate emotional state she was in. He hadn't figured that her state might be delicate in more ways than one.

"Of course," she said. "I'm strong when I need to be." He didn't believe a word of it. "I'm okay, really," she said, and tried to smile. "I just want to see your face clearly enough that I won't forget those rugged good looks."

The conductor leaned out the door, yelling, "All aboard!"

"Come on," Robert said, extricating himself from her arms. "I don't want you to miss it."

The horn blew a long, raucous blast. "Now, ma'am, quickly!" the conductor called.

She still wouldn't move. Robert lifted her up bodily onto the car steps.

"Robert, you have to know, I'm—"

"Don't worry about me!" he said. The conductor took her arm to steady her as the train gave a jolt and began to move. Robert smiled at her. "You take care of yourself now."

The wheels were turning, and the distance between them began to grow. "Robert, I love you!" she called out. "And I'm pregnant!"

If she'd leaned out and punched him in the jaw, she could hardly have stunned him more thoroughly. He stood watching the glittering silver train snaking its way into the distance, trailing its wake of diesel vapor and noise, Eleanor's last words thumping over and over in his head in time with the clatter of the locomotive wheels. *I'm pregnant—I'm pregnant*—Her face shrank to a dot, then vanished; the train accelerated, and soon it was just a sliver on the horizon.

Weeks later, he could still hear the echoes, sitting in the cool quiet of the empty dining hall in the old consular building in Casablanca. He'd come a long way since that parting—much of it sick and barely conscious. All the way, Eleanor's confession had troubled him. She knew him well, and had guessed his feelings. When they flew up to Hamilton to collect their Liberator, Robert had been unable to concentrate, and had to ask Warren to take over the landing.

At first he had felt anger—an unreasoning annoyance, as if she had deliberately got herself pregnant for her own selfish reasons. They had talked about parenthood, and he knew that part of her desire for a baby was so that she would have a piece of him while he was gone. At the same time, he was aware of how selfish *he* was being. The toxic influence of his own father was at work, messing up his feelings in ways that he didn't understand, and wouldn't begin to understand for a good while yet. By the time they flew past the Golden Gate and touched down at Hamilton, his feelings had changed: his heart ached to the point of almost breaking at the knowledge of Eleanor's love for him. But he still didn't feel that it was right to bring a baby into this world—a baby that, like him, might have to grow up without a father.

Recovered from his illness, and enjoying the pleasures of Casablanca, Robert was consumed by guilt, and finally put pen to paper. He wrote Eleanor a long letter describing his eventful journey—the first communication from him since that parting by the railroad track.

It wasn't received in the spirit it was intended. By this time, Eleanor had built up a head of anger of her own. She wasn't enjoying pregnancy one bit, and her anxiety about Robert was exacerbating the effects of chronic morning sickness. The letter might have been the first she'd heard from him, but not the first she'd heard *of* him. Not long before, she had received a letter from a nurse at the hospital at Dakar, who happened to be a Camp Hill, Pennsylvania, girl herself and had taken Robert under her wing. "My name is Loretta," she wrote, "and I am a nurse taking good care of your husband. He is recuperating here in Dakar, and will probably be well enough to continue his mission in a few days." The fact that Robert made no mention of Loretta in his own missive caused Eleanor all manner of suspicion.

She'd had a hard time since they parted. Feeling insecure and alone, she had lugged her suitcases between trains in Chicago, and finally several blocks home to Hummel Avenue. No one offered to help her. No one had been at the station to greet her either; her father, mother, and brother were all dead.

As far as Eleanor could tell, Robert was being pampered by beautiful nurses and had forgotten all about her. She didn't know where he was going, so she couldn't write him yet. She felt she was losing him in every possible way, believing that the next she would hear of him would be the dreaded War Department telegram. She prayed extra hard, night and morning, between bouts of throwing up. She would fall asleep by the radio, humming "Don't Sit Under the Apple Tree" or "Till Then."[11]

Robert, meanwhile, was living out the lyrics to both, crossing oceans to foreign shores—but so far he hadn't held any girls on his knee or given out with those lips of his. And as he sat and wrote his letter in Casablanca, the last trace of his illness was fading away, replaced by a renewed sense of that mingled trepidation and excitement about the adventure waiting for him when he eventually made it to England. Like a million other young Americans heading toward their first taste of combat in that early summer of 1944, he had little conception of what it would really be like, or just how profoundly it would affect him.

A sudden change in the note of the engines, and a simultaneous stomach-lurching drop in altitude, told Robert that the C-47 was beginning its descent, stirring him out of his memories. They were approaching their destination—Marseilles-Marignane Airport, near Marseilles. Peering out the little square window, Robert saw the white-flecked blue of the Mediterranean angling up toward him as the plane banked and turned.

He shifted in his metal seat. The Army really knew how to punish a soldier's rear—he was glad he hadn't been a paratrooper. Maybe the purpose of the design was to make you happy to jump out of the plane into gunfire at the end of your trip. God knew how many more hours of it he'd have to endure before he reached the Ukraine.

Immersed in his memories, he had almost forgotten where he was. Had Casablanca really been only eight months ago? He was a different man now—a father, a combat veteran, and a Lucky Bastard. His feelings about most of those things had changed since the last time he looked down on the blue Mediterranean. Eight months, thirty-five combat missions, and one very perplexing visit to London. The mature, toughened twenty-five-year-old he'd become looked back in wonder at the innocent twenty-four-year-old he had been; the boy looking forward to adventure.

He had survived by luck, and now he was safe, and one day soon he would come marching home, into the arms of Eleanor. That was all he yearned for now—hearth and home. Captain Robert M. Trimble was done with adventure.

Unfortunately, adventure wasn't done with him.

Robert's itinerary ran like a whistle-stop tour of cities recently liberated from the Germans. He'd seen Paris, now Marseilles; from Marignane, the next flight took him to Naples, Italy, and then on to Athens, Greece. In both places his schedule allowed him a little time to gaze in wonder at the sights before being whisked away on another butt-walloping flight. He passed through Cairo, Egypt, and then on to his last stop before entering the Soviet Union: Tehran.

He was held up in Tehran for more than a week. His entry to the USSR was being stonewalled by the Soviet authorities. Pathologically suspicious of any outsiders, they were determined to ensure that every single "i" was dotted, every "t" crossed on Captain Trimble's paperwork before they would allow him within their borders.

Alone in a foreign country, with no friends and nothing to do, Robert spent afternoons idly walking the streets, looking in shop windows and taking in the sights and sounds and smells of the city. He became aware of an unsettling atmosphere of hostility. He wasn't mobbed by beggars and street sellers the way he had been in Cairo, but the groups of turbaned, bearded men who loafed outside the cafés, smoking their bubbling *ghalyans*[12] and drinking coffee, would pause in their conversations and stare at him in a way that made his flesh prickle—a cold, flinty gaze that radiated profound dislike.

Why the Iranians would regard an American officer in this way was a mystery to him. He wasn't aware that he was treading on occupied territory. Iran, after centuries of resisting colonization by the British and Russian empires, had finally succumbed in 1941 to a joint military invasion by the forces of both those countries. The purpose was dual:

first, to secure Iranian oil fields from capture by the Germans (who at the time were driving irresistibly into Soviet territory); and second, to establish a transit route—the Persian Corridor—through which Allied supplies could be ferried into the Soviet Union. The old ruler, Reza Shah, who had resisted Western demands before the invasion, was deposed, and his son, Mohammed Reza Pahlavi, was given the throne. The Persian Corridor had become a busy route, buzzing with military and diplomatic traffic.[13] The café dwellers of Tehran saw the foreign uniforms on their streets and were not pleased by the sight.

A more hospitable atmosphere was to be found in the American diplomatic compound. But even that wasn't free from strange experiences. Weird encounters in embassy buildings were starting to become a feature of Robert's life. It occurred on the Friday evening after his arrival, when he was dining alone in the sumptuous restaurant. The lieutenant in charge of the restaurant approached his table.

"Excuse me, Captain," he murmured. "The shah is dining here tonight, and would like to meet you."

"The who?" said Robert, not sure he'd heard right.

"The shah, sir. The Shah of Iran . . . the king . . . ?" Seeing the light of understanding dawn on Robert's face, the lieutenant explained: "The shah and the queen are dining at that table over there, and wish to be introduced to you."

Robert, dazed, stood up and followed the lieutenant across to a table where a smart-looking couple were seated. They were very young—no older than Robert himself. The man was handsome, with a long fleshy nose, slick black hair, and small, bright eyes—his sharp suit and penetrating gaze gave him the appearance of a Sicilian gangster. The woman was dressed and made up like a movie star. She was undoubtedly the most beautiful woman Robert had ever met—the kind who could stun a fellow dumb just by looking him in the eye. These two exquisite fashion plates were the first couple of Iran—the shah and his consort, Queen Fawzia.

It was the shah's habit to dine here on Fridays (the Islamic day of rest), as part of his efforts to maintain cordial relations with the Western

Allies. Or so Robert was told. What he was not told was why the shah would take an interest in him, a lowly American captain. Only later did he realize that it might have had something to do with the diplomatic status that had been conferred on him. It was also possible that the shah, who was meticulous in gathering information about everything that passed in his nation's diplomatic circles,[14] had picked up whispers about Captain Robert M. Trimble; that he was passing through on some mysterious purpose that was of interest to the highest and most powerful US authorities. (If so, he knew more than Robert himself did at this point.)

The introductions done, the shah, charmingly genial, shook hands and waved Robert to a seat. What followed was the most extraordinary interrogation. From the start, it was obvious that there was a coldness between the shah and his consort, and Robert found himself caught between them, fielding two completely different lines of questioning. The shah had recently been taking flying lessons and was fascinated by pilots;[15] he wanted to know about aircraft, and about Captain Trimble's experiences in combat (he'd clearly been briefed; he seemed to know rather a lot about Robert's record).

"Were you ever in danger?" he asked. "Did you lose men up there? What kind of planes did you fly?"

"We lost many men, sir. Good friends of mine. We had fires, blown engines, and wings torn apart by flak, but we managed to make it back every time."

While he talked, Robert was conscious of Queen Fawzia's eyes on him, and tried to avoid returning her gaze too ardently. It was difficult.

"Captain, are you married?" she asked suddenly.

"Why yes, I am, ma'am. I mean, Your Highness."

"What kind of fashions does your wife wear? Shoes—are they flat or high heels? What does she wear to formal events?"

The shah tried to interrupt, but she talked over him, asking pointedly about the lives of women in America: How were they treated by their husbands? How did they bring up their babies? Where did they shop? How—

"Will you please be *quiet!*" the shah cut in. "I have questions *I* would like to ask."

"I have questions to ask too," she said.

"I have *important* questions," the shah hissed angrily. "This is not any business of yours."

The atmosphere between the two of them went suddenly from cool to icy. By contrast, Robert felt awfully hot. Glancing nervously at the bodyguards at the next table, and trying to keep his eyes respectfully on the shah, he answered the probing technical questions as best he could. He explained that he was really a ferry pilot now—no more combat for him.

Eventually, the uncomfortable meeting concluded with the shah inviting Robert to visit his home. Foolishly, Robert asked for the address. The shah chuckled and said he would send a note with the details.

And so, a few days later, Robert M. Trimble, the boy from Camp Hill, rolled up at the Niavaran Palace—the spectacular sprawl of formal gardens and parkland on the outskirts of the city that contained both the Niavaran Palace and the Sahebqraniyeh Palace, as well as grand pavilions and lodges. He was greeted at the door by a majordomo—an exquisite Iranian version of an English butler. To Robert's disappointment, neither the shah himself nor Queen Fawzia were present. (*Oh well*, Robert figured, *I guess he already got all the information he wanted out of me.* It didn't occur to him that the shah might have *failed* to get the kind of information he wanted.) The majordomo gave him a guided tour of the palace. In a state of awed wonder Robert passed through halls and chambers filled with light from arched stained-glass windows, walled and floored with glittering tiles, and hung with crystal. It was like walking around inside a cabinet of crown jewels.

When he finally found himself back outside, and the palace doors had closed behind him, Robert felt a sense of relief. Although he'd been a little disappointed, he was glad to have been spared the ordeal of a formal dinner. He'd been haunted by an image of himself at one end of a vast dining table, not knowing which fork to use, while the shah and the queen fired questions at him from the far end. (It would come as little surprise when, just a few months later, Fawzia left the shah and went back to her family in Egypt. Robert couldn't believe that the shah could have the poor taste to treat such a woman that way. "A lovely girl," he recalled wistfully.)

Mopping his brow, he put his cap back on, and began to march down the long driveway to the palace gates.

This time the airplane was a Curtiss C-46 Commando rather than a C-47, but otherwise everything was the same: another flight, more long hours of discomfort.[16] Robert was getting his first introduction to a Russian winter. The temperature had got milder between England and Cairo, cooled a little in Tehran, and now plunged below all reasonable limits.

The Soviet authorities had finally run out of reasons to keep him waiting and had cleared Captain Trimble to enter the USSR. Along with three other American personnel en route to Poltava, he was taken aboard a Russian-piloted C-46, and left Tehran behind.[17]

It was an uneasy journey, and he paid less attention to the discomforts and the cold. The first part of the flight was okay, soaring up above the Caspian Sea and turning northwest for Russia. Ahead lay the Caucasus Mountains, which marched across the gap between the Caspian and the Black Seas. As the crew began the long, slow climb to pass over the mountains, it began to snow.

Rapidly a full-scale whiteout developed. The Russian crew couldn't navigate their way through it. They weren't fazed, though; having surveyed what they could see of the landscape, they prepared to put the plane down on a small airfield they knew, at the little Armenian town of Armavir, near the southern skirts of the mountains.[18] As the plane approached the field, the pilot couldn't even see where the runway was. Robert, who didn't think it was possible to do such a landing, was beginning to learn about the techniques of flying in a Russian winter, and about the recklessness of Russian pilots. One day soon he would have to learn how to fly like this.

The landing was tense but miraculously successful. The crew and passengers spent the night at the airfield, where the Soviet commander treated them to a supper of local dishes, including one made with fish eyes (Robert discreetly disposed of his).

Next morning, they pushed on again. Not long after takeoff, the vast range of the Caucasus Mountains loomed up ahead—a great jagged fortress of rock and snow extending from one end of the horizon to the other. The plane began climbing to pass over it. Gradually it pulled up past twelve thousand feet—well above oxygen altitude, which transport planes rarely had to do. Robert watched spellbound as the spectacular barren peaks passed slowly beneath. He'd flown over the Rockies back home, but the spectacle of a great mountain range seen from the air was something you could never tire of—especially from this low altitude, where the peaks were so close you could almost have stepped out onto their snowy caps.

Almost as soon as the plane began its long descent on the far side, it ran into a bank of cloud, dropped down through it, and came out in another snowstorm. It wasn't as dense as the previous day's, so the Russians flew on, heading for the Red Army Air Force base at Rostov, an industrial city sprawling across the marshes where the River Don opened into the Sea of Azov. Like most Russian cities that had been under German occupation, Rostov had seen some fierce fighting, and was in a bad state.

At the air base, Robert got his first insight into the Russian temperament—convivial warmth at one extreme and brutal callousness at the other.

The four Americans were treated as honored guests by their Soviet military hosts. The commanding officer loaded them with as much vodka as they could drink, with the result that the Americans were all half-steamed before they'd even got past the reception. There was a play being performed that night in the base's theater, and the CO took them along as his personal guests. Robert and his compatriots were led in and found rank upon rank of Soviet personnel standing, waiting for the guests of honor to be seated (in the front row, naturally). As soon as their rears touched their seats, without a word of command, the Russians all sat down too.

Robert enjoyed the performance, despite not understanding a word of it (it had wolves in the title, he recalled, but there were none in the play), and passed an altogether pleasant, vodka-hazed evening. The next morning, accompanied by the commanding officer and his staff, Robert, the other Americans, and the flight crew headed out to their plane. A concerned-looking sentry reported that he and his comrades had heard noises coming from the aircraft during the night, and he demanded to be allowed to inspect it. The pilot opened up the cargo compartment and peered inside. There, lurking in the shadows and frozen almost to death, was a teenage boy—he looked to be about fifteen.

The Russian officers interrogated the poor kid fiercely. As far as Robert could make out from the interpreter's commentary, the boy had hopes of being a soldier; too young to enlist, he had stowed away in the belief that the plane was going to the front line and that he would be drafted into the Army as a punishment, in spite of his age. Whether he was a local or had been in the plane since the emergency stopover at Armavir, Robert couldn't tell. It was a brave but foolish act—having spent the night in the plane, the boy was half-dead with hypothermia.

Simmering with suppressed anger at having such an embarrassing scene take place in front of foreigners, the Russian CO proceeded to give the Americans a grand diplomatic farewell. Meanwhile, the boy was dragged away, and the last Robert saw of him he was being taken behind a hangar. "Oh, he'll get his wish," the interpreter said darkly, but whether he meant punishment or a place in the Army, or both, wasn't clear. A few minutes later, against the noise of the C-46's engines starting up, Robert believed he heard a single gunshot from the direction of the hangar.

Feeling a shiver that had nothing to do with the cold, he wondered what the hell kind of a country he had come to.

4.

BEHIND THE CURTAIN

February 15, 1945: Station 559, Poltava Air Base, Ukraine
Headquarters of Eastern Command, USSTAF

With a crackle of breaking frost, the C-46's door pushed open. Captain Robert M. Trimble, stiff and chilled from the long flight, stood in the doorway and looked out at Poltava Air Base.

Instantly he was hit by the wind, a cold slap in the face that made him gasp. Blowing uninterrupted across hundreds of miles of Ukrainian Steppe, it was the coldest thing he had ever experienced. It was a lazy wind—instead of taking the trouble to go around your body, it just blew straight through, taking your breath with it and leaving icicles on your rib cage. Winter in the Alleghenies had nothing on this. Maybe it explained the coldheartedness of the Russians. Robert still hadn't got over what had happened to that boy at Rostov. (Or rather, what he *believed* had happened. The things he would witness firsthand over the next few months would do nothing to shake that belief.)

Catching his breath and hugging himself, he stepped down onto the frozen ground and looked around at Poltava. It didn't look any better from here than it had from the air as they were flying in. Pale rank grass, dusted with snow, stretched to the horizon in every direction. Nearby were some bombed-out buildings, a few flimsy-looking shacks, and, in the distance, new Quonset huts and rows of wooden barracks. Underfoot, the hardstanding on which the C-46 was parked was made from pierced-steel planking—the US Army's all-purpose emergency surfacing material. The runways were made from it too. This stuff was intended to be used as a temporary measure, but apparently nobody had got around to replacing it with concrete. Most of the paths appeared to be surfaced with nothing but frozen mud.

Poltava Air Base looked like Hell with everybody out to lunch.

Until just over a year ago, the Luftwaffe had been flying missions from here, and they hadn't been happy about giving it up. In September 1943, with the Red Army closing in on them, the German occupiers destroyed as many of the base's buildings as they could, and mined others with remote-control demolition charges. The runways too were wrecked. Since then, only the bare essentials had been done to get the airfield functioning again.

It wasn't only the air base that had suffered. The whole Poltava region had seen some of the most ferocious fighting on the Eastern Front. The huge battles of Kursk and Kharkov had been fought just to the east of here in 1942 and 1943, and the battle for Poltava itself had been a savage one. War had plowed through the area twice—once in 1941, when the region was swallowed up in Operation Barbarossa and became part of the Third Reich, and again in 1943, when the Soviet Union clawed it back in the Dnieper-Carpathian Offensive. Millions had fought, and hundreds of thousands had died, in those vast battles. The USSR had lost more than a million men and women killed or wounded in the fight for this region— just a fraction of their losses in the Great Patriotic War.

In the aftermath of this conflagration, the first small group of Americans arrived at Poltava in the spring of 1944: engineers to clear the battle damage and build new facilities, preparing the way for the airmen that were to follow.

It was an ambitious plan that brought them here—to use Poltava as a stopover base for long-range bombing missions. Much of Germany's industry was in the eastern half of the Reich, beyond the reach of British and American bombers based in England and Italy. The four-engine heavies that formed the bulk of the Allied strategic bombing force didn't have the range to hit targets that far away and then make it back to England. They could be fitted with extra fuel tanks, but that would reduce the bomb loads they could carry. The solution was to bomb these remote targets and then fly the much shorter distance onward to bases in Soviet territory. There they could refuel, load up with more bombs, and hit another set of targets on the way back to their bases. This was "shuttle" bombing. It was a bold concept, and totally dependent on cooperation from the Soviet Union.

Despite profound unwillingness on the part of Stalin, Operation Frantic was agreed on. The Eighth and Fifteenth Air Forces (based in Britain and Italy respectively) would be taking part. The base at Poltava was designated the headquarters of the newly created Eastern Command, under the overall control of the United States Strategic and Tactical Air Forces in Europe (USSTAF). Two satellite bases near Poltava were incorporated into the project. American supplies, fuel, and munitions poured in, buildings were put up and steel planking laid down, and soon Poltava was a functioning air base again. The Americans didn't have the place all to themselves—it was under overall Soviet command and was a base for Russian fighter squadrons too—but they had all the facilities they needed. Combat operations began in June 1944.

The Frantic missions were few in number, and the results didn't live up to the planners' hopes. The whole of Operation Frantic quickly began to buckle under the colossal obstructiveness of the Soviet Union. By this stage in the war, Stalin had begun to believe that the USSR could win without its allies. He would take anything the Americans and British could give—such as Lend-Lease supplies—but he had little desire to reciprocate. Moreover, there was Soviet disapproval of the Western Allies' strategy of pulverizing German industry; the Soviet way was to slaughter the people and capture the industrial facilities.[1] Above all, Stalin did not like having foreign military forces trampling around in his front yard, going places and seeing things he didn't want them to see and bringing their alien capitalist values with them. American personnel at

Poltava were kept to a bare minimum, and were watched closely, spied on, and escorted everywhere by Soviet guards.[2]

As the base was under overall Red Army Air Force command, they provided its defenses. The base was surrounded by anti-aircraft guns (which American personnel weren't allowed to inspect closely).[3] The defenses looked impressive, but when it came to the test, they proved pathetically weak. When the Luftwaffe decided to attack Poltava on the night of June 21–22, they had a clear run and easy pickings.

Squadrons of American B-17 bombers and P-51 fighters had arrived that afternoon on a shuttle mission, having bombed targets in eastern Germany. The fighters went to one of the satellite fields; the bombers were split between Poltava and the second satellite. They were parked around the half of the field allocated for American use, and spread out; but the dispersal wasn't as good as it should have been. Regulations set by the Soviet authorities dictated that all parked aircraft must be a certain minimum distance from the runways. As a result, the dispersal space was limited and planes were too close together.[4]

The raid began just after midnight. Luftwaffe aircraft began dropping flares, one after another, until the whole airfield was lit up like a dance floor. As the flares floated down on their little parachutes, there was an eerie pause, filled with the drone of approaching aircraft. When they hit, the impact was like a semi truck through a picket fence. Wave after wave of Junkers Ju 88s and Heinkel He 111s flowed overhead, slamming the base with a barrage of demolition bombs, then raining down thousands of incendiaries and antipersonnel bombs all across the field. "It lasted for an hour or so," the CO of Eastern Command recalled. "They hit us with everything except the kitchen stove, and I'm not sure that I didn't see even one of those when I looked round afterwards."[5] The midnight summer sky turned red with erupting fireballs and filled with mounting columns of black smoke; the fuel and bomb dumps were hit, and half a million gallons of aviation-grade gasoline and thousands of bombs went up in a cataclysm of flame.

The Russian anti-aircraft gunners blazed away with courage and ferocity and hit precisely nothing; Soviet night fighters were scrambled, but failed to shoot down a single plane.

Next morning, the Americans and Russians began to count up their losses. Only two American personnel had been killed, but the Russians had lost thirty, mostly in attempts to fight fires. The majority of the American aircraft had been lost. There had been seventy-three B-17s on the field. Most had been hit, forty-seven of them totally destroyed, reduced to scatters of melted Alclad from which the huge tail fins stood up intact, like gravestones. The airfield was out of action for two days because of unexploded bombs. One of the official historians of Eastern Command would later compare the devastating raid to the Japanese attack on Hickam Field, Pearl Harbor.[6] The Germans were so pleased with their success, they came back again the next night and bombed the satellite base at Mirgorod; again the Soviet defenses were absolutely ineffective.[7]

Official relations between the Americans and their Soviet counterparts deteriorated. For the American high command, the raid was a severe black mark against the viability of Operation Frantic. Only seven shuttle missions were run, and by the end of September 1944 the operation had been put on ice. Eastern Command was reduced to just two hundred men and women—the "Winter Detachment." The only thing preventing the command being shut down altogether was the usefulness of having a foothold in the Soviet Union.

Eastern Command acquired a new role: salvage of American aircraft that had made emergency landings in Soviet-held territory, and evacuation of their crews. Another role was envisaged too: with the Red Army pushing deeper into Poland, the Americans hoped that Poltava would be a good receiving center for the flood of liberated US prisoners of war that was bound to start sometime soon.

But as with Operation Frantic, cooperating with the Soviets would prove frustrating. The entire Soviet system, from Stalin down to the local political operatives, disliked the presence of Americans. The mechanics and pilots who made up the aircraft salvage teams had to venture far from the confines of the base and go deep into the areas behind the Russian front line. The Soviet authorities saw them as nosy, interfering, always poking about, witnessing and commenting indignantly on the Soviet way of doing things, especially in the occupied territory of liberated Poland. The Americans didn't like what they saw in Poland, and some of them had the nerve to say so.

Russian sensitivities about Poland went back to 1939, when the country was divided up between Nazi Germany and the Soviet Union. Tens of thousands of Polish political prisoners were taken away to camps at Smolensk in Russia. They included most of the officer corps of the Polish Army, who were perceived as a source of nationalist resistance. Stalin already had a deep loathing and distrust of Poland and the Poles, rooted in the history of the two nations.[8] The mere possibility of insurrection was more than he could tolerate. In March 1940 Stalin and the politburo authorized the NKVD (the state security and intelligence police) to exterminate the twenty thousand prisoners.

The incident might have passed unnoticed by the outside world if it hadn't been for the German invasion in 1941. German officers stationed near Smolensk discovered that a massacre had taken place. An investigation led to the uncovering of four thousand bodies buried in the Katyn Forest, about twelve miles west of the city. Locals recalled the truckloads of Poles that were taken from the prison and driven out into the forest. The convoys and the gunfire went on for days.

In 1943, facing expulsion from Russian soil by the advancing Red Army, and guessing that they might be blamed for the massacres, the Nazi regime decided to publicize their discovery internationally. They boosted their investigations, bringing in the Red Cross and setting up an international commission. What followed was one of the greatest displays of political hypocrisy of the twentieth century, as two mass-murdering nations pointed accusing fingers at each other.

The Polish government in exile, based in London, had known about the deportations of 1939 and 1940, but the truth about the Katyn massacre came as a hideous shock. They pressed for further investigations and asked that action be taken to bring the Soviet Union to account.

The Soviets responded with frigid hostility.[9] Foreign Minister Molotov indignantly denied that the massacres had been a Soviet deed (as a member of the politburo, his signature was actually on the document authorizing the extermination). It must, the Russians insisted, have been yet another Nazi atrocity. Moreover, the Soviets claimed that the Polish government in exile was now actively collaborating with the Nazis in trying to shift the blame.

Alarmed that the "Big Three" Alliance might be jeopardized, Winston Churchill did what he could to shut the Poles up and pacify Stalin. It was no use. The Poles continued to protest. On April 25, 1943, the Soviet government formally broke off diplomatic relations with them. Western hopes of a restored, democratic Poland were ruined, and the Soviets began preparing to install a Communist-friendly government. As the Red Army pushed across Poland, the NKVD followed in its wake, enacting the plan. The puppet government was established in Lublin in 1944, and the Sovietization of the country, which had been interrupted in 1941, resumed.

It was a brutal process, and Stalin did not want his allies to witness it. He mistrusted them; the Polish government in exile still existed, and Churchill and Roosevelt continued to support it. Stalin believed that the British and the Americans might engage covertly in helping anti-Communist nationalists to resist his puppet. The USSR was busy putting in place its vision of postwar Eastern Europe, and its allies seemed to feel entitled to judge and object to Russian actions.

Naturally, the Americans and the British who witnessed those actions saw it rather differently. They believed they were fighting for a world that was free of repression and tyranny, not a Stalinist empire east of the river Elbe.

Caught up in all of this were the prisoners of war, whose liberation was getting closer and closer as the Red Army pushed across Poland. Added to the callous Soviet attitude to their plight was the problem of getting American help into Poland. Anticipating the difficulties, and the potential risk to liberated prisoners, the men at the top of the American military and diplomatic services secretly made preparations for working around the Soviets.

The first requirement was to have covert personnel in the field in the regions where the prison camps were located. That was a problem in itself. There was no existing intelligence system in place that could be used. Throughout 1944 there had been negotiations between Washington and Moscow about cooperating on intelligence in Eastern Europe, all of which had come to nothing. In early 1944, an idea was floated for America's OSS and Russia's NKVD to run an exchange program, with OSS officers in Moscow and NKVD officers in Washington. The Russians were eager, but the scheme was shot down by President Roosevelt.[10] He was entering an election year, and allowing Soviet agents into the United States would be a propaganda gift to his political opponents.

Throughout the summer, other ideas for getting OSS/NKVD cooperation in Eastern Europe had been suggested, but were all blocked by Stalin and his foreign minister, Molotov. General Pavel Fitin, the deputy director of the NKVD, was enthusiastic. Fitin was the brilliant spymaster who had tried to warn Stalin in 1941 that the Germans intended to invade. His relationship with Stalin and Molotov was uneasy. While their ideological paranoia urged them to keep foreigners out, Fitin saw the value in maximizing all sources of intelligence-gathering. He even used his discussions with General William "Wild Bill" Donovan, head of the OSS, to chisel information out of him about OSS training, technology, and methods—information that Donovan happily (and rather naively) supplied.[11] Fitin was willing to bypass both Molotov and Stalin, and suggested ways of infiltrating OSS officers into Eastern European countries such as Yugoslavia, Hungary, and Romania secretly through diplomatic channels.[12] But in Poland, where the most important German strategic effort was focused (and where the POW crisis was likely to occur), the diplomatic channels did not exist.

As 1944 wore away, Donovan made request after request for permission to put OSS agents into Poland for intelligence-gathering purposes.[13] The requests were denied. In fact, there were so many requests from the OSS, continuing on into 1945, that a dispassionate observer might wonder if they were deliberately designed to distract the Russians from more subtle infiltration efforts.

In November 1944, Major General Edmund W. Hill was posted to Moscow, where he joined the American Military Mission as head of its air division and overall commander of all USAAF units and activities in Russia.[14] Hill's previous appointment had been in Britain, as CO of the Eighth Air Force's Composite Command.[15] Seemingly an innocuous umbrella organization for various specialized units, Composite Command included the 492nd Bomb Group, the unit that provided airlift services for the OSS. The modified Liberator bombers of the 492nd were used for parachuting agents into occupied territories. General Hill was deeply involved in operational planning for OSS mission-drops.[16] If the Military Mission in Moscow had wanted a man who was intimately connected with the operational structure of the OSS in Europe but was not officially an OSS officer, they could not have chosen better than General Edmund Hill.[17]

All the elements that would be needed for a covert operation in Soviet-occupied territory were coming into place.

When Captain Robert M. Trimble stepped out of his transport onto the frozen ground of Poltava on February 15, 1945, he knew nothing about such things.[18] But he was about to begin learning.

Soon he would find out firsthand about the Soviets, including what they thought about Americans and about a lot of other things in this war. He had already seen the bewildering contrast between the wonderful, warm hospitality the Russians could show and the callousness that was the other side of it. What he didn't know was how deep the callousness could run, and how horrifying the effects could be. A seasoned veteran of air combat he might be, but in many respects he was still an innocent in the ways of war. The Eastern Front could teach a man about the uttermost ends of war, and how human beings could become beasts.

There were Russian sentries already on hand as Robert and the other passengers disembarked, and a jeep was waiting to take them to the American camp. The sentries had their bayonets fixed: the long, sword-like Russian type that looked particularly threatening. Robert glanced enviously at the men's fur-lined caps; he'd have to snag one for himself as quickly as possible.

The jeep sped across the snowy field. Drawing into himself against the biting cold, Robert had little attention to give to his surroundings. There were few planes scattered about: a couple of C-47s and two or three battle-scarred B-24 Liberators and B-17 Flying Fortresses bearing a mixture of bomb group markings (presumably these were the salvaged planes that he was here to ferry home). Most of Poltava's aircraft—its squadrons of Russian Yak fighters—were dispersed at the far end of the field. The only thing nearby with Soviet markings was a two-seater biplane that looked like a relic from World War I—a Polikarpov U-2 that the Soviets used for light local transport.

Robert was taken to the officers' quarters—a wooden barracks hut among a cluster of identical buildings lining the edge of a dreary roadway. Looming over it all was a row of old apartment buildings, blackened by fire and bomb-damaged. He had been instructed to report to the commanding officer immediately on arrival, so he deposited his kit and set off for headquarters. Following a sign nailed to a dead-looking tree beside a muddy road, he walked past the broken façades of more burned-out buildings and found the HQ of Eastern Command, which was another wooden shack. It was even less impressive than Debach HQ, which at least had nice trees around it.

Robert went in and, having expected to be kept waiting, was admitted to the CO's office with startling speed. Here he got his first view of the man who was about to turn his life upside down and scare the living daylights out of him.

Colonel Thomas K. Hampton was a man of indeterminate age and even more indeterminate status. His premature baldness made him look older than he probably was, and his heavy eyebrows, solemn eyes, and long jaw enhanced the effect. Robert would know him for quite a while before discovering that there was a good deal of humor and warmth in Colonel Hampton; right now, he had little enough to be humorous about.

The status of his command was uncertain. In terms of its administrative position, Eastern Command was equivalent to formations like the Eighth and Fifteenth Air Forces, and yet it had hardly any infrastructure, no subordinate units, and its complement of aircraft was limited to a handful of transports. In scale, it was on a par with a small transport and maintenance battalion, and yet its senior officers were at the very center of relations between the war's two most powerful combatant nations.

At a personal level, the Americans got on well with the Russians. There were frequent parties at the officers' and enlisted men's clubs, and gatherings at the base's theater and Russian restaurant, to which the Russians brought their vast talent for lively celebration and a real air of hospitable warmth. But then there was the official relationship, which was policed by the NKVD and colored by two sets of values and principles which were worlds apart.

About half of Colonel Hampton's time was devoted to diplomatic liaison with his Soviet opposite number, Major General S. K. Kovalev, overall commander of the Poltava base. Besides being an enthusiastic reveler, Kovalev was a cunning diplomat, whereas Hampton didn't really have the temperament for it. He regarded it as his duty to put the interests of American service personnel first and had no patience with Soviet obstruction and little ability with diplomatic doublespeak.

There were one or two officers in Eastern Command who, while not exactly sympathetic to the Soviets, empathized with the Soviet viewpoint; they regarded Hampton as needlessly antagonistic.[19] He had been barred by the Russians from flying into Poland because they believed he was gathering political intelligence (which was how they viewed reporting on Soviet misconduct).[20] He never neglected to stick up for his men. There had been sporadic incidents in which unknown Russian soldiers had shot dogs belonging to American servicemen. Hampton informed General Kovalev that his men took "a very serious view of such cruelty to animals," and warned that if the men ever caught a Russian soldier injuring a dog, "I refuse to take any responsibility for what might happen to the Russian."

Robert would grow to like Colonel Hampton, and eventually learned firsthand about the stresses of his position. He greeted Robert with a sour smile. "Welcome to paradise, Captain Trimble," he said.

Robert laughed, and murmured something about being keen to

take up his duties. Hampton looked oddly at him and asked if he understood fully what his duties were.

"Why yes," said Robert. "I'm here to ferry those salvaged aircraft back to their groups." He guessed that the Forts would be going to England, and the Libs to Italy, and wondered if they'd all have to go via the tortuous Tehran route.

Hampton frowned sternly at him. "You're not here to be a ferry pilot," he said. "Didn't they brief you in London?" He demanded to see Robert's passport, and studied it closely while Robert felt the first prickles of cold sweat. "When the clearance request came through from Tehran saying you were down for temporary duty only, we had to query USSTAF about your appointment, to be sure we had the right man.[21] Seems we do. Have you taken a look at this passport, Captain?" Hampton said. "This is a diplomatic passport, identifying you as a United States government official." He handed it back. "You should've been briefed on this back in England."

Robert had a dizzying sense of déjà vu; suddenly he was back in that office in the US Embassy in London, objecting stridently while they tried to hustle him into being a spy.

"You're not here to be a ferry pilot," Hampton repeated. "I have enough pilots for the work we do here. That was just a ruse to get you out here. Your appointment comes from the Military Mission in Moscow. You'll be working with the OSS, Captain Trimble; you're going to be our agent in Poland."

When Robert bunked down that night, his head was spinning. He was exhausted; it seemed like days had passed since setting out from Rostov that morning. Whole days of bewilderment, briefing, and suppressed indignation. He'd been lied to, right from the start. He could excuse his old commander, Colonel Helton—he'd almost certainly been just as dumb about this as Robert himself. But somebody somewhere, in the shadowy upper reaches of the chain of command, had cooked up a lie and made him eat it.

His course was set, and there was nothing he could do about it. They'd caught, plucked, and basted him without him even realizing it. How could he have been so stupid? The thought that he had traded the opportunity to go home to Eleanor—even if it was just a couple of weeks—for *this* . . . this nightmarish mission that sounded like a one-way ticket to a garrote or a firing squad, it was enough to make a man weep.

Robert's first impulse when Colonel Hampton delivered his dry-gulching was to rebel, to refuse as he had in London when they'd tried to make a spy of him (as he thought). But he suppressed the urge; it wouldn't do here, in this back-of-beyond place, with this dark-eyed nemesis staring at him. So he bit back his indignation and asked what kind of "agent" he was meant to be, what his task was, and what the OSS had to do with it.

"Don't worry," said Hampton, "we're not going to parachute you into Berlin or anything like that."

Robert was glad to hear it. But when he heard what *was* going to be done with him, he almost choked. He listened dumbly as Colonel Hampton gave him his first unsettling glimpse behind the curtain.

Eastern Command, the Military Mission, and the United States government were facing a humanitarian crisis. All across the disintegrating territories of the Third Reich, millions of prison camp inmates were being turned loose. Rumors were coming through that they were being abused, enslaved, and massacred. How true these stories were, nobody could tell.

First had come the death camps, many of which were in the east of the Reich. In July 1944, the Soviets had liberated the death camp at Majdanek in eastern Poland, and even they were shocked by what they found there. In this instance they took their human responsibilities seriously, giving aid to the survivors and beginning trials of captured Nazis. By the end of 1944, they had even established a small museum at Majdanek memorializing what had been done there. Journalists from around the world were brought there to witness it.[22] Behold the nature of fascism, the Soviets declared.

Other kinds of camps were less horrifying, and Soviet sympathies were not moved at all. When Red Army units began encountering the dozens, then hundreds, of satellite camps and forced labor camps, they wanted no responsibility for them. The Poles and the Ukrainians could at least try to get home. The inmates from other nations had no hope at all.

On January 12, 1945, the Red Army, having halted on the Vistula River to build up their strength, launched the massive Vistula-Oder Offensive, pushing deep toward Germany. The Soviet Union's Western Allies watched anxiously as the Russian front line drew closer to the prisoner of war camps that were clustered around the German-Polish border. The stalags and oflags were filled with thousands upon thousands of American and British prisoners, as well as French, Dutch, Polish, Canadian, Australian, and every combatant nationality.

Russia's own people were also imprisoned, some in POW camps, many more in concentration camps, where they had been murdered in their thousands along with the other victims of the Holocaust.

The Soviet attitude toward soldiers who had allowed themselves to be taken prisoner was well known. It had been articulated in Marshal Stalin's infamous Decree of the Stavka of the Red Army Supreme High Command, Number 270, of August 1941, which declared that Red Army officers and commissars who became prisoners were "criminal deserters" who had "breached their oath and betrayed their Homeland." They should be shot by their commanders if possible, and their families would be arrested. The order, together with Stalin's preamble to it, which equated all acts of surrender with cowardice and desertion—colored the attitude of Russian soldiers toward POWs for the rest of the war, and beyond.[23] So did Stalin's declaration, when asked to comment on the order, that "there are no prisoners of war, only traitors."[24] A further order, No. 0391, reiterated that deserters and traitors must be put to death.[25] These decrees were made in the climate of shock and fear that came with the German invasion of the Soviet Union and were designed to encourage Red Army troops to fight to the death. The views they embodied took root.

Would this attitude be limited to the treatment of liberated Russian POWs, or would it also lead to mistreatment of Americans, British, and others? In military and diplomatic circles in Washington and London, and in the British and American Military Missions in Moscow, they suspected that it would. They began to lay plans, and Poltava—that fragile little island of America in the vast Communist bloc—was their focus.

Officially they professed to believe that the Soviet regime would do right. Accordingly they prepared transport, supplies, and contact teams for transfer to Poltava and on into Poland. As soon as the camps started being liberated, contact teams would round up American and British POWs and transfer them to holding centers where they could be given emergency care. Then they would be flown promptly to Poltava, where a hospital and accommodations would be established. From there, they could be transferred as quickly as possible via the Persian Corridor or the Black Sea ports, and shipped home.

Such a plan had worked before. The first mass liberation of POWs in Eastern Europe had occurred with the fall of Romania in August 1944. Their evacuation was arranged quickly by the American and Romanian governments, before Soviet forces took control of the country.[26] There would be no such opportunity in Poland. The Soviets were eating it up in swathes, and already installing their Communist-friendly government.

So things stood in mid-February 1945, when Colonel Hampton sketched out the situation to a bewildered Captain Trimble in his office at Poltava. Robert couldn't imagine what all these vast political matters had to do with him. What could he possibly be expected to do about all those thousands of prisoners? It sounded like either there would be a massive airlift evacuation of POWs or a huge diplomatic fight between the Allies. Other than maybe flying a plane as part of the airlift, there didn't seem to be anything he could contribute.

He wondered when Hampton would get around to explaining his hair-raising allusions to Robert being some kind of agent, working with the OSS, and not being parachuted into Berlin.

The official plans and preparations depended on Soviet cooperation. Theoretically, there ought to be no problem. Only four days ago, the latest "Big Three" conference had ended at Yalta in the Crimea. (Poltava had experienced a brief resurgence of activity, with Eastern Command providing air transport services for the British and American delegations attending the conference.) Roosevelt, Churchill, and Stalin had signed their names to an agreement which included provisions on the treatment of liberated prisoners of war.[27] They must be kept separate from enemy prisoners; they must be fully cared for, sheltered, fed, and clothed; and full access must be given at all times for repatriation officers representing the POWs' home nations to inspect the camps and evacuate their people.

Stalin had signed the agreement, but it was doubtful whether he would even give permission for the Americans to conduct their own evacuation and welfare program, let alone cooperate actively with it. Hence the covert American preparations for an alternative way to get their men out. Whistling innocently, the Americans smiled benignly at the Soviet Union, while behind the Soviets' backs the Military Mission and its contacts in the OSS arranged to bring in an unsuspecting outsider to do their work.

"You're being appointed assistant operations officer," Hampton told Robert. "Officially your role will be aircraft salvage and aircrew rescue. But that's just your cover. What you'll really be doing is penetrating into Poland to make contact with POWs. It's your job to gather 'em up and get 'em to safety."

Robert was assured that the Soviets would tail him relentlessly and do whatever they could to track and restrict his movements. But they couldn't touch him. His diplomatic passport, plus his status as an authorized US officer on sanctioned aircraft salvage business, should give him immunity from arrest and detention. That was the theory. As he would learn later that day, when his briefing got down to details and he met the two men who were going to be his contacts out in the field, his diplomatic status would actually put him in greater danger.

He would just have to ensure that the Russians didn't discover what he was doing, and watch them even more carefully than they watched him.

5.

A BRUTAL AWAKENING

A jeep roared along the road leading toward the village of Brzezinka, swerving to avoid shell holes and scatters of rubble. Its passengers clung on, bracing themselves against being flung out. Every fifty yards or so, the Russian driver had to slam on the brakes and lurch off the road to allow vehicles to pass the other way. The road was busy with traffic going both ways—artillery, supply trucks, ambulances, and troops going to and from the front line, creating a series of stop-go jams that went on for mile after mile.

During each pause, Robert Trimble, sitting in the backseat of the jeep, noticed that the sounds of gunfire had grown a little louder. Almost immediately after he had disembarked from the plane at Kraków, the faint rumble had been perceptible. It had grown gradually to an intermittent thunder that sounded like it was coming from just over the next hill. Now, as the jeep halted on the edge of the village, it was just possible to make out the burr of machine guns in between the booms of Russian artillery and the thunder of German shells exploding. The sweeping Soviet advance that had begun a month ago had slowed to a halt a few miles from here, and the Red Army was fighting for every foot of ground.

Robert looked about him. The jeep had halted to let through a column of Red Army troops, all dressed in their long greatcoats, some with white winter smocks. Most carried the distinctive submachine guns with round magazines that they called *Papasha*—"Daddy." A column of roaring, squealing tanks rolled by with squads of soldiers riding on them. Robert was astonished to realize that some of the tank commanders, standing up in their turret hatches, were women.

The jeep squeezed through the village streets. Despite the damage done by the battle that had passed through here a couple of weeks ago, it looked like a pretty place, with winding streets and tall, quaint, timber-framed houses.

It was his first day in Poland, and Robert had been diverted from his main mission. He had been brought to this place because there was something here that his superior officers at Eastern Command wanted him to look at and report on. Unusually, the Soviets were keen that an American come here to see it. Therefore, Colonel Hampton had regarded it as the perfect opportunity to get his agent rapidly into Poland, without the usual delays and stalling. Accompanied by a Russian escort and interpreter, Robert had set off from Poltava. He was in a daze, having had no chance yet to digest the intensive briefings or get his bearings.

His interpreter, sitting beside him in the jeep, was a young woman in Red Army uniform, with a second lieutenant's star on her shoulders. Her name was Maiya, and like many of the female interpreters the Soviets provided for Eastern Command, she was rather pretty. She had large, doe-like eyes, accentuated by Slavonic cheekbones and a plump underlip. Her hair was blond and glossy, worn in a neat, militarized Betty Grable style. Robert had been warned to regard Maiya with suspicion. The Soviets used pretty women as interpreters for the simple reason that they were liable to tempt unwary, sex-starved American personnel into being malleable and indiscreet. The interpreters—and the male officers provided as guides—were all, despite their Red Army ranks and uniforms, attached to the NKVD, the political police, the Soviet equivalent to the German Gestapo.

It had been founded under Lenin, in the turmoil that followed the 1917 Revolution. The Cheka, as the internal security police force was originally called, instantly became a byword for terror. Under Stalin's rule the People's Commissariat for Internal Affairs (*Narodnyy Komissariat Vnutrennikh Del*, or NKVD) acquired all the roles of a police and emergency service, and became the most powerful instrument of repression in the Soviet Union, responsible for purges and mass murder.

The NKVD policed every boundary—physical and ideological—between the Soviet Union and the outside world. It was Stalin's guard dog, and along with the Foreign Office it controlled every aspect of American experience in Soviet territory.

Women were a favorite conduit for the NKVD's spies. Around Poltava, the organization used local women in attempts to seduce information out of American servicemen. It was such a prevalent practice, the GIs joked that NKVD stood for "no ketch venereal disease."[1] The Red Army translators and officer escorts were a more subtle means of spying. The Americans at Eastern Command called them "bird dogs." They followed you everywhere and were adept at trailing.[2] Maiya seemed pleasant enough and struck Robert as entirely genuine. She had a coquettish little smile, which was very charming, and Robert was rather susceptible.

She wasn't smiling now, as the jeep passed the last house in the village. She looked rather apprehensive and unhappy. Maiya evidently wasn't looking forward to seeing what they had come to see. Neither was Robert. Based on the sketchy information he'd been given, it sounded like something that nobody would want to look at.

They had almost reached their destination. The jeep rounded a bend; there was a long straight ahead, beyond which Robert could make out wire fences with guard towers and brick buildings. Beyond were rows of barracks buildings. From the road it looked vast, the fences marching on and on into the distance.

The road was converging with a railroad track which split away from the nearby main line and curved round in a great arc. Together the road and rail track headed toward a long, low building made of brick, with a tower in the center and two archways through which road and railroad passed.

In answer to Robert's query, Maiya told him the name of the village they had just come through: Brzezinka it was called in Polish. In German they called it Birkenau. The neighboring town, which could be seen on the other side of the main railroad, was Oświęcim, which the Germans called Auschwitz.

The previous day

Your area of operations will be in this triangle encompassing the cities of Lwów, Lublin, and Kraków."

Put like that, it sounded simple. But when he began learning the details of what he was expected to do in that triangle, Robert's already rattled nerves took another hit. In fact, it wasn't so much the details as the *vagueness* of the details. It sounded like he was going to be relying on his own initiative an awful lot.

He studied the map on Colonel Hampton's wall. It was marked with colored pins and ribbons indicating aircraft crash-landing sites, transportation hubs, and the current German/Soviet front line. Most of the positions were approximate, based on information that had come in from Soviet and Polish sources via Moscow, plus intelligence from rescued aircrews and a fair amount of guesswork.

"Major Kowal will have more accurate information," Hampton said. "He's our operations officer. Officially, you'll be subordinate to him, but in practice you're answerable to me and to Moscow."

Robert understood that "Moscow" meant General Hill, who was CO of the Air Division, and General Deane, who was overall commander of the American Military Mission at the US Embassy.

The information on prisoners of war was even vaguer than that on downed aircrews. It was known that the recent Soviet advances had liberated some camps, but so far there had been no direct contact with any American or British POWs, and no information was forthcoming from the Russians. Nonetheless, the Military Mission in Moscow had many sources of intelligence, including agents and diplomatic channels, as well as sources in the Polish provisional government. The Polish authorities were happy to cooperate, despite being Soviet puppets (the process of Stalinization was in its early stages still). Information even came from within Germany, via the Swiss legation in Berlin, who passed on Wehrmacht reports of American POWs being left behind in the retreat.[3]

Then a breakthrough came. Just two days ago, while Robert was still en route from Tehran through the snowstorms of the Caucasus, a message had come through to General Deane at Moscow. Relayed from Lublin in Poland, the message confirmed everybody's fears—there were already thousands of liberated American prisoners wandering loose and uncared-for. The message originated from two officers who had escaped from a German POW camp, crossed German lines into Poland, and spent weeks there trying to find their way to freedom: paratrooper Colonel Charles Kouns and OSS Colonel Jerry Sage.[4] It was the first definite information that the Russians were not honoring their obligations under the Yalta agreement.

But in spite of all the leads and reports coming out of Poland and Germany, there was no information from the Soviets themselves: just glib denials.[5] All was fine, they insisted; liberated prisoners would be well cared-for in the reception centers that were being established in major towns at this very moment.

General Deane, alarmed by the message from Kouns and Sage, immediately briefed two of his senior staff officers to prepare for a trip to Lublin. On arrival, they were to inspect the Russian facilities in Lublin and any other Polish towns that were being used for receiving POWs, and arrange for their prompt evacuation by air to Poltava. Deane received assurances from the Soviet government that his two officers would have full and free movement in Poland and access to POW facilities.[6] Orders were sent to Poltava to begin preparing to receive hundreds of POWs, who would need to be accommodated and then sent on by air to Tehran.[7]

Deane's two officers, Lieutenant Colonels Wilmeth and Kingsbury, accompanied by an American interpreter, traveled from Moscow to Poltava on February 15, arriving on the very same day as Captain Robert Trimble.[8] Two very different branches of America's plans for POW evacuation—the official and the strictly off-the-record—were now in place and ready to be put into action. General Deane, despite all he knew about the Soviet way of doing things, professed high hopes for his little inspection team, and also for the POW contact teams, which had been assembled at the recommendation of the Military Mission and were currently supposed to be en route to Poltava from London. Privately, though, he thought the plan unlikely to succeed.[9]

Eastern Command applied immediately to the Soviets for clearance for the two colonels and their interpreter to fly from Poltava to Lublin to begin their tour of inspection.

Permission was denied.

So began a pattern that recurred frequently over the coming days and weeks. While Captain Trimble entered Poland with the Russians' assistance, clearances for Wilmeth and Kingsbury were repeatedly sought and repeatedly denied. Less than a week had passed since the signature of the Yalta agreement, and already the Soviets were failing to honor it. General Deane had consciously played soft with them on the POW issue prior to Yalta, for fear of provoking them.[10] In the weeks that followed, he began to grow impatient and angry.

He wasn't the only one.

Beyond General Deane, the US ambassador in Moscow, Averell Harriman, took a keen and close interest in the welfare of POWs in Soviet hands. So did Ambassador John G. Winant in London. Ambassador Winant had a personal interest in the matter; his own son was one of the prisoners likely to be liberated at any moment by Soviet forces.[11] The President of the United States, reflecting the feelings of all those American families with menfolk in German prison camps, also regarded the matter as profoundly important.

Fortunately for his nerves on that first day in Poltava, Captain Robert M. Trimble had little notion of how high and how far the chain of concerned parties went, or just how much hinged on his performance of the mission that was being entrusted to him. He was just meant to be a backup, an emergency sideline, but he might end up being the only way out for the POWs.

It had been made clear to him that it was a mission of extraordinary diplomatic sensitivity. He must never speak of it to anybody, even within military circles. If the Soviet government discovered that the United States was deliberately putting agents inside Soviet-occupied territory for the purpose of counteracting NKVD and Red Army procedures, it could lead to a diplomatic incident that could affect the course of the war, or even alter the geopolitical shape of postwar Europe. Even the OSS could only provide back-door support.

After his short but stunning introductory briefing by Colonel Hampton, Robert had walked out of the headquarters building an older, wiser, and significantly more worried man than he'd been when he went in. He was given no time to reflect. From headquarters he'd been herded off to the Operations Office, housed in yet another wooden shack, where he met Major Michael Kowal, the man whose assistant Robert was ostensibly going to be.

The two men hit it off immediately.[12] Like Robert, Mike Kowal was a veteran bomber pilot. He had completed his combat tour with the 94th Bomb Group, flying B-17s out of Rougham, Suffolk, back in the dark days of 1943, when the Luftwaffe was stronger and the Eighth Air Force fighter escorts only went halfway to the target.[13] Kowal believed in a brotherhood of bomber pilots, a breed apart from other airmen.[14] At twenty-seven, he was a couple of years older than Robert. A native of Passaic, New Jersey, Kowal was a lively spirit; he'd been an air-show stunt pilot before the war,[15] and was the beau ideal of an Air Force flyer: handsome and dark-eyed, with a chiseled jawline and a winning grin. His features were a little askew, as if his maker had set out to create a matinee idol but got the proportions slightly off. A good-looking fellow, though. He had Slavic ancestry, and spoke Russian, which was how he'd ended up on the staff at Poltava in the early days of Operation Frantic.

As operations officer, Kowal was responsible for coordinating aircrew rescue and plane salvage work in Poland. He had been taking part in the work himself until a few months ago, but was now grounded. The Russians disliked and distrusted Major Kowal intensely, bracketing him with Colonel Hampton as an illicit gatherer of political intelligence (back in November, he'd written a report on Soviet misconduct in Poland). Along with Hampton, the Soviets had barred Major Kowal from flying into Poland, and he was now restricted to Poltava.[16]

Robert was given a hasty briefing on salvage and aircrew rescue. American bombers and fighters, damaged in combat and unable to limp back to their bases in Britain or Italy, often made crash landings in Poland. It was Eastern Command's job to rescue the crews and salvage the planes, and bring both back to Poltava for transfer back to the crews' home units.

The Soviets were happy enough to help with aircrew evacuation, because they had no reason to be suspicious of the crewmen: they were in uniform, carried identification, and their landings had usually been observed by troops. A few crews had been subjected to interrogation, and Russian care was often rough and simple, but they were mostly treated as fellow warriors against the common enemy. The American rescue workers had little trouble getting them out of Poland, so long as they could get to wherever they were being quartered.

Aircraft were a little trickier. The War Department and USSTAF wanted them picked up and returned without delay. Not only were they very expensive, they were also classified technology which the Soviets were eager to acquire. Preaching what he hadn't managed to practice himself, Major Kowal briefed Robert on the importance of being diplomatic with the Russians, but at the same time ensuring that they didn't steal or wreck American aircraft. (Either was possible, depending on whether Air Force intelligence personnel or drunken soldiers got there first.) The practice was to send out a salvage team comprising an American flight crew and mechanics, plus Russian helpers and an interpreter. The Russians were supposed to help, but were likely to look for opportunities to seize the aircraft once it had been repaired.

Kowal's briefing was supplemented by a talk from the intelligence officer, Captain William Fitchen, a tall, serious fellow with blunt features and a vaguely cheerful demeanor. Another pilot turned staff officer, Fitchen knew more about the current situation on the ground in Poland than anyone. His job was to interrogate rescued aircrews, and he had helped furnish Hampton and Kowal with a detailed picture of how Soviet-American-Polish relations were working out and how the Russians were treating Polish citizens (badly). As a result of his role, Captain Fitchen was another man whom the Soviet authorities in Poltava regarded with deep suspicion.[17]

As he took in these briefings, Robert began to understand why the decision had been made to use this work as a cover for aiding POWs. It gave the officers involved a fairly free run of the country, albeit in company with bird dogs, and an excuse to travel to remote areas. It also allowed for intelligence-gathering, since the information about landing sites that came through from the Red Army was vague, and inquiries had to be made to find the exact locations of planes and crews. Under cover of this activity, Robert's mission was to contact and exfiltrate wandering prisoners.

That, of course, was the real trick, and he had no idea how he was supposed to achieve it.

He began learning the answer to that question in the last of his series of whirlwind briefings. Taking on an even graver air than he had shown so far, Colonel Hampton took Robert aside and escorted him to an office in the headquarters building. "I told you you're not going to be dropped into Berlin," he said. "Well, I have two men in this room who were trained for exactly that."

Robert was warned that the imperative for secrecy applied doubly from this moment on. The men he was about to meet were at Poltava unofficially, clandestinely, without the knowledge of either Russian or American personnel. They were the OSS agents he would be working with, and if their presence became known, a catastrophic diplomatic incident might ensue. Hampton opened the door, and with a sense of trepidation, Robert followed him into the office.

There were two men seated there, and after the dramatic buildup, they looked about the most unimpressive pair you could imagine. They were nondescript; their clothing was civilian, utilitarian, neither expensive nor cheap, smart nor shabby. They could have passed for tradesmen, shop workers, or laborers. Their faces were unremarkable, not particularly memorable. You wouldn't glance twice at them.

But of course, that was their aim. Their dull jackets and coats, worn-looking pants, and slightly frayed shirt collars had been painstakingly fabricated to German or Polish patterns at the OSS clothing depot in Brook Street, London, where they had the resources and skills to fake anything from a laborer's overalls to a German army uniform or a Gestapo suit, using materials brought in from the OSS office in Stockholm, where German-made articles of clothing, luggage, and personal effects could be purchased.[18]

How these two men had got to Poltava past the NKVD, Robert had no idea.[19] He was told nothing about the men other than Colonel Hampton's allusion to parachuting into Berlin.[20] Possibly they had been seconded from the Eagle project. Eagle had been set up to train Polish soldiers as behind-the-lines agents to infiltrate German industry in the guise of workmen.[21] More likely the two men had been drawn from the pool of Joes who formed the more highly developed Operation Tissue, also trained to infiltrate Germany. They were tasked for intelligence-gathering rather than sabotage, and their training was in communications, cryptography, espionage, forgery, lock-picking, and surveillance; their specialist combat training was limited to self-defense, which they received on top of core agent training in close combat and weapons. The agents were fed into the country from the OSS Westfield Mission in Stockholm, from where they went via sea routes into Denmark and on into Germany. Agents from the Tissue project were infiltrating enemy territory at this very moment.[22]

All Robert knew about the two men was that they were OSS, and that they had been diverted from their original mission to be his contacts.

Their purpose was to go deep into Soviet-occupied Poland, making contact with locals and gathering intelligence on liberated Allied prisoners of war: their condition, health, the locations where they had concentrated, and what, if anything, the Russians were doing to help them.

The two agents gave Robert an intensive, efficient briefing. Completely free of the camaraderie and military etiquette of his previous briefings, it was nothing but business: straight and concise. There wasn't the time, nor were there the facilities, for any kind of practical training, so their advice had to be sufficient. They instructed him on contact procedures and codes, providing him with a basic system of communications protocols, which he had to memorize there and then. They advised him on outdoor survival and gave him tips on fieldcraft. He believed that his upbringing ought to equip him for the job—all those winter weekends spent deer-hunting in the Pennsylvania hills had given him an understanding of outdoor living. What was entirely new to him was the instructions on avoiding pursuit, throwing off a tail, and most crucially of all, how not to get yourself killed.

Above all, he was told, the most important thing was not to antagonize the Soviets, especially not the NKVD. And if he sensed that he *had* antagonized them, he should on no account accept any kind of hospitality or transportation from them. There were all kinds of hazards in an occupied zone that had recently been a combat area, and it was only too easy to explain away a sudden death as an accident or the work of German agents. Robert's passport made him immune to arrest, but all the more vulnerable therefore to murder.

Robert didn't sleep well when he eventually hit his bunk that night. His mind kept going back to his talk with Colonel Helton at Debach, and the scale of the lie they'd both been told. So much for being "safely out of the combat zone." He wondered if there was any way out of it, any reason or excuse he could give that would make it clear that he couldn't possibly undertake this mission, that they'd got the wrong man. But everything that made him unsuitable—the fact that he was a pilot, not a spy, his lack of familiarity with the country and its politics—made him precisely the man they needed.

His course was set.

I n front of the brick gatehouse, the road crossed over the railroad just before the track ran in under the larger of the two archways. The jeep bumped over the sunken rails and followed the road through the smaller arch, waved past by the Russian sentries standing by.

What Robert saw inside that place would stay with him for the rest of his life.

He knew what the camps here had been used for. Everyone knew about Majdanek, and this appeared to be more of the same. And yet Auschwitz had attracted little attention in the Western press since its liberation—it was just "another Majdanek," and was overshadowed in the news by coverage of the Yalta Conference.[23] Few people had seen it with their own eyes. What was unprecedented about this place was its sheer scale. The Auschwitz-Birkenau camp was vast. Beyond the gatehouse, the road and the rail tracks ran on and on, straight as a die, the tracks dividing to straddle a long station platform. On either side, behind more layers of barbwire fencing, stood rank upon rank of barracks buildings. A few appeared to have burned down, but most were standing, hundreds of them in rows that stretched out to the left and right and marched away into the far distance.

There had been a thaw here lately; the snow was thin on the ground and turning to slush, adding to the air of grim, gray misery that pervaded the place. The jeep drove slowly on. It was hard to believe that this camp was just one part of a complex of dozens of camps that had sprouted in this corner of Poland like a malignant infection.

For Robert, Auschwitz-Birkenau remained in his memory as a collection of disjointed images. The shed where bodies, thin to their bones, naked, frozen stiff, were piled up, spilling out of the broken door—prisoners who had died of starvation, whose corpses the SS hadn't had time to destroy in their retreat. In another building Robert saw stacks of cans with bright red-and-yellow labels. The initial impression that this was a store of canned food was dispelled by the skull-and-crossbones symbol on the labels.

Robert picked one up. "Giftgas!" the label said, and "Zyklon." He asked Maiya to translate the label. "*Giftgas* means poison gas," she said. "This here is saying, 'To be only opened and used by experienced persons.'" There was a manufacturer's logo on the other side, beneath which was a warning that the product was authorized for use only in regions of the Reich east of the Elbe River, in Poland, the Baltic states, Scandinavia, and Sudetenland. The Nazis who had been captured and interrogated were claiming that the gas was used for disinfecting the inmates' clothing. But as Maiya told Robert, its true purpose was the extermination of human beings. They went to look at the place where it had been done.

Screened by birch groves at the far end of the camp stood the remains of the "crematoria," the death houses where victims had been gassed, hundreds at a time, and their corpses burned. The SS had tried to destroy the evidence; the "Krema" buildings had been half-demolished and set on fire. Reduced to slabs of broken concrete and brick, the gas chambers lay open to the sky and the sleet. Scattered about were more of the yellow-and-red-labeled canisters, open and empty.

It was almost unbelievable that there were still people living in the camp, nearly three weeks after its liberation. Thousands of inmates had chosen to stay behind when the others were force-marched westward by the Nazis, and the SS squads had only had time to murder about six hundred before fleeing the approaching Russians.

Just a few hundred people now remained in the barracks blocks, those too sick or scared to be moved. After liberating the camp, the Soviets had done all they could to alleviate the suffering of the thousands of survivors. Red Army medical teams, together with the Polish Red Cross, had set up a hospital in the main labor camp, in the town of Auschwitz itself, where the buildings were larger and more suitable for the purpose. Even now, a convoy of horse-drawn carts was taking weakened inmates, living skeletons bundled up in blankets, down the main road through the Birkenau camp, heading for the hospital.

The Russian doctors and the Red Cross had saved many, but others were beyond help. There had been 7,650 survivors in the Auschwitz complex when the Red Army arrived on January 27. By February 6, only 4,880 were still alive. Many left of their own accord, hoping to get home. Hundreds died, mostly of exhaustion.[24] Some were killed by kindness; Russian troops in the front line sent gifts of food to the camps, on which the starving survivors gorged themselves, and died.[25] Conditions were almost indescribable; shortly after the liberation, a thaw set in, and the thousands of frozen bodies began to rot.[26]

By the time Robert viewed Auschwitz-Birkenau, the cold had resumed, and the worst was past, but it left him with images that would live in his nightmares for decades to come.

In all his guided tour, Robert heard little mention of the Jews. As with Majdanek, the Soviets affected not to recognize that the mass murder had been focused primarily on the destruction of the Jewish race. The Communist view was that the camps represented the ultimate obscenity of fascism and capitalism: an industrial system which incarcerated and murdered its workers.[27]

But it could not be denied that the Soviet authorities had reacted promptly, efficiently, and humanely to the plight of the thousands of prisoners. Was it possible that American fears for their liberated POWs were misplaced? Might the Russians actually honor their obligations?

Robert didn't know. But when he got back aboard the jeep for the return journey to Kraków, he felt a grim resolve that had been absent since his briefing at Poltava. His lingering feeling that this mission wasn't for him, that they had chosen the wrong man, had dissipated. Whatever happened, he would do whatever he could to save his fellow men from suffering, and to bring them to safety and freedom.

On the same day that Captain Trimble visited the Auschwitz-Birkenau complex, three American ex–prisoners of war arrived at the US Embassy in Moscow, having made an extraordinary journey on foot and by train across Poland, the Ukraine, and Russia. The three officers told their story to an amazed General Deane.[28]

They had been in Oflag 64, a camp for officers at Szubin in western Poland, liberated on January 21. With no help from the Red Army, the three officers had traveled by themselves, and encountered hundreds of fellow Americans, all wandering, all wary of going to the camp that the Soviets were said to have established at Rembertów. Dodging the NKVD, the three officers headed for Moscow. They were the first ex-POWs to tell their stories in full to the American authorities. From them came the first detailed eyewitness testimony of the Russian failure to honor their obligations to Allied prisoners of war.

Soon, more and more stories began to filter through: stories of neglect, stories of abuse. Liberated prisoners had been fired on by Russian troops, robbed, herded with captured Germans; sick POWs had been force-marched along with their comrades, and hundreds were abandoned in the wilds of Poland or incarcerated in squalid camps.

It seemed that in the Soviet mind, the victims of fascist capitalism formed one category; soldiers who had surrendered to the enemy were still firmly in an entirely different one, a category for which no human sympathy was reserved.

6.

RUNNING WITH THE BIRD DOGS

February 1945: Somewhere in southeast Poland

The atmosphere inside the little stone-built barn was one of aching cold infused with the sour smell of damp, filthy clothing and unwashed bodies, almost strong enough to override the animal odors of the livestock. For the two-dozen men who had taken up residence in it, the barn was better than being outdoors in this cruel weather, where the wind could cut to the bone; and if the rumors were true, it was better than being under the care of the Russians.

Some of the men lay sleeping uneasily on the straw; others sat huddled against the walls, wrapped tight in their greatcoats, swaddled in rough blankets, with mufflers and hoods made from woollen rags, anything that could provide a layer of protection against the subzero temperature. There was warmth as well as a feeling of security in numbers, and men who had been utter strangers until a week ago bonded like old friends. The instinct for comradeship that had kept each of them going in combat now held them together in adversity.

The men, mostly Americans, had come from Stalags III-C in eastern Germany and XX-A in the north of Poland, both liberated by the Red Army at the end of January.[1] Of the thousands of prisoners set loose, with hardly any aid from their liberators, and nowhere else to go, many had hidden out in the local countryside for a while and then returned to the camps, desperate for shelter.[2] Hundreds of others, without food or transport, were force-marched by the Russians to towns and villages away from the front line, then abandoned there.[3] They were told to make their own way to Warsaw, where they would be collected for repatriation. Warsaw was more than two hundred miles away.

The bolder spirits struck out right away. A tiny handful made it out of Poland all the way to Moscow, or to the American outpost at Poltava. Hundreds were diverted from town to town, trying to get aid from the Soviet authorities and find some way home. Eventually they ended up in camps that the Russians had set up in cities such as Lublin, Lwów, and Rembertów, where they were kept under guard in unspeakable squalor, worse than the prison camps they had come from, without heating or sanitation and on starvation rations.[4] In some cases they were subjected to prolonged interrogation by Soviet NKVD officers.[5]

As small groups and pairs of ex-POWs drifted through Poland, news and rumors spread among them. Already, many were wary of venturing into the towns or coming into contact with Russian troops. They took refuge in small villages and farms, where they found Polish citizens willing to give them shelter and what little food they could spare.

Twenty-three of them had gathered in this small barn. They were a burden on the farmer, who attempted to feed them but couldn't provide more than a fraction of what they needed. They were also a potential danger to him. If the NKVD found out that Poles had sheltered foreigners, who could potentially be spies, they could face serious trouble.

Day followed day, and the men in the barn grew colder and weaker. A few had fallen sick. Sooner or later they would have to make the decision to give themselves up to the Russians. Each time it was discussed, they decided to wait a little longer. Perhaps some miracle would happen. Surely the American or British authorities must come for them soon, to take them out of this purgatory? The men hunkered down, huddled together, and waited.

Robert was woken by a gunshot. He lurched upright, gasping for breath, the loud bang echoing through his skull.

For a second he couldn't think where he was, or why, but then it came back to him. The pleasant dark tones of the Victorian furniture, aglow with polish, the ornate wallpaper, and the soft bed under him. He was in his room at the Hotel George in the Polish city of Lwów. Arriving late in the evening, dog-tired, he'd fallen asleep across the bed, half-undressed.

He looked blearily at his watch. Eleven o'clock. The gunshot was still reverberating in his head. He must have dreamt it, though he couldn't recall any dream. He stood up to finish undressing, and was startled out of his skin by another bang—as loud as if it were in the room with him. This time it was unmistakable—the sharp report of a rifle, echoing in the street outside. It was followed by raised voices, and laughter.

Edging back the curtain, he peeked out. At first he couldn't see anything alarming, just a couple of Russian soldiers loitering near some trash cans on the sidewalk below. One of them was holding his rifle in the crook of his arm, and both men were looking at the trash cans and laughing. By the dim glow of a nearby window, Robert could see something in one of the cans: something that seemed to be moving. With a cold, creeping horror, he realized that the thing was a person. A woman.

She had been forced into the trash can, with her upper body and lower legs sticking out the top. The soldiers were taking turns to swig from a bottle, and chatted idly, occasionally directing a taunt at the woman. She struggled weakly and moaned, but all she got in return was more abuse. She appeared to be naked from the waist down, and there were wounds visible where she'd been hit by rifle shots.

Trembling—either with horror or fear, he couldn't tell which—Robert reached for the washstand, where he'd left his belt; he unclipped the holster

and drew out his Colt. Glancing out the window, he saw that the two soldiers had been joined by a third, who shared in their little party. Robert
looked up and down the street. There was nobody about. There was a curfew, and citizens weren't allowed out after seven in the evening. Did he dare
to intervene? It was unthinkable. Even if he survived—one pistol against
three rifles—what would the consequences be for his mission, for all the
souls depending on him? Not to mention all the organization and secrecy
that had brought him here. The sights he had seen at Auschwitz flashed into
his head (they were hovering on the edge of his thoughts constantly). Would
he have raised a hand to stop that happening, if he'd had the chance? He
gripped the Colt, his finger trembling on the guard, and tried to force himself to act. He had to do *something*, didn't he, no matter what?

The decision was taken from him. One of the soldiers raised his
submachine gun and fired a short burst. The woman jerked, and then
was still. The soldiers went back to their liquor bottle.

Robert stepped back from the window, shaking from head to foot,
and sat down heavily on the bed. After a moment, he realized that he
was still gripping the Colt. He laid it aside.

Again he found himself wondering what the hell kind of world he had
come to. The boy in Rostov, the horrors of the Nazi camp, and now this.

He wouldn't be sleeping any more that night, so he sat for a while,
regaining control of himself. Then he went back to what he'd been doing
before dozing off. Laid on the nightstand were some slips of paper on
which he'd noted down the messages he'd already begun receiving from
the OSS agents out in the field. He picked them up. Forcing himself to
concentrate in spite of the scene he'd just witnessed, which kept replay-
ing itself in front of his eyes, he read through the messages again, sepa-
rating out the originals from the decoded versions he'd been working on.

The system was simple enough. With no way to maintain direct
contact, the agents communicated their intelligence bulletins to him
via Moscow. Robert had been given a phone number which put him
through to an office at the US Embassy. Once he had checked in and
confirmed his identity, the voice (he had no idea who the person was, or

what position they occupied) dictated the information. He then had to decode the message, which was designed to appear routine or trivial. It wasn't an ideal way to communicate, but it was all they had.

He was under observation most of the time. The George, like most hotels in Soviet territory, was owned by the Intourist organization, the USSR's state travel agency, which was run from Moscow by the NKVD.[6] He had been advised to use it as his headquarters. It was commonly used by Americans on salvage missions, so he could be reached easily there, and the Russians were comfortable with the arrangement.

The seemingly uninteresting, apparently routine communiqués from Moscow contained vital information on POW numbers, locations, and rendezvous points.[7] Armed with the information, it was up to Robert to do the rest.

To help him, he'd been supplied with money. A lot of money. It was stashed in a special vest worn under his jacket, an uncomfortable garment with multiple pockets that he would grow to loathe as his mission progressed. It had given him a shock earlier that evening when he'd shut himself in his room (the first time he'd been alone since leaving Poltava) and taken the vest off. Opening one of the pockets, he found a wad of bills, so fresh they had to be peeled apart. Opening a couple more pockets and adding it all up, he figured the vest contained about ten thousand dollars' worth. A disturbingly large sum to carry around in a violent, seemingly lawless place like this.

He recalled being told the amount when he'd been issued with it, but it hadn't really sunk in at the time. His head was still reeling from the briefings he'd been subjected to. The final stage of Robert's preparation at Poltava had been his designation as a class B agent officer. It was a far more mundane position than its name implied. In this context, an "agent" was simply an officer authorized by the War Department to spend US Army money. An agent officer could pay soldiers' wages, settle their expenses, and purchase supplies. There were two grades: class A were usually the finance officers of army units; class B agents were appointed by them to act on their behalf.[8] (Eastern Command had an agent officer who visited Poland periodically to pay the expenses of rescued air-crews.)[9] Robert was made an agent subordinate to Eastern Command's finance officer, who would issue him with whatever cash he needed.[10]

Some of the money was in US dollars, some in rubles. There was a thriving black market in Poland, where dollars could be exchanged for rubles at very profitable rates. The Russians took exception to this and had insisted that American personnel be stopped from taking US dollars into Poland.[11] The dollars Robert had brought with him were for distribution to POWs; as nonexistent entities in the eyes of the Soviet authorities, they could exchange them if they wanted and get enough back in rubles to take good care of themselves. If necessary, Robert could do the same, but it was strictly inadvisable. Anything that might irritate the Russians was to be avoided.

At some point in the night, fatigue caught up with him, and Robert dozed off. Next morning he went down to the lobby—a rather grand affair with marble tiles and elegant pillars—and reported the previous night's incident to the assistant manager. She was a large, very friendly lady who went out of her way to befriend her American guests. He asked for another room, on the other side of the hotel.

He hadn't been able to shake the feeling that the atrocity he'd witnessed had somehow been intended to intimidate him. It was an absurd thought, but it nagged at him. He learned later that the trash-can torture was often meted out to civilians caught on the streets after curfew, a combination of punishment and intimidation for the citizens and entertainment for the soldiers who perpetrated it.

Seizing his opportunity while the Russian escort officer who'd accompanied him from Poltava was still in bed, Robert left the hotel. He had arrangements to make, and places to go.

Near dusk, a car pulled up at the edge of a stretch of lonely, snow-bound woodland. The solitary passenger got out, handed some money to the driver, and slammed the door. The ramshackle car drove off, rattling and smoking. As the taillights dwindled into the distance, the passenger hefted his heavy pack onto his shoulder and started walking up and down beside the road, stomping his boots in the snow as if to shake some life and warmth into them. He pulled his fur-lined hat lower on his head and tugged the collar of his parka tighter. The sky was steel-gray with stored-up snow, and the first flakes were already nipping at his face.

When the car was out of sight, he stomped up and down a couple more times, then took one huge sideways stride away from the road; one more step took him under the boughs of the pines. Drawing a knife from an inner pocket, he cut a branch and, using it like a broom, brushed snow into the prints he'd just made. Walking backward, obscuring his tracks as he went, he worked his way deeper into the wood. When he'd gone about thirty or forty feet, he turned and walked on normally, throwing the branch away. The snow would start falling soon and do the rest of the work for him.

Back before the war, when Robert first left his mother's home in Camp Hill to join the Army, he'd dreamed of one day becoming a pilot. Without a college education, he knew it would be hard to get a transfer from the infantry to pilot training, but he'd had no trouble imagining it. What he could never have imagined in his weirdest daydreams was that he was setting out on a path that would end up with him creeping through a forest in the wilds of Poland, covering his tracks to throw off the Russian secret police.

As strange as it seemed, in some ways it was closer to his upbringing than most of what he'd been through since enlisting. Secret police were a novelty, but moving stealthily through a snowy forest was almost as familiar to him as strolling on a downtown sidewalk. The Polish countryside reminded him of his home country and the boyhood weekends spent stalking deer in the woods of the Juniata and Susquehanna Valleys above Harrisburg or fishing in their slow waters.

Robert glanced back toward the road. It would take a hell of a tracker to catch up with him. First they'd have to discover that he'd hired a ride from Lwów, then tail him to this spot, then notice that the car had stopped. With any luck, the tracker would see the pattern of footprints and assume Robert had got himself another ride or walked on down the road.

Satisfied that he'd done a good job, he strode on. Before long he had vanished into the gloom among the trees, invisible from the road. Reaching the far side of the wood, he struck out across a field. In the gathering gloom, he could make out a farmhouse about a mile away, a dark patch against the white landscape. Taking a bearing on the house in case he lost sight of it in the dusk, he set out toward it.

The faint sound of an automobile came from the road behind. It was a quarter mile away, but Robert dropped to a crouch and remained motionless. The lights of a car moved slowly east to west, disappearing beyond the screen of trees. The glow seemed to stop at about the spot where Robert had left his ride. He waited, heart thumping. The bird dogs were even better trackers than he'd feared. After an agonizing couple of minutes, there was the faint sound of an engine revving, and the glow of lights moved on, fading into the distance.

Robert breathed again. Standing up, he located the distant outline of the farm once more and carried on walking. After about twenty minutes of crossing ditches and climbing fences, he came to a dirt road which led into the farm homestead. He climbed the gate and looked around. It was almost fully dark now. There was a glow in the window of the farmhouse. Off to one side were some outbuildings and a small barn. If his information was correct, this should be the place.

Not wanting to alarm the farmer, Robert made straight for the barn. Pausing to listen, he could hear a murmur of voices. The door was barred from inside. He thumped on the timber, and the voices fell silent. "I'm American!" he called hoarsely. "American. Open the door."

There was a sound of a bar being withdrawn, and the door opened a little, revealing a dim glow of candlelight within. A face appeared—hooded, bearded, wary.

"I'm an American. I'm here to help you," Robert said.

There was a pause, then a clamor of surprised voices; the door opened wide, and he stepped inside. He felt himself being seized and embraced; his nostrils filled with a powerful reek of human filth. Looking around, he saw a scene from a Victorian slum—haggard, unshaven faces illuminated by a candle, bodies wrapped in frayed, shapeless coats and mufflers—everyone looking at him like he was the Second Coming. Some stared dumbly, while the rest talked simultaneously, swearing in delight, smiles breaking out on the dirty faces.

Robert took off his pack and opened it up. First things first. Fending off questions about who he was and where he'd come from, he began sharing out the food he'd brought. It was mostly K rations, from a supply that had come with him from Poltava—pocket-size packs of luncheon meat, pork loaf, tinned cheese, biscuits, malted milk tablets, oatmeal, and sugar. He had brought as much as he could carry, but it wasn't going to be enough. He counted twenty-three men, and there were only enough rations for about twenty decent-size meals. Anticipating the problem, he'd filled up space in his pack and pockets with extra D-ration chocolate bars, which he shared around.

There were ironic groans at the sight of the ration packs. As a flyer, Robert had no experience of K rations, but they were a bugbear to combat infantrymen: always the same stuff and never enough of it. There wasn't a man there who'd thought he could ever be so deliriously glad to open up a K-ration pack.

As the men ate, Robert studied them and listened to their talk, occasionally asking a question of his own. Many of them scratched themselves intermittently; they were alive with lice. How could any honorable nation allow this suffering to happen to its allies' people? Some had escaped from forced marches westward when their camps were evacuated, and Robert heard stories of prisoners being used by the Germans as human shields. Much good that did the Germans against an enemy like the Red Army, who just fired regardless. Those who had been freed from their camps by Soviet forces told of incidents of Russian POWs being murdered by their liberators. American and British prisoners were either ignored or marched to the rear and abandoned. Some had managed to get rides on trains or trucks, but none had any real idea where they were going, or why.

It was said that those who went to the Russian camps were as bad off as they had been in the stalags, and there were rumors that the Russians would simply keep the liberated prisoners captive forever. Asked if the rumors were true, Robert had to admit that he didn't know. But he was here to do what he could to get them to safety. They'd soon be out of here and on their way home.

There were little packs of Camel cigarettes and matches in the ration packs, and soon the barn was filled with a fog of tobacco smoke and cheerful conversation—between them they dispelled the nauseating atmosphere of filth and despondency. One voice broke softly into song, and the others joined in. The only men who didn't enter into the jubilant mood were the sick and injured. Robert did what little he could for them, but he was no medic, and all he had was a few first-aid supplies and a bottle of vodka.

They would need to depart before dawn. Robert settled down to spend the night in the barn, feeling like a shepherd with his flock. So far, so good. Tomorrow the real test would come. Somehow he had to get this scarecrow band into Lwów. He had a plan worked out, but it was a risky one.

In the hour before dawn, Robert rose from his bed on the straw. Accompanied by the couple of men who seemed to be the de facto leaders of the group, he went to see the farmer. Communication was difficult, but the farmer agreed readily enough to Robert's request for a ride to the outskirts of Lwów. With a generosity that Robert would learn was common among the Poles, the farmer was only too glad to help the Americans on their way.

In the dark, he began hitching his horse to the cart, while Robert assembled the POWs. The sick were put aboard first, and the rest climbed in and settled down wherever they could. The cart, creaking under its unaccustomed weight, rolled out onto the farm track in the first glimmer of dawn.

It wasn't many miles to Lwów, and it was still early when they approached the outskirts. Robert was anticipating that any Soviet sentries or patrols who were about would be hungover from the previous night's drinking, and wouldn't be inclined to question travelers. The Russians were addicted to the local liquor, a powerful brew made from beets, and he'd seen them consume large quantities of it—on duty and off.

At the edge of town, the farmer reined in, and the Americans climbed down from the cart. Robert offered the farmer money for his trouble, but the man smiled and waved it away. Then he bade his friends farewell, shook the reins, turned in the road, and trundled off the way they'd come.

Taking turns to support the weaker men, Robert and his party of fugitives walked the last quarter-mile into Lwów. It wasn't far to the main railroad station. Robert had visited it the day before to check the times of trains, and had bought two dozen tickets for Odessa, the main port city on the Black Sea coast.

Robert had learned from Moscow that the Soviets were establishing a transient camp at the port. The intention was that all liberated POWs (subject to being properly screened in Soviet camps) must be sent there to await evacuation by sea. There were to be no exceptions.

At Poltava, optimistic preparations to receive airlifted POWs were still going on.[12] The Americans objected to the Odessa plan. Odessa was a three-day rail journey from even the nearest Polish cities, and there was no telling what kind of facilities the Soviets would put in place, or what kind of delays and maltreatment the POWs would experience along the way. At the very least, the Americans argued, the sick must be evacuated by air via Poltava and Tehran, where they could receive proper hospital treatment.[13] The Russians refused.

General Deane cabled Colonel Wilmeth, who was still stuck at Poltava awaiting clearance to enter Poland with his contact team. Deane notified him that his mission had finally been approved by the Russians in Moscow, and that he would be permitted to go to Lublin to inspect the POW facilities there. Colonel Hampton applied immediately to General Kovalev, the Soviet commander at Poltava, for clearance for Colonel Wilmeth and his team to fly to Lublin.

The request was denied.[14]

While his superiors protested, cajoled, and argued with the Russians, Captain Robert M. Trimble walked into the suburbs of Lwów leading a ragged band of ex-prisoners. There was a guard post at the edge of town. Robert's pulse quickened as they approached it. There was nobody about. It looked like they might get through without being challenged. Then, just as Robert's hopes were rising, a soldier came out of a nearby house and challenged them. He was every bit as bleary-eyed as Robert had hoped, and blinked suspiciously at the crowd of men.

Without giving him a chance to speak, Robert held his passport in front of the soldier's face and said, "*Ya amerikanets*,"[15] one of the handful of Russian phrases he had memorized for just such an occasion. "I am a representative of the Embassy of the United States of America," he added in English.

Whether he understood it or not, the Russian seemed satisfied by the sight of the passport, but he gestured threateningly with his rifle at the POWs. "*Nemtsy?*" he said. Robert recognized the word—he thought the men were Germans. "*Yavlyayutsya li oni fritsev?*"[16] he added, looking decidedly hostile.

"No, no," said Robert. "*Amerikanskiy*. Like me. Americans. They were prisoners of the Germans."

The soldier seemed to accept this, but didn't lower his rifle. One or two of the POWs were looking like they were bracing themselves to make a run for it. The soldier directed a stream of Russian at Robert. He didn't understand any of the words, but knew enough by now to recognize it as a demand for identification papers. Robert tried to explain that the men had no papers—they had all been taken by the Germans.

In a last bid to overcome the guard's resistance, he pointed to his watch and said, "*Poyezd*." Train.

The soldier shook his head. Hangover or no hangover, this was one Red Army grunt who was determined to be awkward. He ordered them to stay where they were and turned, rather unsteadily, back toward the guard post. The next move would be a phone call to the city commandant's office, followed by detention in the POW holding camp, and the end of their hopes of imminent freedom.

Casting around desperately for a way out, Robert spotted a bottle of beet liquor on a table outside the guard post. He called to the soldier, who stopped and turned back. Robert gestured to the bottle, indicating that he would like to have it. The soldier shook his head and snatched the bottle, holding it protectively against his body. Robert dug in his pocket and pulled out a wad of dollar bills. He fanned them out under the soldier's nose.

Immediately he sensed the man wavering. Liquor might be precious, but dollars were better than bullion in this city. Robert stuffed the bills into the guard's coat pocket and pried the bottle from his grubby fingers. Simultaneously smiling and bracing himself, he took a swig of the blue liquor. It was like methanol. Wheezing, he offered the bottle back. The soldier took a slug, and soon they were like old buddies, passing the bottle back and forth. The Russian smiled, Robert smiled, the POWs tried to smile.

At last, Robert announced, "We go now, bye-bye." With a cheerful gesture, the guard stood aside and waved his American friends through, then went back to his post to sit down and continue sweating off his hangover.

They made it to the station without any more hindrance, and with plenty of time to spare before the Odessa train was due. Like the rest of the city, Lwów Station was a grand piece of nineteenth-century architecture, with great, echoing halls. But the POWs didn't look as out of place as they might have expected. There were millions of displaced persons in Poland, and people were accustomed to seeing ragged strangers in their midst.

While the men waited, Robert hurried off to the shops, and returned laden with food. He shared it among them, along with handfuls of dollars. When everything was safely stowed away, he hurried the men up to the platforms and onto the train. As they boarded, they shook him by the hand, some of them seizing hold of him and hugging him; some had tears in their eyes.

As the train pulled away, Robert stayed to watch it go. With a sudden, almost painful, clarity, he recalled the last time he had waved someone away on a train journey—Eleanor, at Riverside in California, when she set off on the long journey to Chicago. It had been the very last time he had seen her, a year ago now. It felt like a lifetime. But he could still conjure up the look in her eyes and hear those last words she called out . . .

He wondered if he would ever see her again. He wondered if those twenty-three men would find their way home to the people they loved, whoever and wherever they were. Robert had done all he could to see them on their way to freedom. How many others would there be before he was done? In his pocket, his hand touched the slips of paper—each one a location, a number, a set of directions to the next group of lost.

The caboose disappeared beyond the bend, and Robert turned on his heel, walked back through the station, and out into the streets of Lwów. He had places to be, and time was short.

7.

FIGHTING BASTARD OF THE UKRAINE

U.S. PLANES RAP TARGETS DOZEN MILES AHEAD OF REDS ADVANCING ON DRESDEN

CLOSEST DIRECT AIR RAID SO FAR. Cottbus lies only 12 miles west of Red Army Spearheads. . . . American Flying Fortresses and Liberators more than 1,180 strong smashed today at targets only a dozen miles ahead of the advancing Red Army. . . . The heavy bombers had an escort of more than 430 Mustang fighters, bringing the total air force hurled at Germany today to 1,530 planes. . . .

Dresden has been under almost continuous assault by British and American air forces for two days and nights. This vital hub of German rail and supply connections which is only about 43 miles distant from the most advanced Red Army column has had one of the heaviest plasterings of the war.

Cottbus, 53 miles southeast of Berlin, is a target of almost equal importance. It is a big rail junction point from which highways radiate in all directions. The American assault followed a double blow by 717 RAF four-engined bombers at Chemnitz . . .

The News-Herald (Franklin, Pennsylvania), February 15, 1945

February 15, 1945: Near Staszów, Poland

Engines screaming, losing altitude, a B-17 Flying Fortress burst through the cloud base at four hundred feet, struggled to level out, then flew on southeast, heading into a gathering snowstorm. Two engines dead, her silver body peppered with holes, bleeding oil and gasoline, she raced on above the treetops. Laborers in the fields and travelers in the country lanes looked up in alarm as the wounded beast roared overhead.

In the cockpit, Lieutenant Arnold A. Tillman worked to keep the Fortress airborne and level. At the same time, he and his copilot, Lieutenant Stan Neese, scanned the ground below for a place to land. She had no name, this Fort; she was just B-17G 43-37687, call-sign BX/Y. And yet to Lieutenant Tillman and his crew, "687" was home, a little piece of America. At this moment she was a rather fragile, broken piece of America that looked likely to get spread across half a mile of Polish countryside.

The Fort had been part of a huge force sent to bomb the marshaling yards at Cottbus, Germany. The flak barrage was intense, fragments slapping and zinging through 687's skin. She lost an engine while they were still over the target, and flew on with the prop feathered. During the turn off the target to head for home, a second engine died, and 687 began losing altitude. They weren't going to make it. The only option was to turn back east and make for Poland.[1] Losing power and altitude, the crew began jettisoning everything that wasn't bolted down: machine guns, ammunition, flak jackets. But still 687 kept losing height.

They had been struggling on for nearly an hour when they came out of the clouds and began looking for a place to crash-land. As Tillman and Neese scanned the landscape, a third engine was stuttering. If they didn't find a spot to put this crate down immediately, they were finished. They were in a broad, shallow valley with great tracts of woodland everywhere, and the fields were all small, separated by hedgerows. While the pilots searched and fought to keep the plane in the air, the rest of the crew gathered in the radio operator's compartment, hunkered down in crash positions; some of them began to say the Lord's Prayer. At last, Tillman spotted what looked like a suitable field, just below a line of trees on a gentle rise. He made a snap decision to put down there.

Neese flipped the switch for the landing gear, and there was a tense few seconds—the gear was almost certainly damaged, and if it was shot, they'd have to do a belly landing. Miraculously, the light came on indicating that the wheels were down and locked.

With the snowy field racing up to meet them, Tillman leveled the Fort out and dropped her down, drawing back the throttles on the two remaining engines to let the wheels hit the ground. It was instantly clear that the field wasn't going to be long enough. The tree line was racing toward them. Tillman rammed the throttle levers forward and pulled back on the control column. One of the engines, already running rough, gave a final stutter and died. With her last dregs of speed and power, dragging herself by her one surviving engine, the Fort bounced upward, brushed through the treetops, and sank down on the far side. There was an instant's glimpse of another small field, then she hit the snow, skidded, and eventually slewed to a stop, straddling the boundary between the field and another copse, wheels in a ditch and her nose among the trees.

The last engine rumbled on for a while, whipping up a little blizzard across the ground. Then it too was shut down, and silence settled over the field.

It was broken by the squeak of the escape hatch opening. One by one, the officers dropped out onto the snow. The gunners emerged from the fuselage door. Together they milled around the bomber, looking at the holes in the skin, the ruined engines, gazing back toward the trees, wondering how in the world they had survived.

Lieutenant Tillman quickly organized the destruction of all the classified materials on board—the navigator's maps, the bombardier's data charts, target list, pilot's notes, and finally the Norden bombsight, which they pulverized with pistol fire. They had barely finished when they saw a squad of Russian soldiers heading across the field toward them, rifles at the ready.

"Amerikanski!" the crew shouted. "Amerikanski!" To the men's astonishment, as the soldiers drew near it became apparent that they were all women. They looked the Americans over, glanced at the stranded plane, then turned about and walked back to the road.

"Guess none of us took their fancy," said Sergeant Echola, the tail gunner.

There wasn't a soul in sight. The Americans, alone in the snowy landscape, wondered what they were going to do now.

815 Hummel Avenue, Lemoyne, Pennsylvania

> AIR ATTACK PLANNED AT YALTA. . . . Dresden, an important railway and industrial city, was already in flames from raids yesterday and Tuesday night, when it was the main target of an assault force totaling some 8,- (*Continued on Page 6.*)

Eleanor Trimble pushed away the newspaper with a sigh. It all sounded awful, even though America was winning. She could scarcely even imagine what a bombed city in flames would look like, or envisage all those thousands of airplanes, or the dangers faced by the men flying them. All she could do was thank the Good Lord that Robert wasn't a part of it anymore. No longer would she suffer the anguish of seeing those news reports and wondering if he had been involved, and whether he was one of the dead or missing.

She shifted Carol Ann on her lap and sat back from the breakfast table. Gazing lovingly into the little face, Eleanor told her baby once more that her daddy was safe now and would soon be home. Carol Ann, with no idea what she was talking about, smiled back, gurgling happily.

Ruth, Robert's mother, was standing by to take the baby in her arms while Eleanor got ready to go to work. It was a comfort to both of them to know that Robert was out of danger for the rest of the war, and that his daughter wouldn't grow up without a father. It was about time somebody in this family had a father they could love and always recall with affection. It had been such a weight of worry for Robert. But it was all past now. He was safe.

He had to go back to Kraków. There was no way around it; he was needed there.

The very thought filled him with dread. Only a few days had passed since his visit to the camp at Auschwitz-Birkenau, and his mind had had no chance at all to come to terms with what he had seen there. The thought of going back to that area, even if only to the city of Kraków, was unbearable. He had tried to draft a report on the visit for Eastern Command, but it had all been too vivid. The frozen bodies were the worst. Even more than the pathos of the barely living survivors, it was the skeletal corpses, bent and huddled in the shadowy interior of the shed and lying in the freezing slush on the ground. Especially the children. There was nothing in all of creation so pitiable, so bitter, as that. Attempting to articulate the bestiality of what he had witnessed, to convey even a fraction of that briefest of glimpses into the abyss, made him break up inside.

To the world, Captain Robert Trimble presented a placid, even cheerful, countenance, never short of a smile. But inside, the wounds were raw, not yet hardened into scar tissue. Combat had left deep marks on him. Mission after flak-torn mission had stretched his nerves and left them permanently taut. And now he was learning that the world was even worse than he had believed it to be. He had to hold it in, fight his way past it. And to do that, he had to go on with his mission, and go wherever it took him. Right now, that meant back to Kraków, where the OSS agents had identified several groups needing help.

After seeing his first batch of POWs safely off from Lwów, Robert had briefly felt heartened, and he hurried back to the hotel, packed up his kit and a big batch of rations, then headed for the airfield on the outskirts of the city. He had official, aboveboard business to attend to, which would take him a big part of the way to Kraków and enable him to make

use of Russian transportation. There was a crash-landed aircrew from
the 96th Bomb Group in need of evacuation at Staszów. Eastern Command had told them to hang in there while an officer was sent to pick
them up. Normally it would take a lot longer—at least a week or more—
to arrange an evacuation, but Captain Trimble was nearby, and he
needed his cover story. Whoever they were, they were lucky guys.

With the grudging assistance of the Soviet officer who served as
interpreter, NKVD escort, and watcher (still upset about Robert's sudden disappearance from Lwów the previous day), Robert secured a
place on a Soviet flight going west.

The flight from Lwów to Rzeszów—the nearest airfield to the
crash-landing site—was only about eighty miles, but from there it was
fifty miles more to Staszów, along winding roads in a Russian jeep, with
only his escort to keep him company. It was a long journey for a man
who'd had hardly any sleep.

Robert was driven to a farm about five miles outside Staszów, close
to the spot where the B-17 had made its forced landing. There was a
sense of déjà vu—the snow-dusted homestead just like the one near
Lwów that he had trekked to in the dusk. But in every other way it was
as different as it could be. For one thing, the place was full of Russians,
who appeared to be there to guard the American flyers.

Lieutenant Tillman and his officers were accommodated in the
house, and the enlisted men in the barn, accompanied by Russian
minders. It was almost a shock to see the crew—they looked so clean
and well dressed. Not quite fit to go out on a date, maybe, but fresh and
healthy in their rumpled flying gear, clean-shaven and cheerful. The
contrast with the ex-POWs couldn't have been more stark. But they
were still delighted to see a fellow American climb out of the jeep, and
they greeted Robert as if he were their brother, shaking his hand and
telling him over and over how good it was to see him. They were also
pleased to see his sack of rations. The Russians had fed them, but it
wasn't much.

Robert couldn't help feeling a bond with the nine men—a sensation he hadn't felt since leaving Debach, of being among combat airmen, bomber boys, with all the shared experiences that implied. But they seemed so young to him now, even though there was barely any difference in age. Tillman himself was short and slightly built, and as fresh-faced and bright-eyed as a schoolboy. He had the cockiness of a born hotshot who believed he was hell on wings. Only a few months ago Robert had been much the same.

The Russians and the Polish family were sorry to see their American friends depart. They had grown close in the past few days. Again Robert witnessed the cordiality of Russians toward people they saw as comrades in arms, and marveled at the contrast with the flip side, the harsh detestation of anyone outside that group. One of the Russians, a rather lugubrious, gentle-looking captain with the Order of the Red Star pinned to his tunic (Soviet soldiers wore their medals even in combat), had given Tillman a signed photo of himself. He'd written an inscription on the back in English: "A token in remembrance for friends in fight against German Nazis."[2]

Some of the American sergeants weren't quite so fond of the Russians, claiming that their soft cotton underwear had been filched by soldiers while they were bathing in the cedar tub in the yard.[3] There was also some tension with the Russians because of the way they regarded the Poles. Tillman and his men had been warned not to mix with the locals;[4] they ignored the advice, and found that most of the Poles detested and feared the Russians, and dreamed of escape to America or England.

Of all the farewells, the most heartfelt was from the Polish farmer's family. Their son Tadeusz was an airman too, far away in England, and they had lost touch with him during the German occupation. Tadeusz Kratke had been a fighter pilot in the Polish Air Force and had fought in the defense of Warsaw in 1939. Escaping the country after the German and Soviet conquest, he had made his way to France, and eventually to Britain, where he joined the RAF.[5] The family believed that Tadeusz was based somewhere near London, but they were hazy about English geography and they'd had no word of him for three years.

Seizing her opportunity, the farmer's young daughter had written a letter to her beloved brother, and she pressed it into Lieutenant Tillman's hands, imploring him to deliver it.[6] *Your colleagues in trade from America are our guests,* she wrote. *They are going to London in a few days, maybe my letter will reach you. Beloved Tadzik,[7] thanks to the Highest God we are glad of peace and good health, still living on the old place. We are uneasy about you. . . . Embracing with love, your sister, parents, and Hela.*

In order that the Americans should recognize him if they found him, she gave them a photograph of Tadeusz: dashing in Polish flying gear, he was a fine-looking, boyish young man with a huge sunshine grin; just the sort who would be idolized by his kid sister.

Pocketing their missives and mementoes, Lieutenant Tillman and his crew took their leave of their Polish hosts. To Robert's eyes the departure from the homestead was about as different as could be from the last one he had witnessed. A happy parting of friends. The number of men was similar, though; now that their custodial duty was over, the Russian soldiers were going back to their barracks at Staszów, and they piled aboard the transports along with the ten Americans.

The vehicles rumbled off down the icy farm track, the family standing at the gate to wave them off. The young girl was breathless with joy at the prospect of being in touch with her brother again.

Unfortunately, the Kratke family had been right to be concerned about Tadeusz. The letter never found him. It remained in the possession of Lieutenant Arnold Tillman for the rest of his life, along with the photograph of the smiling young Polish pilot. In March 1942, almost three years earlier, while his family was still living under Nazi occupation, Tadeusz's Spitfire squadron had been sent on an escort mission to France. Forced to turn back due to bad weather, and with hardly any fuel left, they found the southwest of England blanketed in thick fog. It was impossible to locate their airfield; the pilots couldn't even see the ground. One flew right over the airfield at low altitude without knowing it was there. Ten of the twelve Spitfires crash-landed; the squadron commander hit a cliff and was killed. Flying Officer Tadeusz Kratke crashed badly and was pulled from the wreckage injured and almost blinded. It was said that his face was so cut up, it lived up to his name (*kratke* means "grille" or "checkered pattern").[8] By the end of 1944, his squadron had been posted to Belgium, and he was no longer a part of it.

Whether he ever returned home to the farm near Staszów, whether his sister and parents ever saw him again, is not known. Most Polish veterans did not go back to Poland. By the end of the war, the country was no longer the same homeland they had left behind, and expatriates who had served with the Western Allies were regarded with suspicion by the Communist authorities, as a potential source of nationalist resistance. This was not the country the Polish veterans had fought for, that they had been driven from in 1939, and to which they had yearned to return in triumph. Most of them turned their backs on it in bitterness and regret, feeling that they had been betrayed by the Allies with whom they had served, who had signed away their independence at Yalta.

When the convoy of vehicles reached the town of Staszów, Robert parted from his new friends and went on with the Russians. He still had his onward journey to make and would have to bunk at a Red Army barracks that night. He gave Lieutenant Tillman and his men a per diem and a share of the rations he'd brought, and told them to take his ride back to Rzeszów. There would be a C-47 there to take them on to Lwów. Robert gave them directions to the Hotel George, where an officer from Eastern Command would collect them and arrange a flight to Poltava.[9]

In exchange for their rescue, Tillman's crew bestowed a new nickname on Robert Trimble. In their conversation during the journey from the farm, Robert had mentioned that the people of Eastern Command, aware that they were way off the map of public consciousness, called themselves the "Forgotten Bastards of the Ukraine."[10] Somebody—

Robert couldn't recall who—suggested that it didn't suit him; he was more like the Fighting Bastard of the Ukraine.

It was the kind of thing men say when they're young and flushed with optimism, and whoever said it had no idea that they were talking to the one member of Eastern Command who really was on the front line, with a battle to fight. Captain Trimble hoped he could live up to the nickname. He believed in that minute that there was no length he wouldn't go to to save the vulnerable and defy Soviet interference. As long as they didn't kill him, he would go on until everyone was free.

8.

KASIA

February 22, 1945: Lemoyne, Pennsylvania

Ruth Trimble stood by the parlor window, her little granddaughter clutched in her arms. Together they peered up and down the length of Hummel Avenue, looking out for the paperboy. It wasn't something they did every day, but today was a bit special.

Here he came, pedaling his bicycle along the sidewalk under the trees, head down against the sleety drizzle. As he flashed past, the folded *Evening News* sailed across the small front yard and landed with a thud on the porch. Ruth stepped out, scooped it up, and hurried back into the warmth.

Setting Carol Ann down, Ruth shook the slightly soggy paper open and started eagerly scanning the columns. On page 4 she found what she was looking for, and sat back with a contented sigh.

LEMOYNE, Feb. 22. Mrs. Robert Trimble, 815 Hummel Avenue, has received word that her husband, Captain Trimble, has been awarded the Distinguished Flying Cross. Previously, he was awarded the Air Medal and two Oak Leaf clusters. He was stationed in England and is now in the Far Eastern War Theater. . . .

Ruth frowned at that last sentence. Eleanor had clearly told the reporter that it was "Eastern," not "Far Eastern." But maybe the Harrisburg *Evening News* wasn't aware that there were Americans in Russia. Everyone was obsessed with the Far East and Germany; the news was all about Iwo Jima and the push to the Rhine, and nobody paid any attention to obscure little corners of Eastern Europe.

Eleanor had been so startled when the letter came; it looked so official, and she thought for a terrifying minute that it portended something awful. It was just over a year since her brother Howard had been killed in combat, and Eleanor was jittery over every communication.

The citation said that the medal was awarded to Robert because he had "distinguished himself by heroism or extraordinary achievement while participating in an aerial flight." It was a belated recognition of his service as a pilot with the 493rd Bomb Group.

Heroism . . . extraordinary achievement . . . Ruth recalled the distraught boy he had once been, his heart breaking when his father abandoned them. It hadn't been so many years ago. He'd been forced to grow up fast, and just look at him now! As with so many other young boys who'd been transformed into men, it was a wonder what he was able to bear, and how much he was expected to give for his country.

Ruth wondered where her boy was this minute: whether he was as safe as she and Eleanor hoped, whether he was warm and comfortable, and what he was thinking about.

Near Kraków, Poland

Scooping the snow out from a deep drift at the base of a tree, Robert fashioned a burrow about three feet deep and five feet long. Wrapping his bedroll around him, he fastened it at his middle, pulled up the fur-lined hood of his parka, and crawled into the burrow, curling into the confined space and pulling his pack after him to close off the hole.

At last he was out of the savage wind that was whipping across the frozen fields. His stiffened limbs began to relax, and the warmth he had built up in his core by trekking into the forest and digging the burrow spread to his extremities.

Clicking his pocket flashlight on, he rummaged in his pockets for the D-ration candy bars he had stashed there. With his head cradled on the wall of his cave, he unwrapped an almond Hershey bar and munched it down. Cheeks still bulging with chocolate, he unwrapped another. With the cold and the exertion, his body craved calories, and it was hard to stop once he started.[1] Restraint had to be exercised. There were others who needed the nourishment more than he did. His heavy pack was stuffed with K- and D-rations, but he guessed from experience that it wouldn't be enough.

Getting out of Kraków hadn't been difficult. He was short on time because of the diversion to Staszów, so he hadn't even bothered checking into the hotel; he'd simply paid for a ride out of town. This time he'd created a diversion by making conspicuous arrangements for transportation to pick him up from the front of the hotel. Meanwhile he slipped out of a side entrance. The bird dog who'd been with him since Rzeszów didn't even know he'd left the building. At this stage in his mission, the NKVD still had no suspicion that Captain Trimble was doing anything other than authorized aircrew recovery operations. However, the more frequently he disappeared, the more likely they were to guess he was up to something. This was a mission that was going to get harder as it went along.

Finishing off his second candy bar, Robert put his mittens back on and settled down to try and get some sleep.

As so often in this environment—as so often for all the scattered people in the world—his thoughts drifted homeward, and he wondered what the women in his life would be doing this minute. Eleanor would be finishing work, riding the bus across the Market Street Bridge, the endless line of lanterns flicking hypnotically past the windows. In the house on Hummel Avenue, lamps would be alight in the windows, casting a warm glow onto the street, and his mother would be lighting the stove and starting the dinner, and . . . and he almost saw his father sitting at the kitchen table, his tie loosened, leafing through the evening paper. But he wasn't in the picture anymore. That was an image from a long-dead era. Instead there was the figure that Robert couldn't quite see—the tiny shape of the child.

What did she look like? What was this life that had come from him but that he had never seen? It was no good—he couldn't see her, couldn't conjure the feelings that he imagined ought to be there when he thought of her. All he had was a kind of longing that he could do nothing with.

But he could picture the house, and picture Eleanor going up the steps to the lighted porch. The lights—the lanterns on the bridge and the glowing windows of the houses along the street—evoked the very essence of home. In blacked-out England there were no lamps in the street, there was no welcoming glow in the windows. In Poland, you rarely saw a town at night; it was too dangerous to be out after dark

. . . And so he thought of home. And in the comfort of those thoughts, he found sleep at last.

He awoke a little after dawn to discover that there had been a fresh fall of snow during the night, and the clouds had cleared. Pushing his pack ahead of him, Robert emerged from his burrow into a brightening world. Light was growing among the trees, and the sky was a pale blue-gray. The forest was filled with a close, hugging silence, in which the creaking of snow was like the grinding of boulders.

It was amazing how well you could sleep in a snow hole if you were tired enough. Rubbing his eyes and loosening his limbs, Robert packed up his bedroll, hoisted his pack, and set off through the forest. He had a map, a compass, a grid reference, and a goal. That was all he needed. So long as there was something to aim at, something good to do today, he felt he could win through this war, and find his way home.

He hadn't been walking long when he saw movement among the trees ahead. Two men, wearing the familiar ragged, bulked-out clothing of refugees, were standing in a clearing, faces turned toward the sky, apparently taking a moment to enjoy this rare interlude of morning sunshine.

Robert approached, thinking they must be from the POW group he was looking for, despite the fact he was still some way from the rendezvous. But as he came closer, he noticed that one of the men had on blue-striped trousers beneath his overcoat—the same kind of stuff he recalled seeing on the inmates in the camp at Birkenau. The Auschwitz complex was only a few miles from here.

Suddenly the men noticed him, and began to back away nervously. Robert called out, "I'm American! It's okay!" They didn't seem to understand. Robert guessed that all they were seeing was the military clothing and the Red Army fur hat. "American," he said again, pointing to himself and then spreading his hands to indicate his peaceful intentions.

The men stopped and let him catch up with them. One of them spoke a little English, and Robert managed to make them understand that he wasn't a Russian, and that he was looking for prisoners of war. A light of recognition dawned, and they broke out smiling. Shaking him eagerly by the hand, they indicated that he should follow them.

Neither of the men was in good health—one was a little unsteady on his feet and had a racking cough—so it was a slow trek through the woods. Robert reckoned they had gone a quarter mile or so when they came to a scatter of abandoned farm buildings. The two men called out a greeting, and Robert watched in astonishment as, in ones and twos, timid, ghostly figures emerged from the broken-down doorways of the sheds. There must have been dozens of them, some wearing the distinctive striped Auschwitz clothing, most dressed in the usual mess of salvaged coats and filthy-looking blankets.

It gave Robert a shiver when one of the men stepped forward and spoke in English, with an American accent. It never ceased to seem alien, hearing the voices of New York, Texas, Pennsylvania, California, issuing from the mouths of emaciated, peasant-clad ghosts in some out-of-the-way corner of Poland.

Robert explained that he was here to help get them out of the country. The news was received like a divine revelation. The POWs had no idea that the outside world knew about them. (The OSS agents, who couldn't compromise their own cover, did not necessarily contact the ex-prisoners they gathered intelligence about and gave out minimal information about their purpose.) Robert asked how many of the people here were POWs. He'd been notified to expect a group about the same size as the one near Lwów, but there must be twice that number here.

Only about half of them were Allied POWs. The rest were refugees from Nazi labor camps, as well as some Jews who had escaped from the SS during the terrible death marches from Auschwitz in January. Some of the POWs were also death-march escapees, having cut loose from the march out of Stalag VIII-B at Lamsdorf,[2] about fifty miles to the west. Aside from the American and British POWs, there were civilian ex-prisoners. Their nationalities were mixed: French, Dutch, a handful of Poles. They had attached themselves to the POWs in the hope that they might help them to salvation, not realizing that the Americans were as firmly trapped in Soviet Poland as everyone else.

They had been living on a small stock of canned food looted from a storehouse in an abandoned camp, but it was almost exhausted. Robert looked at the circle of faces—some despondent and sick, others regarding him with hope and delight—and felt a flutter of panic at the thought of sneaking this many into the city and onto a train.

But there was no time to waste on worry. It was a long way back to Kraków, and with fifty mouths to feed, Robert's supply of rations wasn't going to last to the end of the day. He explained that he only had a little food but could give them plenty of money to buy more. He could only take responsibility for the Allied POWs, but he was willing to put all the civilian men who wanted to leave Poland onto a train for Odessa along with them. From there, they would be on their own. He had no idea whether the Soviets, or indeed the Americans or the British, would give them passage out.

There was a short discussion among the civilians, and they agreed enthusiastically that they should go with the American. There was an outburst of jubilation, and Robert was shaken by the hand and embraced. Tears of joy were shed at the good providence that had brought them this opportunity to escape from this frozen hell.

Amid the joy, there was anxious muttering. Some asked, "What about the women?"

"Which women?" somebody asked.

"In the camp, of course," said somebody else.

"And the little ones," someone added.

A few voices were raised in protest, arguing that if they were to make it to Kraków they needed to get going now and not waste time with trifles. Other voices spoke angrily against them.

Bewildered, and with a rising anxiety, Robert was persuaded to go with a small group of men to meet these women. Another mysterious walk ensued, across fields and woods. He could feel the situation slipping out of his control and wondered what surprises were still in store for him—an extremely unpleasant one, it turned out.

The trek brought the little party to the edge of an industrial area and a road that led to a concentration camp.[3] It looked just like the one at Birkenau, with layers of barbwire fencing surrounding rows of barracks blocks, but much smaller, just a fraction of the size. The place had been abandoned; there wasn't a soul about. The men led Robert in through the broken-down gate. He had prayed that he would never have to set foot in such a place again. With a rising sense of horror, heart thumping, he walked among the barracks, some of them burned, some demolished. Unlike his visit to Birkenau, fresh falls of snow had softened the scene a little.

Passing by an open space, Robert noticed a big ditch. The men with him averted their eyes as they passed it. Robert realized that what he had taken for a snow-covered mound of earth beside the ditch was a stack of frozen corpses, sprawled and entangled, naked limbs protruding rigidly. As at the main camp, the work of destroying the survivors and the evidence of the murders had been left half-done by the SS. Robert looked away, feeling sick, and hurried after his guides. They led him to a barracks hut in the middle of the camp, where one of them knocked on the door, called a greeting, and entered, beckoning Robert to follow.

It took a moment for his eyes to adjust to the gloom inside after the glare of the sunlit snow. A long, low table ran the length of the room, and along both walls were wooden structures that looked like shelves in a freight warehouse. The place seemed deserted, but then he noticed some faces looking out from one of the shelves. Women, together with a couple of children. More female faces appeared, peering at the stranger.

"They come with us?" one of the men asked Robert.

At a rough count, he figured there were twenty-five of them. He already had fifty people to manage. It wouldn't be possible. No, he couldn't do it; it could put the whole operation in jeopardy. But how could he tell them that? He glanced around at the miserable interior of the hut, and an image of the bodies outside flashed into his head. He looked again at the faces of the women and children.

"They come with us," he said.

Fishing the last half-dozen chocolate bars and the remaining tins of cheese and luncheon meat out of his pack, Robert handed them out to his companions, who began dividing them up into tiny portions and distributing them among the people.

Since he and the men had shepherded the women and children from the camp and met up with the others, the ragged column of refugees had covered several miles across the snowbound countryside. They could only go as fast as the children and the sick could manage. It wasn't fast enough. The food was gone, and they still had a long way to go. Robert figured he could head to the nearest town and buy food, but time was pressing, and he couldn't afford to attract too much attention.

He walked around restlessly, watching the gathered people as they savored their morsels of food. His attention was caught by a small knot of people gathered near a young woman sitting on the ground with a bundle of rags lying next to her. Looking closer, Robert realized that the rags were wrapped around a baby. The woman was listless, exhausted physically and emotionally. The people with her were trying to talk to her, but there was no response. The baby appeared to be asleep; the tiny face was gaunt, with a bluish tinge.

She was a girl, somebody said in answer to Robert's query, born in the camp. Her name was Kasia. Robert picked up the bundle of thin rags. Kasia stirred and opened her eyes, then closed them again. This wasn't a healthy infant. Even to Robert it was obvious that she was on the threshold of death. Quickly he took off his thick woollen muffler. Discarding the rank blanket she was wrapped in, he wound the muffler round the little body, and placed her inside his parka, against his chest. She seemed to revive a little, opening her eyes, and this time seemed to see him. There was a ghost of a smile.

A woman explained that Kasia's mother had too little milk; she was sick and had lost the will to live.

It was time to move on. The weak were helped to their feet by the strong, and the trek resumed. Kasia's mother was helped along by some of the other women, while Robert kept the baby inside his coat. Her eyes had closed, and he prayed that she could cling on to life. Maybe they could get medical help in Kraków. Eastern Command's money would buy the best possible aid. But they had to get there first, before darkness fell.

As he walked, Robert was hard-pressed to keep his emotions in hand. Every so often he glanced down to check that Kasia was still breathing, and each time he couldn't keep the thoughts of home out of his mind. Thousands of miles away, Eleanor would be holding their baby in her arms, chuckling and playing peekaboo. And the baby, plump and rosy-cheeked, would smile back, unaware that there were such things in the world as war, and death, and camps, and starvation, and . . . and save for an accident of birth, this could be Carol Ann here in his coat, emaciated and close to death; this could be Eleanor trudging along listlessly, unconscious that her flesh and blood was dying beside her.

All the while, Robert felt these people's overwhelming hopelessness. He thought he'd had it bad when his father left, but he was wrong. These people still survived when there was nothing left to live for. And he wondered how they could ever feel normal again, with their families and homes all dispersed and destroyed.

There was nothing he could do but hold baby Kasia to him and keep walking with the others—and follow the plan.

An hour later, they reached the main road. There was a farm where transport had been prearranged. The farmer was known to be anti-Russian; he had been contacted by one of Robert's agents and had agreed to put his cattle truck at their disposal. He was a little surprised to see the number of people who showed up, and that they weren't just Americans. But he recovered and brought out his truck.

With some difficulty everyone was loaded aboard, and the truck pulled out onto the road to Kraków. It was a short distance, but a slow, laborious journey. Eventually, as darkness was falling, the truck reached the outskirts of town. It pulled over, and the people dismounted, stiff and exhausted. Robert thanked the farmer and offered him money as a reward, but of course it was refused.

It wouldn't be safe to go into town now. Kraków was close to the front line still, so the town garrison would be much more alert to curfew-breaking and treat it even more violently than they did in Lwów. So the men and women all found places to huddle up, away from the road, and wait for morning. They were accustomed to it. With luck, they wouldn't have to endure it anymore after tonight. Robert entrusted Kasia to one of the women. In the morning he would attempt to put them all aboard the Odessa-bound train.

At dawn, the people roused themselves for one more walk. Robert went alone into the city and made his way to the railroad station. His refugees had been instructed to wait awhile and then begin following him in small groups of no more than two or three at a time, setting out at intervals. That should give them the best chance of not arousing the suspicions of Russians sentries; and if some were stopped, others might still get through. Unlike Lwów, the railroad station in Kraków was right in the heart of the city, so it might be harder to reach.

Arriving at the station, Robert bought the tickets and waited anxiously. Gradually the men, women, and children drifted in. Miraculously, none had been stopped. There were Russian soldiers at the station, but they didn't seem to object; as long as the American officer was responsible, they didn't care what he did with the refugees. (Had they known that there were POWs in the party, it might have been different.) Kraków's proximity to the front line made it a more dangerous place to be at night, but it also meant that there was a constant flow of refugees—mostly Poles, Russians, and Ukrainians—passing through. And it meant that the NKVD had less of a foothold. There was a lag between the movement of the Red Army's front line and the appearance of the full apparatus of state security. As Robert would learn, in some towns it was surprisingly easy to get Russian approval for channeling liberated prisoners to the railroad—until the NKVD moved in and leaned on the town commandants.[4] After that the barriers would come down; there would be no more blind eyes.

For a second time, Robert went through the happy ceremony of departure, accepting the hugs and blessings and fond farewells and watching the train as it steamed out of the station, beginning the long haul to Odessa and freedom.

Over the next couple of days, he went through the ritual several more times. At least one of his contact agents was still in the area; seizing the opportunity presented by the circumstances in Kraków, the agent dispatched small groups to the edge of town, where Robert would pick them up and put them through the same routine, drifting inconspicuously through the city to the station. Most were POWs, but there were a few refugees from the death camps as well. He lost count of the numbers but figured that he must have put at least a hundred and fifty souls aboard trains during those couple of days at Kraków.

But the soul he had most wanted to bring to freedom—the ticket he had most wanted to buy—was not among them. Baby Kasia had not made it through that cold night on the outskirts of the city. Robert's heart had come close to breaking as they laid her to rest, still wrapped in his scarf, on a secluded patch of ground near the roadside and raised a little cairn of

stones over her. She had found a different kind of freedom from the pain of
the world.

The little stock of rations was long gone, and his money vest was
almost empty. It was time to go back to Poltava and replenish his
supplies. The thousands of dollars Robert had brought had been spent
in a few days; he would need to bring more next time. Altogether, the
money had set almost two hundred people on the road to freedom, but
there must be thousands more out there.

Robert had almost completely forgotten about the bird dog who'd
accompanied him from Rzeszów and was surprised to find him still at the
hotel. Like his predecessor in Lwów, the man was annoyed at being abandoned, and probably worried about his neck if his superiors found out.
Robert spun him a tale about following up a report on a downed bomber
which had turned into a wild goose chase, and the man seemed satisfied.

The bird dog got them places on a flight to Lwów, where they managed
to pick up one of the regular Russian transports going to Poltava. Robert
had a hard time believing that less than ten days had passed since he'd
taken off from the base, still confused, innocent, and rather naive for a combat veteran.

When he gave his various reports to Colonel Hampton, Major
Kowal, and Captain Fitchen, it was difficult to recall some details, and
impossible not to fixate on others. Describing the inside of the Birkenau
camp, he broke down, and had to pause and collect himself before going
on. It wasn't just what he'd experienced personally in Poland that had
affected him, it was what he had learned about the world and about
human nature. Something in him had altered, and would never be quite
the same again.

Kowal and Hampton had seen for themselves some of the things
Robert described—the atrocities committed by Russian troops against
Polish citizens, in particular—and sympathized with the emotions he
felt. But Auschwitz was altogether outside their experience.

To Robert's surprise, Hampton told him that he would be taking a break from his mission. Hopes were high at the Military Mission that the Soviets had had a change of heart about POWs. Colonel Wilmeth and Colonel Kingsbury, having been kept confined to Poltava for the past ten days, had been joined two days ago by a second small team from Moscow, led by a Major Paul Hall, which was intended to go to Odessa and inspect the reception facilities for POWs there. The Soviets had blocked Major Hall as well. However, word had now come through that both teams were definitely going to be allowed to proceed.[5] A Russian plane was being provided to take Colonel Wilmeth's party to Lublin in Poland, and Major Hall would be flown to Odessa. Both officers were busily preparing the huge quantities of equipment and supplies that would be needed.

It sounded too good to be true, but the Americans had decided to treat the Russian concession as being in good faith. Meanwhile, Captain Trimble was going back into Poland with a team of his own—a salvage team. Lieutenant Tillman's B-17 was still on the ground at Staszów. Robert knew the location, was familiar with the general area, and had been commended by his former commanding officer as a pilot who was skilled at getting bombers into the air from tight spots.

Robert didn't know what to think. He suspected that the Russians wouldn't play nice for long, and his heart went out to all those people who would remain stranded while he was tinkering with broken bombers.[6]

There was a little piece of consolation. Having lagged behind him all the way from USSTAF headquarters via the War Department and England, the news finally caught up with him—he had been awarded the Distinguished Flying Cross. A token of appreciation for thirty-five combat missions' worth of outstanding service.

Robert's spirits couldn't be kept low for too long; he was cheered to discover that Lieutenant Tillman and his crew were still at Poltava, as large as life and full of beans. They were still waiting for the transport that would take them on the circuitous route back to England. They greeted Robert even more like an old friend than they had at Staszów. Tillman had a camera, and was making a record of his adventure. He snapped Robert's picture on the step outside the Operations Office. Robert, enjoying the atmosphere of bonhomie, gave the camera a big smile, but the weariness in his eyes couldn't be disguised.

A dollar bill was produced—possibly one of the ones Robert had given them—and made into a short snorter, passing from hand to hand for everyone to put their signatures on. The tradition had begun back in the 1920s but had caught on in a big way in World War II. A traditional short snorter was meant to commemorate a journey by air; everyone on board would sign the bill, and the owner would preserve it.[7] During the war, servicemen had begun using them as autograph books, picking up the signatures of people they met on their travels, scrawled any which way, all over the back and front of the bill.

Tillman signed the front "Lt A. A. Tillman, Air Corps,"[8] and copilot Stan Neese added his name beside it. Next came navigator Cornelius F. Daly, squeezed into the gap along the top edge. Robert inscribed "R. M. Trimble, Capt. A.C." on the back, and in the margin, in commemoration of the rescue from Staszów, he added "Fighting Bastard of the Ukraine—25 Feb 45."[9]

Only the officers signed the snorter. (There were social barriers even among combat airmen.)[10] Robert didn't notice who had produced the bill, and didn't see who kept it. The snorter went on its way, gathering more signatures, and eventually vanished and was forgotten, along with the other human minutiae of the war.[11]

That day in 1945, Robert was again conscious of the gap that separated him from these other young men. Horsing around, posing for pictures, they seemed so carefree. Physically they were hardly more than boys, with the innocence of childhood still in them; but they were also men of war. Their bombs had inflicted death and devastation. They had seen friends die; they had faced death themselves and withstood it, and would go on to face it again and again before this war was done, and maybe succumb. And yet they were still youths at heart, each man believing himself the immortal center of his own universe.

It was only when you saw the suffering and the aftermath up close, lived among it, and knew that your own world and everything in it was just as vulnerable to the inferno—only then did you discover your place and your purpose. Robert Trimble had been to the abyss, and looked over the edge, and could never see anything the same way again.

9.

NIGHT OF THE COSSACKS

March 17, 1945: Poltava
Three weeks later

I n a pool of light cast by a single desk lamp, Captain Trimble sat alone
in the gloom of the deserted Operations Office. He took a sheet of
paper and fed it into the typewriter.

```
                    HEADQUARTERS
                 EASTERN  COMMAND
       US  STRATEGIC  AIR  FORCES  IN  EUROPE
                     APO  798


                     RMT/rte
                  17  March  1945

    SUBJECT:  Report  on  Flight  to  Rzeszow,  Staszow,
              Lwow,  Poland.
```

He paused and stared at the row of place names. How innocuous
they looked on paper. Yet the memories associated with them were still
raw, and would never entirely heal—wounds on top of wounds.

It was late, and Robert was dog-tired. It had been a tough flight back from Lwów. His ears still rang with the din of the B-17's rough-running engines, and he could still feel the vibrating controls in his hands. Everyone else had gone to their bunks, and he longed for his, but HQ wanted this report instantly. He'd be stuck in front of this typewriter all night if need be.

Captain Trimble was in hot water, and they wanted his side of the story. He'd pushed his luck this time, and his mission was hanging in the balance.

After his reunion with the Tillman crew, Robert had been back at Poltava only forty-eight hours when the time came for him to load up and leave again. He put his kit together, drew rations for his team, got a batch of cash from the finance officer, and prepared to head back to Poland to begin salvage work on Lieutenant Tillman's B-17 Flying Fortress.

Colonel Wilmeth and his team were simultaneously preparing to fly to Lublin and inspect the POW facilities there. Moscow was holding its breath. If the POW situation started to rectify itself, Robert's mission might not need to be continued. Personally, Robert wouldn't lay a bent nickel on it, and he wasn't the only one. It was maddening to have to suspend his work just when it was getting going, when he knew there were thousands of lost souls still out there in the cold wilderness. . . .

He forced his attention back to the typewriter. Where to begin? The events of the last three weeks were a confused and bewildering sequence of vivid memories and blurs, many of which had no place in an official report. The bullets pinging through the fuselage in the dead of night; the grinning, bearded giant thrusting a cup of rotgut liquor at him; the drag marks in the snow and the freshly turned earth in the quiet woodland; the terrifying flight into a snowstorm; the feel of the pistol in his fist; and the pitiful looks in the eyes of the emaciated prisoners.

Always the POWs; it always came back to them. Whatever headquarters might say, there was no escaping his true mission; it had pursued him and caught up with him even when he was diverted to other duties.

It was getting late, and the report still wasn't written. Again, he focused his attention. Begin at the beginning.

One of the base's C-47s had been made available for the salvage operation. Robert and his team loaded their gear aboard. There were seven men altogether, including Captain Trimble as pilot and leader.

Lieutenant Tyler E. Jessee was a seasoned navigator. He had come to this part of the world when he and his pals bailed out of their B-24 over Poland back in December. He had a good knowledge of the lay of the land and knew firsthand the political tensions, having been picked up by Polish partisans before being handed over to the Russians.[1] Rather than being evacuated back to his unit (the 460th Bomb Group, based in Italy), he had joined the staff of Eastern Command.

First Sergeant John Matles was from the Military Mission in Moscow.[2] A very smart Romanian-born New Yorker, he had been an engineer before the war, a skill which would make him useful on this operation. His greatest value, though, was as an interpreter. Aside from English and his native Romanian, he spoke good Russian and Polish. It was his linguistic talent, his intelligence, and his commanding personality that had raised him—a mere sergeant—to a position of distinction in the US military-diplomatic service.

In addition, there was a crew of four mechanics to fix up the downed B-17, under crew chief Sergeant Picarelli, another New Yorker. There were also two Americans catching a ride as far as Rzeszów. Aside from their personal kit and rations, the salvage crew filled up the C-47 with tools, spare parts, and a supply of gasoline. Then they waited for the Russian flight crew.

Americans were not permitted to fly transport planes in and out of Poltava. Sometimes mixed crews were allowed, but the pilot had to be a Soviet officer. It was with sinking hearts that Robert and his men learned that their pilot for the trip to Staszów was to be Lieutenant Roklikov.

Roklikov was notorious. He was careless, arrogant, and dangerous. Many military pilots had a daredevil streak (Robert himself was no exception, as RAF Balloon Command personnel could testify), but Roklikov was truly crazy—and incompetent with it. Colonel Hampton and General Hill had tried many times to persuade the Soviets to suspend him or transfer him elsewhere, but they never would. Maybe he was the son of somebody powerful, or had some nefarious role at Poltava; whatever it was, the Soviet commander, General Kovalev, would not accept that Roklikov was anything other than a brilliantly skilled, courageous pilot.

It had required a determined stand by the very highest authority to remove him from just a single flight. Back in January, he was scheduled to pilot a C-47 from Moscow to the Crimea, carrying a group of senior officers from SHAEF headquarters to the Yalta Conference. They included General Eisenhower's deputy, Air Chief Marshal Arthur Tedder. Tedder had heard about Roklikov from Colonel Hampton.[3] Using the full weight of his authority, he argued with the Russians—taking it all the way to a marshal of the Soviet Air Force—and refused to be flown by the mad lieutenant. They relented, and Colonel Hampton piloted the plane to Yalta, with Tedder himself as copilot.

Lesser authorities than the deputy commander in chief could try to go against the will of the Soviets, but they'd be wasting their time. And so Roklikov carried on flying routes in and out of Poltava. His attitude never changed, and his skills did not improve.

Thinking about Roklikov got Robert sufficiently annoyed to overcome his tiredness as he wrote his report. The Russian's misbehavior had begun the moment the C-47's wheels left the runway. Robert began punching the typewriter keys:

```
On take-off, Lt. Roklikov improperly flew over
headquarters building, very low, with eight (8)
barrels of 100 octane gasoline on board and nine
(9) American personnel.

The trip to Rzeszow was uneventful. At Staszow
there was question as to whether the field was
suitable for landing.
```

That was when the fun really started. Having been to the crash-landing site, Robert knew the situation. The field was five miles outside the city. With no reliable road transport available to haul the parts and fuel, there was no choice but to locate a farm field big enough to land in, as close as possible to the Fortress.

Robert, sitting in the freight compartment with his team and their mountains of stuff (several of the men, including Robert, were using the gasoline barrels as seats), could feel the C-47 descending and circling. His pilot's sixth sense told him something wasn't right—which was par for the course with Roklikov.

Maiya, the Red Army interpreter, appeared in the forward doorway, looking anxious. It was a look she did well, with her large, expressive doe eyes. This was the first time Robert had traveled with her since the journey to Auschwitz. "Captain Trimble will come to the cockpit, please?" she shouted over the noise of the engines.

Captain Trimble came to the cockpit, and didn't like what he found there. Lieutenant Roklikov was experiencing an uncharacteristic moment of doubt. Through Maiya, he indicated that he would like Robert to take a look at the field and say whether it was suitable for landing. The copilot stood aside, and Robert took his seat.

"What do you think?" Roklikov asked through Maiya. "Can we land?"

Robert surveyed the landscape. It wasn't as flat as the Ukrainian Steppe, but it was fairly level, and some of the fields, although narrow, were long. With all the snow, it wasn't easy to make out the boundaries, and the fields were interspersed with patches of woodland and what looked like fishponds or small lakes. He made out the shape of the stranded B-17, lying with its nose in the trees, and the gouges it had left in the field and hedgerow as it made its emergency landing. Robert instructed Roklikov to pick a field he liked the look of and "drag" it to test its suitability.

The Russian couldn't even do that properly. He picked a field and, instead of dragging it at low altitude, just above stalling speed—a dry-run technique to test the length—he buzzed it, tearing through at high speed, almost brushing the treetops.

"I don't know," Robert said. "I didn't even see it. What do *you* think?"

Roklikov shrugged. "It's all right, I think."

Figuring there wasn't much point asking him to drag it again, Robert gave his consent to land. What followed was one of the worst displays of incompetent piloting he'd ever experienced. A cadet would have been ashamed of it. He was just glad he was strapped into a proper seat when it happened.

Instead of turning into the wind—the simplest, most fundamental principle of landing a plane—Roklikov made his approach with the wind behind him. Robert could see the direction of the wind from the smoke of a distant factory stack. Not only was the direction obviously adverse, it was also a stiff breeze, about twenty miles per hour. Moreover, Roklikov had picked the very field the B-17 had tried to land in.

Ignoring Robert's warning, Roklikov carried on, preventing the C-47 from stalling out by extending the flaps to their fullest and keeping the speed up. They were going far too fast. Roklikov hit the treetops at the edge of the field, then dropped the plane down sharply into it. The wheels hit the turf with a savage jolt that shook the whole aircraft to its uttermost nuts and rivets. Hurtling and bouncing up the field, rapidly running out of space, Roklikov jammed both feet hard on the brake pedals; the C-47 lurched forward violently, almost tipping over on its nose, before settling tail-down and slewing to a shuddering halt, just forty feet short of the pines at the end of the field.

The crew and passengers emerged from the plane physically and emotionally shaken. They were in the midst of a featureless, snow-covered field, and dusk wasn't far away. Robert and his team inspected the C-47 and found that both flaps and both elevators had been damaged, probably where they'd hit the treetops on the approach. Wonderful—now they had *two* planes to fix. Lieutenant Roklikov seemed to think he'd done a pretty decent job in the circumstances.[4]

Maiya approached Captain Trimble. "Where will you and your men sleep tonight?"

He'd made up his mind about this before leaving Poltava. He'd stayed at the Red Army quarters at Staszów before, en route to Kraków, and didn't fancy repeating the experience. "We'll sleep in the plane," he said.

There was shock and a trace of anxiety in her eyes. "You will not come into the town with us?"

No, they wouldn't. Aside from the fact that they had no transportation for their personal luggage, it was a five-mile walk. Also, the plane was full of valuable parts, tools, and gasoline. Maiya tried to persuade him, but he insisted: the Americans would stay in the plane.

While this conversation was going on, one of Robert's men, who had wandered off toward the road, had met a Polish woman who lived nearby. Hearing about their situation, she invited the whole crew to stay the night at her home. Robert agreed gladly, and dispatched two of his men to go with her and get a cart to transport the luggage.

What happened next still made Robert seethe. The typewriter keys clacked loudly as he typed . . .

```
While they were gone, the Russian crew left for
Staszow, walking. The Russian crew went into this
lady's house while the two Americans were there
and informed her that if the American personnel
stayed there it would mean trouble for her,
therefore, the first night was spent in the C-47.
```

They arranged themselves as best they could inside the cargo compartment, and after a meal they bedded down. Robert, who was growing accustomed to improvised sleeping conditions, arranged himself a bunk by laying out his bedroll on top of the fuel barrels. Some of the other guys lay on the benches or the stretcher supports that were fitted for transporting wounded. It was going to be a cold and uncomfortable night.

How long they had lain there when the first faint rumbling sound began, nobody was sure. It came from somewhere in the distance, growing rapidly, a thumping, grumbling sound that was unmistakably that of horses running—lots of them. Peering out the window, Robert could make out the shapes of horsemen in the silvery light of the full moon—Cossacks, two dozen of them cantering in a circle around the plane, brandishing their weapons and whooping like a Sioux war party. That was worrying enough. Then they started shooting.

It was a sound that every combat airman knew and hated: the ping of bullets piercing the Alclad skin of an airplane. Who were these guys, and why were they shooting? Was this an enemy raid? There were Cossacks in German service as well as in the Red Army. But this was a hell of a long way from the front line. As another round zinged through the fuselage, Robert became acutely conscious of the eight fifty-five-gallon barrels of high-octane fuel he was lying on. One bullet in the wrong place, a spark, and they'd all go up in one almighty fireball.

Something had to be done. Defense was out of the question; between the seven of them they had only their sidearms, against more than twenty Cossack riders armed to the teeth. A couple of the men hastily improvised a flag from a pole and a white rag, opened the cargo door an inch, and waved it. There was a distant shout, and instantly the firing stopped. The thundering hoofbeats slowed and came closer.

A few of the Cossacks trotted up to the door and dismounted—a little unsteadily. One of them was clutching what appeared to be a liquor jug. He was a huge man, like an unholy hybrid of Santa Claus and Genghis Khan, with a great black beard, a fur hat, and bandoliers across his broad chest. He barked an incomprehensible inquiry in slurred Russian.

"*Ya amerikanets*," Robert said. "Americans."

"Amerikantsy?" Genghis repeated. His hedgerow beard opened up in a broad grin. "Amerikantsy!" he cried. He turned to his men and shouted: "Amerikantsy!" They all laughed uproariously. Robert wasn't sure if that was a good sign or not. They were a forbidding band. They all wore heavy fur caps and long riding coats, but all different (the Cossacks had a casual notion of uniform when on active service), and all were armed to their grinning teeth.

Genghis tilted his head back, took a slug from his liquor jug, and thrust it at Robert with a grunt that could have been a threat or an invitation. Guessing it was the latter, Robert took the jug. He recognized the stuff: the local blue-colored beetroot liquor they called "three beets." Looking around the ring of satanic faces, he felt like it was *drink or die*. He drank. Genghis was delighted. More jugs were produced and passed from hand to hand. The Cossacks drank; the Americans drank. There seemed to be no shortage of the stuff.

By this time, some of the Cossacks had a campfire going. The Americans were exhorted to come out of their plane and join them at the fireside. A couple of the Cossacks brought out instruments, and soon there was singing and dancing. To the accompaniment of the wild, fiery music, clapping, and laughter, the riders took turns at the *hopak*, the Ukrainian folk dance, squatting and kicking in the firelight. Robert and his men, who by now were half-plastered, were not allowed to sit out the dance, and there were roars of laughter all round at their attempts to mimic the squat-kicking steps. Presiding over it all was the bearded bulk of Genghis, with his ever-present jug of three beets.

It was an image from a dream, burning itself into Robert's memory: the Slavonic faces in the flickering firelight, beards split by demonic grins. Most wore crossed bandoliers, some with an extra one as a belt; they sported rows of *gaziri* across their chests, the cigar-like pouches that had originally been for gunpowder cartridges but were now just decoration. In the Russian tradition, they displayed their medals on their coats. Every man was heavily armed—aside from their rifles, each had a *shashka* at his belt—a huge weapon like a cross between a cleaver and a short sword. With the heady music, the reek of liquor and woodsmoke, and somewhere off in the darkness, the snorting and chafing of the hobbled horses, a man could imagine himself having strayed into another age of the world. . . .

The next morning, Robert woke facedown in the snow beside the embers of the fire. Luckily, his parka and the dying warmth of the fire had saved him from hypothermia. His head was out of bounds, and his tongue seemed to have gone AWOL. He looked up just in time to see Genghis emerge from the door of the C-47, where he'd apparently spent the night on a very convenient bed made up on top of some fuel barrels. He spotted Robert, strode over, and embraced him. He slapped him on the back, and laughed as Robert stumbled to his knees and puked in the snow.

Around them harnesses were jingling as the horsemen mounted up. Genghis swung into the saddle, called an order, and they wheeled about. Spurring their horses to a canter, they took off across the snowy field and were gone, like smoke on the wind.

10.

RUSSIAN ROULETTE

Memorable as it had been, the night of the Cossacks was best left out of the report. Skipping discreetly over it, Robert inserted a fresh sheet of paper in the typewriter and continued his sanitized version of the narrative:

```
The next day quarters were arranged at another
Polish house, and the remaining nights were spent
there.
```

This time they ensured that the Russians didn't know about the arrangement.

By the time Maiya and the Russian crew returned from Staszów—having walked all the way—it was one o'clock in the afternoon, and the Americans' hangovers had faded. This turned out to be the pattern every day (the late arrival of the Russians, not the hangovers). Robert suggested they get up earlier in the morning. They were supposed to be helping with the salvage operation, but couldn't be much use if they only put in half a day's work each day. But nothing changed, and in customary Soviet fashion they contributed more in the way of obstruction and irritation than practical aid.

Meanwhile, Robert and his crew got on with the task of making the

B-17 airworthy. They walked over to the field, and there she was, the nameless "687," right where Tillman had left her, with her wheels in a ditch and her Plexiglas nose among the trees. An inspection showed that work needed to be done on the engines, props, and landing gear, all of which had suffered damage either in combat or in the forced landing. Three engines were dead, and the fuselage was peppered with flak holes, some as big as baseballs.

With limited tools, no lifting gear, no transportation or power, it was going to be a hard slog. And the weather was deteriorating too. The sky, which had been bright for a couple of days, was growing sullen with snow.

As pilot, Robert's second concern was how he was going to get this bird off the ground once it was patched up. The field it was in was no good at all: far too short. He searched around and found a neighboring field that might be just about big enough—if they were lucky. In order to get there the Fort would have to be taxied, which would burn up precious fuel. Also, between this field and the other was a ditch, which would have to be crossed somehow. Robert assigned the Russians the task of building a small bridge across it. And a path would need to be cut through the trees.

There was also the C-47 to be repaired, thanks to Roklikov. The flaps could be fixed in situ, but the elevators couldn't. New ones would have to be flown in from Poltava. Maiya said they could be fixed at the Soviet air base at Rzeszów, but unfortunately the bridges between here and there had been blown. And they had no transportation anyway. Maiya asked Sergeant Picarelli, Robert's crew chief, if he could give the Russians some oil from the C-47 so that they could fix up a truck they knew about in Staszów, which they could use to make their daily journey in reasonable time.

Robert overheard the suggestion, and intervened. Not a chance. Every drop of oil was going to be needed for the planes. He had learned (from the Polish farmer with whom they were staying, although he kept that quiet) that Russian soldiers had been coming at night and stealing oil and gasoline from the stranded bomber. The Americans actually caught them at it one night; the soldiers were threatened with arrest and stayed away. But oil would need to be drained from the C-47 to replenish the B-17. There wasn't any to spare for trucks.

"How much oil?" Maiya asked at the prompting of the Russian mechanic.

"Forty gallons," Robert said. "Ten gallons per engine."

"That is too much," said Maiya, translating the mechanic's reply. "You do not need that much."

"I have considerable experience with B-17s and Wright engines," Robert said firmly, "and so does my crew chief. *You* do not."

Over the course of the following week, poor Maiya was the mouth-piece for a regular stream of interference and objections from the Russian crew. She even disputed the field that Captain Trimble had chosen for takeoff, insisting that it was impossible to take off from there. Although he had grave doubts of his own, Robert assured her that it would be fine.

He had walked it several times, pacing out the distance. It was about a thousand feet long, down a slope, leveling off in the last hundred feet, at the end of which was a frozen stream with a bank about two feet high. Robert had flown off short runs before, on turf and soft surfaces, but nothing as short as this. *What the hell have I taken on here?* he asked himself. *I'm an idiot.* One thousand feet. A B-17 Flying Fortress, fully laden with crew, guns, ammunition, fuel, and bombs, weighed in at sixty-five thousand pounds, and needed thirty-five hundred feet of good runway to get airborne. Even unladen, a Fortress was a monster, and would have trouble taking off in under twelve hundred feet—on turf it would need more. And on a surface like this one, with eight inches of snow . . . it was anybody's guess.

As if that weren't enough of a challenge, there were limits to how good a repair job could be done. They fixed two of the damaged engines and replaced some propeller blades, but Sergeant Picarelli had discovered that one of the prop shafts was a little bent. There was nothing they could do about that. "She'll run," he said, "but she'll vibrate like hell. Might need to shut her down once you're airborne."

So the Fort was going to be underpowered. One thousand feet. It was going to take some skillful piloting. And this Fort was going to have to lose a little weight.

While work on the B-17 was slowly proceeding, an order came through from Poltava—a report of another downed plane that might need retrieving. This one was a little outside Robert Trimble's experience: a P-51 Mustang fighter. But it was nearby, and needed checking quickly before the Soviets could get a team to it.

Red Army Air Force intelligence was keen to get its hands on all American aircraft types, and had formed top secret test squadrons to evaluate stolen examples.[1] Some aircraft were more prized than others. In general, the US government was liberal about giving aviation technology to the Soviet Union: several aircraft types were supplied to the USSR under Lend-Lease, and the USAAF was generous with technical data on others.[2] But there were exceptions. None of America's cutting-edge technology (such as the Norden computing bombsight) was made available, and the AAF's core combat aircraft were likewise off-limits. That included B-17 and B-24 bombers. It also included the new, ultra-secret B-29 Superfortress, which at that time was taking the war to Japan in the Pacific. The Russians would do almost anything to get their hands on a B-29, and by 1945 their spies had already accumulated a lot of data on the type. They were equally determined to capture examples of America's state-of-the-art fighter, the P-51 Mustang.

The Mustang was a wonder of Anglo-American cooperation. Designed by North American Aviation company, to a British specification, named "Mustang" by the British, and powered by the same Rolls-Royce Merlin engine that drove the Spitfire, the P-51 had become the USAAF's most successful escort fighter, the only one with the speed and range to take on the Luftwaffe in the farthest reaches of the Reich. Aside from the revolutionary new jet fighters that the British and the Germans were now bringing into service, the Mustang was the most advanced frontline fighter in the world. Whenever one was forced down intact in Soviet territory, there was a race to get to it.

Although the distance from Staszów to the reported landing site wasn't great, it was much too far to walk. Robert managed to secure transport, and set off with First Sergeant John Matles as interpreter. Maiya and her comrades were left behind, under the watchful eye of Lieutenant Jessee and the repair crew.

In the deteriorating weather, it was a slow journey to the area where the Mustang had supposedly come down. They hadn't been given precise coordinates, just a local area. After some hours of searching the fields, Captain Trimble and Sergeant Matles hadn't found any trace of the fighter. Robert wasn't altogether surprised. Reports of crash-landed aircraft came in all the time from local Soviet units, and were routed to Eastern Command via Moscow. The reports weren't always reliable, and often salvage teams would go to the landing site and find nothing there.[3] But it was annoying.

By this time, it was too late to travel back. Robert spotted a farmhouse and decided to ask if they could bivouac in the barn. It was a small, poor homestead, just a shabby little house and some outbuildings clustered around a dirt yard with a horse trough. But the farmer was friendly. Waving aside the request to sleep in the barn, he invited the two Americans into the house and gave them a bed.

They paid for his hospitality with news of the war, which he was eager to hear. He lived alone, having lost his wife during the German invasion. They sat long into the evening, talking. The kitchen was cold, with no fire, and it quickly became obvious that the farmer had no food to offer his guests. They offered him a share of the rations they had brought with them. The old man looked embarrassed. Yes, he could use a little, he confessed. He had lost his cow and his chickens recently, and his stock of beets and potatoes from the last harvest was almost gone. Still, at least he had a home, he said, which was more than a lot of Poles could say right now.

While the food was being shared out, Robert took the opportunity to ask about the American plane that was said to have come down near here.

Did the farmer know anything about it? No, he didn't, and he quickly changed the subject. A little later, Robert brought the matter up again; this time the old man pointed out that it was getting late and they should turn in. He brought them a small dish of icy water to wash in, saying apologetically that it was all he had: his well had stopped working, and all his water had to be carried from a stream half a kilometer away.

Robert felt desperately sorry for the old man. His wife gone, and his livestock, his food, his well. It seemed all he had left was his house and himself. From the way things looked to Robert, neither of those seemed likely to survive much longer.

In the morning, the two Americans bade the farmer farewell, having shared their breakfast with him and left him their surplus rations. It might keep him going for a week or two.

As they drove down the cart road from the farm, Robert happened to notice some marks in the snow in the next field: long ruts like the wheel tracks of a small aircraft. Exactly the right size for a single-engine fighter. No sign of a plane, though—just an expanse of snow between the stands of trees with the wheel tracks disappearing into the distance. He pulled up and walked to the gateway.

Following the tracks across the field, the two men came at last to an area where the snow had been trampled down. There were footprints everywhere, and tire tracks from a vehicle too—a large truck had been here. At this spot the aircraft's wheel ruts came to an end. If this was the Mustang they were looking for, it had long gone, presumably loaded onto the truck. But you wouldn't be able to maneuver a plane the size of a P-51 through the narrow lanes hereabouts—it would have to be dismantled. Maybe the salvagers had left evidence behind that would identify it. Robert searched the ground, and at last he found it: barely discernible among the trampling, two thin parallel lines of dots melted in the snow, about ten feet long and eight feet apart, with a metallic residue in the bottom. There was no doubting what had caused the grooves: they were the drip runs of molten metal where the wings had been cut off with an oxyacetylene torch.

What had happened to the pilot? To have brought the plane in to land—even the bouncing crash-landing that the tire marks indicated—he could not have been mortally wounded. If the Russian salvagers had taken him away, they hadn't reported it to Moscow, despite several days having gone by. So what had they done with him? Robert felt he could guess, but without evidence, there was nothing he could do.

Robert looked across the field toward the farm; it was more than half a mile away, on the far side of a copse, but the noise that must have been made here would have been unmissable . . . Robert and Sergeant Matles exchanged a look, then set off back to the homestead.

For a moment they thought the farmer might have fled; there was no answer to their knock on the house door, and he was nowhere to be found in the outbuildings. Then he appeared, struggling along with two buckets of water.

"May we come in?" Robert asked, more formally this time. The old man seemed to sense what they were here for, and motioned for them to come in and sit down.

Once they were settled in the cold kitchen, he began to tell the story that he had withheld the previous night.

About a week ago, he had heard the noise of an airplane passing very low overhead. He hadn't heard it land. Sometime later, he saw Soviet jeeps passing on his road, headed for the site where he learned later the plane had come down. He knew to remain invisible when the military was near (German or Russian, they were all the same), but he watched from his window as the vehicles passed by, traveling another three-quarters of a mile down the road to the field on the other side of the copse. Not twenty minutes after they had passed, he heard two gunshots.

An hour later, the jeeps came back and stopped at the farmer's house. The officer in charge banged loudly on the door. The farmer opened it and peered out fearfully. The Russian officer wished to know if the farmer had seen or heard anything unusual recently, such as enemy activity. The farmer said no, which was true. They ransacked his house nevertheless, and of course found nothing. They eyed him sternly once more, and then ordered him not to leave his house until further notice. If he did, he would be shot. The officer got back in his jeep and the little convoy sped off up the road.

The terrified farmer obeyed; all that day and the next he stayed indoors, hardly daring to peep out the window. He had no idea what was happening, and was glad of it. In recent years he had learned the hard way that it was better to see nothing, to know nothing, and to fear the worst. One's life might depend on it.

Early the next morning, another convoy of military vehicles passed by, heading toward the field on the other side of the copse. Whether they were the same ones or not, the farmer couldn't tell, but there were two large flatbed trucks with them this time. By the middle of the afternoon, the noises from the field had stopped and there was a sound of motors working hard. Eventually, as the light was growing dim, the old Pole, peeking through a gap in the drapes, was astounded to see one of the large trucks passing by, with the fuselage of an airplane on its flatbed. A moment later, the second truck passed by with two long forms on it—the wings.

What kind of airplane it was, he had no idea. What did he know of airplanes? Nothing. The whole thing was a mystery—hopefully a mystery that was over now, and could be forgotten.

Unfortunately for the farmer, it was not over. A squad of Russian soldiers showed up at his door a few minutes after the trucks had passed by, demanding that he put them up for the night. They were also hungry. They quickly ate whatever meager food he had available, although they did give him some of their rations too; he hoped this was a sign they meant him no harm. After all, he had kept his promise and hadn't left his house. He spent an uncomfortable, sleepless night huddled under a blanket in front of the kitchen fire, the two Russian officers having taken his bedroom and all his spare bedding.

In the morning, the Russians arose and breakfasted; the officers ordered the farmer to get them water for their ablutions. He went to his well near the house and pumped enough to serve their needs, thinking to himself that they could wash all they wanted and never be clean. Before leaving, the senior officer interrogated him about what he knew or thought he knew. He confessed complete ignorance. The officer looked at him sternly; he was not convinced. Two soldiers seized him by the arms and rushed him out into the yard. On the officer's orders, some of the other soldiers went into the barn and brought out the farmer's solitary cow. They asked him again to tell the truth or they would kill his livestock. He again told the truth, that he knew nothing. In front of his eyes they put two bullets into the cow's head. They wrung the necks of the chickens and left the dead animals where they dropped. They were not done.

They placed a grenade next to the water pump, pulled the pin, and took cover. The explosion broke the pump and bent the pipe beyond repair. The Russian officer told the farmer that he must not mention anything at all about the events of the last two days; if he did he would suffer the same fate as his animals. Finally, their work done, the soldiers got into their vehicles and sped off up the road.

Ever since, the farmer had lived in fear of the Russians returning to obliterate what was left of his livelihood. They might as well take his life too.

Robert listened to the story in silence as Sergeant Matles translated it. He was saddened, but not surprised. Robert had seen and heard so many heartrending things recently. The man seemed numb, unable to show emotion. It was clear that he was broken, and that all he had left was a proud refusal to lie down and die.

Robert came back to the one remaining question: did the farmer learn anything about the pilot? Without speaking, the old man stood up and motioned for the Americans to follow him. They walked down the dirt road in the direction of the crash site, until they reached the pine copse that stood between the fields. The elderly Pole led them into the woods. About forty feet from the road they came to a small clearing, where a pile of pine branches concealed a freshly dug patch of earth. Removing the branches revealed a low mound about six feet by three. The farmer had discovered it two days ago.

Was this the last resting place of the pilot? If so, was he killed in the crash or murdered? For the time being, the question would have to remain unanswered. The soil was frozen, and they had nothing to dig with. The Russians had "borrowed" the farmer's tools and never returned them.

They had nothing: no plane, no pilot, no body, no hard evidence that anything at all had happened here. All they had was the word of this old Polish farmer, some marks in the snow, and a patch of dug earth. If the pilot survived the crash-landing, he might have left the scene before the Soviet troops arrived; the "gunshots" could have been anything.

For that matter, even if the pilot was dead, he might not have been shot by the salvagers. There had been cases of stricken American aircrew being mistakenly killed by Soviet troops. Faulty identification and Soviet paranoia were a lethal mix. It was later noted in the official history of Eastern Command that damaged US planes and their crews "were forced to run the whole gamut, including Russian fighter attacks, flak hits, attacks after bailing out, attacks after landing, being shot at or being threatened with shooting . . . mauling and beating" at the hands of Soviet troops who were suspicious of Nazi tricks.[4] Everybody was a potential spy, and life was dirt-cheap.

All Robert could do was radio a report on the incident to Poltava. Right now he had a salvage operation to complete, and his own set of problems with Soviet interference.

Captain Trimble and Sergeant Matles returned to Staszów to find the B-17 almost ready to go.

To bring down the weight, every unnecessary piece of steel had been removed. Every seat other than the pilot's and copilot's had been taken out, along with the armor plating in each crew station, the bomb racks, and the navigator's table. The heavy steel machine-gun mountings had been taken out (the guns themselves were long gone), and the ball turret under the Fort's belly was unbolted and lowered to the ground. Everything that could be dispensed with had come out, strewing the snow with discarded components.

On the afternoon of the seventh day, the B-17 was as ready as she would ever be. The fuel had been funneled in—400 gallons sloshing pathetically in the aircraft's vast 2,780-gallon tanks. Enough for around two hours' flight in good conditions; it wouldn't get them to Poltava, but there should be enough to make Lwów. On the positive side, the lack of fuel would keep the takeoff weight down. So would the minimal crew, which would be limited to Robert as pilot, Lieutenant Jessee as navigator, Sergeant Picarelli as flight engineer, and Sergeant Matles as passenger. The salvage crew would be flying out in the repaired C-47, once more placing their lives in the hands of God and Lieutenant Roklikov.[5]

Around four o'clock on the last afternoon, with the light fading and dark clouds building, before heading back to their quarters Robert and his team made a final inspection, checking and double-checking every nut and bolt. The repairs to the engines were adequate, but far from perfect. That bent prop shaft would be a real problem.

Their attention was drawn by the sound of vehicles from the road that passed by the bottom of the field. A couple of jeeps pulled up, and a group of Soviet officers got out. They were led by a colonel Robert had never seen before, and accompanied by Maiya. It was clear the colonel wanted to speak to him, so Robert walked down the hill.

Evidently a man of little patience and even littler manners, the colonel was already starting up the hill toward him and began talking when Robert was still a hundred feet from him. Poor Maiya had to jog along behind him, shouting her translations.

"Captain, how is the repair work progressing?"

Robert considered his reply carefully. It might not be a good idea to let them know that the plane was ready to fly, but on the other hand, they might get hostile if they thought the Americans were prolonging their stay in Poland. He opted for the truth: the bomber would be ready to attempt takeoff the next day. He also prevaricated: "But I'm not completely sure yet."

"You are doing good work, Captain. Are you flying it to Rzeszów first?" the colonel asked.

"No, sir," Robert said. "The plan is to head straight for Lwów." *As you well know*, he thought.

"Indeed." The colonel nodded, then dropped his little bombshell: "You will of course need to have one of our pilots fly the airplane, as is the rule. You and your men can return with the transport. This will be best for you."

Robert could hardly believe the gall of it. The colonel's interpretation of "the rule" was not an officially sanctioned one for salvaged combat aircraft. "Thank you for the offer," Robert said diplomatically, "but I have strict orders to take this aircraft to Lwów myself, then on to Poltava."

The Russian looked put out. He wasn't accustomed to having his orders contradicted by a mere captain. "I will have to check on this," he said. There was a muttered consultation in Russian between the colonel, his officers, and Maiya. Robert had the distinctly uneasy feeling that he was the subject of their discussion.

Maiya approached him and smiled. "You look tired," she said. "But happy I guess, since your work is all done." She was all smiles, and something was different about her. Robert noticed the smell of perfume. Were Red Army women allowed to wear perfume, or just interpreters? She didn't look half-bad to a homesick soldier. "The colonel has some good news!" she said. The colonel was smiling too. "We have a wonderful offer. As you are to fly away tomorrow, we wish you to be our honored guest for dinner in town. We will arrange for you to spend the night in a hotel. A very good hotel." Maiya added (and Robert had the strong impression that the words came from her rather than the colonel): "I will personally assure that you are comfortable, Captain. What do you say? We must be getting on, it will be dark soon."

Robert was mesmerized by the invitation—the thought of good food, a nice hotel, a soft bed . . . and the promise of female attention. For a young, lonely soldier—even a faithfully married one—it was more than flesh and blood could resist. He hesitated.

As he looked into Maiya's lustrous eyes, a voice echoed in his head.

Don't go with them, it said. He couldn't place it for a moment, then he remembered it as the voice of one of the OSS agents, that first day at Poltava. *They'll try to get you to go with them. Don't do it. You will be traveling along, and you'll pass some woodland. Suddenly they stop the car. "Everybody out! There are Germans there, in the trees!" There will be confusion; you'll jump out and take cover. Meanwhile, two of their guys circle around behind you. . . . You'll be found with a bullet in your back, from the "German ambush." The Soviet authorities will buy it—they're paranoid about German paratroopers and spies everywhere. And believe it or not, there are pro-German partisan groups in Poland. The Americans might not believe it, but there won't be a damned thing they can do. . . .*

Robert tore his eyes away from Maiya. He looked at the colonel, and the little knot of junior officers and enlisted men behind him. Their faces were impassive. Would they murder him to get their hands on a B-17?

"No," he said. "Thank you for your offer, but we'll stay here tonight."

"Captain, it is late. Come with us now, you'll be happy you did," the colonel insisted.

"No thank you, sir."

The colonel's face darkened angrily. "I am a colonel; you are only a captain. You must do what I tell you to do. You will come with us now, and tomorrow a Soviet pilot will fly the airplane."

He turned away for a second and gestured at his men to escort the American captain. Robert, acting on instinct, drew his sidearm; when the colonel turned back he found himself looking into the muzzle of a Colt .45.

"I'm telling you something right now," Robert said, his voice hard. He leveled the pistol at the colonel's gut. "I'm not going anywhere with you. But I would invite you to come up right now and talk to all of my men. They'll say the same. They'll tell you what we're here for, and what we're gonna do. We're gonna fly this plane out in the morning."

He stared into the colonel's astonished, enraged eyes, but there was no reply. Satisfied, he turned his back on the Russians and walked back up the slope toward the Fortress, where his team was watching the drama unfold.

Behind him the colonel yelled furiously, and Maiya translated (leaving out a few ripe curses, Robert guessed): "You'll hear about this! When you hear, it will be from Moscow! I will report your behavior. I don't take this kind of talk!"

With his dignity sorely wounded, the colonel marched back to his jeep, his entourage flocking behind him, including Maiya, whose linguistic skills had been sorely tried by the whole episode. It hadn't been a good day for US-Soviet relations.

Thinking back on the incident later, Robert could hardly believe his own bravado. The colonel was as good as his word; he did report it to Moscow, and the reprimand came back down the line all the way to the US Military Mission. It would do Robert no good to give his side of the story, and so he left it out of his report, along with the night of the Cossacks and the tale of the Mustang and the farmer. He merely noted that there were frequent arguments in which Maiya was caught between his decisions and the desires of the Soviets.

Having made that note, he fed a fresh sheet of paper into the typewriter, and went on with his story. He wasn't done with it yet, not by a long way.

The Americans were on-site early the next morning. After a thorough inspection to ensure that no tampering had occurred in the night, Robert and Sergeant Picarelli installed themselves in the cockpit. Picarelli was a mechanic, not a copilot, but Robert needed him to help manage the aircraft's engine controls. With mounting apprehension, they began the routine of bringing the sleeping beast back to life. One by one, with gentle coaxing, the engines were started up, coughing and spluttering great clouds of gray smoke and settling down to an uneven grumble that Robert didn't like the sound of at all. Once they were warm, they were run up to high revs; they showed no sign of seizing or catching fire, so Robert eased back and began the slow, extremely awkward job of taxiing 687 to her takeoff strip.

She was one sad-looking B-17, leaving behind a scatter of discarded parts in the snow. Battle-scarred, with sheets of plywood covering the holes in the fuselage where the gun turrets had been removed, and rags stuffed in the larger flak holes, she didn't look like much of a prize for either side. They eased her over the little bridge the Russians had built across the ditch, and entered the takeoff field.

With careful use of brakes and throttles, Robert maneuvered the B-17 into position as close to the top field boundary as he could, to maximize the run-up. He swung the nose round to face down the slope, then he and Picarelli locked the brakes and walked the throttle levers up to the stops, opening everything up to maximum emergency power. It was a method used on maximum-load missions, with fuel tanks brim-full and an overload of bombs, when even three-quarters of a mile of concrete runway might be insufficient to get the bird off the floor. Here the bird was stripped to the bone, and they had one-fifth of a mile of ankle-deep snow. With the engines roaring, blowing up a hurricane of snow and whipping branches off the trees, Robert held the control column hard back against his belly, fighting to prevent the Fort pulling herself over on her nose.

"They're coming!" yelled a voice in his headphones. He glanced out the window and saw two jeeps pulling in at the field entrance. Russian soldiers jumped out and ran toward the plane.

"Brakes off!" Robert ordered. Picarelli released the brake handle, and they both took their feet off the pedals. Anticipating the powerful surge he had experienced countless times before, Robert was startled at the way the lightened Fort leapt forward and raced down the slope. The soldiers, guns raised but not shooting, were left behind instantly. She ate up the space at an alarming rate, and the line of the frozen stream was rushing toward them, jolting and shaking, before they'd even reached minimum takeoff speed. The indicator rose past one hundred miles per hour. For an instant Robert felt they weren't going to make it—they'd smash into the hedgerow, slide across the field beyond, and end up pancaked against the fifty-foot pines.

The wheels hit the stream bank with a violent jolt that sent the Fort leaping upward. Miraculously, she stayed airborne. Engines howling, she struggled, accelerated, and began to climb. Tucking up her wheels, she cleared the pines, the very tops just brushing her belly.

Robert's stomach flipped over, and he felt the familiar thrill of flight more intensely than at any time since his training. Once again he marveled at the miracle of the Flying Fortress. As one of his fellow pilots from the 493rd said, recalling the group's transition from Liberators to B-17s, "After all of the trouble we had getting the B-24s off the ground with three times as long a run, it was a real pleasure to be flying an airplane that seemed to want to fly."[6]

Captain Trimble kept one eye on the compass as he put the Fort into a gentle bank, turning her onto a bearing for Lwów.

The operation on which they had set out from Poltava just over a week ago was still not over, and Robert's true mission was about to make an unexpected reappearance.

11.

SUFFER THE LOST PRISONERS

February 23, 1945: Refugee camp, Czarnków, Poland

The pace of the war had changed. To the people in the town of Czarnków, it seemed that the distant thunder of the guns had paused for a
while, then resumed—farther away and firing in a different tempo. The
news eventually came through: at long last, the city of Poznań had fallen to
the Red Army. It had been a stubborn point of resistance at the heart of the
Soviet advance, which had been surging forward north and south of it,
punching a corridor toward Berlin. Now the city was freed.

To one American, the news was particularly welcome. Sergeant
Richard J. Beadle from Louisiana, formerly of the 45th Infantry Division, ex-inmate of Stalag III-C, could continue his journey to freedom.[1]
Along with thousands of displaced persons, military and civilian, he
had been living in the refugee camp at Czarnków, waiting for the route
southeast to clear.

Sergeant Beadle's odyssey had begun just over three weeks ago,
when he and his fellow POWs were liberated. Stalag III-C was a camp
for enlisted men located near Küstrin, about fifty miles from Berlin. At
the end of January, with the spearhead units of the Soviet divisions
closing in, the Germans decided to evacuate the camp. The prisoners
would be marched to a new location fifty miles to the west.

The fifteen hundred prisoners were roused from their huts and herded at bayonet point into a long column. Many of them were malnourished, some were sick, and all were reluctant to be force-marched.[2] It was hours before the column was ready to set out. The evacuation had barely begun when the leading battalions of the Red Army arrived. The Soviet troops, fighting as they came, were entirely unaware that there was a POW camp in their path. Thinking the stalag was a barracks, and that the prisoners were Hungarian troops (or so they later claimed), they poured mortar fire onto it. As the column of POWs marched from the camp, they were hit with shells and machine-gun fire by Russian tanks.[3] Men rushed for cover, many seizing the opportunity to escape from the column. By the time the Russians realized their error and ceased firing, fifteen prisoners lay dead in the snow, and another twenty-five were wounded.

Of those who survived, some scattered into the countryside, while others took refuge in the camp buildings. Most were rounded up by the Soviets and marched to the rear, away from the combat zone. Some were taken the twenty or so miles to Landsberg.[4] The group into which Sergeant Beadle had been herded was marched just a short distance from the camp, to the tiny village of Quartschen.[5] They were given no food and nothing to protect them from the freezing weather; their liberators simply turned them loose and told them to head for Warsaw.

Sergeant Beadle was in better condition than most. As a medic he knew how to take care of himself, and as a combat veteran who had served at Anzio he was used to harsh conditions. He also had the advantage of having been a prisoner for a relatively short time; captured the previous September,[6] he had suffered the privations of the camp for just a few months, and his health was good. He set out, making his way toward Warsaw as best he could.

Warsaw was more than two hundred miles away, and the route was a fraught and dangerous one. The Red Army's northern divisions, forcing the Germans back into their fatherland, had pushed the line of the Eastern Front hard, swinging it like a vast double door, opening up a broad corridor from east to west. The hinges on which the doors had swung were two of the fortress cities designated by Hitler as *Festungen*: strongpoints which were not to be surrendered, where the soldiers of the Reich were ordered to fight to the last man.

In the middle of the open doorway, isolated as the Soviets advanced around it, stood the *Festung* city of Poznań. Known to the Germans as Posen, it was an ideal place for a siege. An earlier generation of German occupiers in the nineteenth century had built a vast, impregnable network of fortifications—the *Festung Posen*, and it was in these redoubts, forts, and tunnels that the Nazi forces held out for week after week against the Red Army, which pounded the city with massed artillery and sent Guards regiments to infiltrate the defenses.

To Sergeant Richard Beadle, the siege of Poznań was an impassable obstruction on the route to Warsaw. Keeping a safe distance from the front line—the walls of the corridor—he found his way to the town of Czarnków, where there was a refugee camp. There he settled down to wait for the siege to break.

It happened on February 22, when the fanatical Nazi commander at Poznań committed suicide and his surviving men surrendered. The Russians flooded through, and the road to Warsaw was clear. Sergeant Beadle left the refugee camp and headed south.

It was a doubly significant date for him. Exactly one year ago he had been in Italy with his unit, I Company, 180th Infantry Regiment, at the Anzio beachhead. On February 22, 1944, I Company and its neighboring units were the focus of savage German assaults. One of the men who were instrumental in fighting off the attacks that day was Beadle's platoon commander, Second Lieutenant Jack C. Montgomery.[7] With his platoon reduced to half its strength, Montgomery, a Cherokee from Oklahoma, launched a series of single handed assaults which killed eleven Germans, captured more than thirty more, and knocked out two machine guns. His actions earned him the Medal of Honor. Later that night, Lieutenant Montgomery was caught in a mortar barrage and severely wounded. As he lay alone in the dark, he had faith that help would come. "It wasn't very long before my medic found me," he recalled. "Your medic was one person that you had to have confidence in. I knew Beadle would find me."[8]

Now, exactly a year on, Beadle needed to have that same kind of faith in himself, and in his ability to find his way to friendly forces. And if he was lucky, onward to his home in Louisiana—a little place called Reserve, on the Mississippi between New Orleans and Baton Rouge. Home seemed more like a different world than merely a different country.

When Beadle passed through Poznań, it was a living nightmare, a city of death. Almost the whole of the city center was in ruins, and much of the outlying districts too, pounded to rubble by Soviet and German artillery. Despite the devastation, the Soviets had quickly got the railroad working again (the Poznań route was a vital artery connecting the front line to the supply system), and Sergeant Beadle managed to get aboard a train to Warsaw. He rode the whole way in a boxcar with no source of heat, and again the Russians refused to give him any food.

If Poznań had been a sad place, Warsaw was worse. The scene of uprisings by the ghetto Jews and by the Polish Home Army, it had been attacked ferociously by German forces and the Red Army. Despite having been instructed to come here, Sergeant Beadle found no assistance, and quickly moved on. There were no trains available, so he set off walking toward Lublin, where he had been told there was a reception center for liberated POWs. It was more than a hundred miles from Warsaw to Lublin, and Sergeant Beadle covered about half of it on foot, managing to catch a ride on a truck the rest of the way. If it hadn't been for the fact that he was fit and healthy to begin with, and received help and food from Polish people he met on the way, he might never have made it.

In Lublin he found the promised reception center—or what passed for one. Dozens of his fellow American and British ex-POWs had gathered. Some of them were survivors of the Russian assault on Stalag III-C. There was a small contact team of American officers in the town, led by a Colonel Wilmeth, recently arrived from the Military Mission in Moscow. They were doing what they could to organize the men's relief and evacuation. For a brief time, it seemed like Lublin might be the end of Sergeant Beadle's odyssey. In fact, it would turn out to be just a way station on a journey that was far from over. Things were not going well for the Americans in Lublin.

March 7, 1945: Europa Hotel, Lublin, Poland

Lieutenant Colonel James D. Wilmeth stared out of his hotel window across the snow-covered rooftops and the open spaces beyond. How many men were still out there, he wondered; how many still lost or hiding in the vast reaches of Poland's countryside? Intelligence he had heard from the tiny handful who had made it to Poltava and Moscow indicated that there were thousands. There was nothing he could do for them unless they came to him, here in Lublin. He was trapped here. And even if they came to him, what he could do was limited.

He had been in the town just over a week and was already bowing under the weight of the task he'd undertaken. The work itself was far beyond the capacity of one small group of men, but it carried a moral imperative that drove Wilmeth and his two companions onward. But the constant, bullheaded resistance from the Soviets at every level was utterly demoralizing.

After the way he'd been repeatedly stymied before even leaving Poltava, it was pretty much what he ought to have expected. For two weeks he'd been stuck at the air base while the Soviets responded with refusals and excuses to his requests to be allowed to fly to Poland. He and Colonel Hampton even discussed the possibility of loading up an American plane and flying Wilmeth to Lublin without Soviet permission.[9] It would undoubtedly result in Soviet rage and some kind of punishment against Eastern Command, but Colonel Hampton was willing to risk it. He started readying a plane. Wilmeth persuaded him to abandon the idea. Instead, he advised that Eastern Command start preparing facilities and air transport for the large numbers of POWs who would undoubtedly be coming to Poltava soon, once he got into Poland

and started liaising with the Soviet repatriation authorities on the ground. It was sure to happen; they just had to be patient.

On February 27, Captain Robert Trimble set off with his salvage team to Staszów. On that same day, almost two weeks after coming from Moscow to Poltava, Colonel Wilmeth was finally allowed to fly to Lublin.

Wilmeth and his two companions—Lieutenant Colonel Curtis Kingsbury, who was a surgeon, and interpreter Corporal Paul Kisil[10]—boarded a Russian-crewed C-47. The plane was loaded with supplies, plus a jeep that Wilmeth intended to use to travel around seeking out and contacting stray POWs. The little team was accompanied by three Russians: a "chauffeur" for the jeep, an interpreter (unnecessary, since Kisil spoke excellent Polish and Russian),[11] and an officer as their "escort." All three were known at Poltava to be NKVD bird dogs.[12] This wasn't a good sign. And for all the use it would be, they might as well have left the jeep at Poltava, and saved themselves the trouble of maneuvering it in and out of the C-47's cargo doors.

The obstructions, restrictions, and inconveniences started almost the moment the plane touched down at Lublin.

On that first day Colonel Wilmeth met with the town commandant and the Soviet officers in charge of evacuating Allied prisoners of war. All five men regarded him with cold hostility.[13] When he announced that he had come to help with the task of locating ex-prisoners, caring for them, and evacuating them, they told him that they needed no help. The process was in hand. His presence was unnecessary and—they implied—deeply unwelcome. Besides, they said, the Soviet officer in charge of the ex-POW repatriation group, Colonel Vlasov, had moved his headquarters to Praga the previous day. Praga was a district of Warsaw, about a hundred miles away.

In that case, Wilmeth said, his patience still in abundant supply, he too would move to Praga, if that was acceptable? No, it was not. Permission would have to be sought from Moscow.

Very well, Wilmeth said; could they seek permission for him? They told him grudgingly that they could. In the meantime, Wilmeth was eager to visit the liberated prisoners of war who were currently in Lublin. If somebody would be so good as to take him to the camp . . .

That would not be possible, he was told. Taken aback, Wilmeth asked why not. The Russians pondered a moment, and declared that it was because he didn't have a permit to show that he had a right to be in Lublin.

Colonel Wilmeth was puzzled. He had arrived on a Soviet-approved plane, accompanied by Soviet officers. Wasn't that sufficient evidence that he had permission to be here?

No, it was not. He should have a written permit from the ex-prisoner repatriation headquarters. Which, they reminded him, had just moved to Praga, a hundred miles away. Without it, he would not be allowed to visit the ex-prisoners.

Colonel Wilmeth's stock of patience remained considerable, although depleted somewhat. Very well, he said; perhaps they could obtain a permit for him? Along with the permit to go to Praga? And could he send a telegram to General Deane in Moscow?

He was told to bring his message to the town commandant, who would send it on. With that curt instruction, the meeting ended.

An hour later, Colonel Wilmeth returned to the office with his message for General Deane, summarizing the meeting. The commandant told him the message could not be sent until all the people who had been at the meeting had gathered again; they would have to read it and clear it for sending.

A less placid man might have started tearing his hair at this point. James Dudley Wilmeth was, as far as any man alive could be, a placid man. At West Point he had been known as "Uncle Dud" and regarded as a rather dull, plodding, banal young man.[14] That temperament now stood him in good stead.

Later that evening, he was suddenly summoned back to the commandant's office and told that permission had been granted for him to visit the ex-prisoners. It was 10:30 P.M. All the Soviet officers from the earlier meeting had to be present for the visit. It took three trips by jeep to get everybody—Russians and Americans—to the building near the university where the ex-prisoners were housed.

Until a few days ago, the Russians had been accommodating the ex-POWs at Majdanek, the former Nazi death camp on the outskirts of Lublin, but now they had been moved into the town. Whatever Majdanek had been like, the new quarters didn't look like an improvement. The building was in an appalling state.[15] It had walls and a roof, but that was about all that could be said in its favor. The windows were broken, and there were no doors. All the toilets were blocked up and overflowing; there was no hot water, and no bathing facilities or medicines. Into this squalor were crowded more than 200 men: 91 Americans and 129 British. Nearly half were infested with lice. They slept on straw-covered wooden pallets. Each man had one blanket. The only source of heat was a single coal-burning stove.

Colonel Wilmeth and his companions had previously heard firsthand accounts of how Allied POWs were being treated by their Soviet liberators, and they heard more now as they moved among the men, taking their names, listening to their stories; but seeing it in the flesh was something else again. The stories were sickening and heartbreaking. The worst treatment began once they were passed back from the front line to troops in the rear areas. They had been starved, robbed, herded with captured Germans; many of their comrades had gone into hiding in Polish homes to escape this treatment. It was as if the liberated POWs were regarded as spoils of war, to be plundered or discarded at will.[16]

An American lieutenant told Wilmeth that if there was no transportation out of there soon, many of the men who were fit enough were thinking of slipping away and making their way south or east on their own. They had been on the verge of giving up hope, but seeing Colonel Wilmeth had revived them. At last, they believed, they would get some real help.

Wilmeth went back to his hotel and prepared a cable for General Deane in Moscow, asking him to send supplies for two thousand men, plus $10,000 to supplement the $4,000 the colonel had brought with him, so that urgent supplies could be purchased in the town. It was absolutely obvious that the Russians were not going to provide anything. All supplies would have to be bought on the black market. The message to General Deane did not get through.

That first day at Lublin proved to be a foretaste of Colonel Wilmeth's entire stay in the town. His messages to Moscow were garbled or blocked. He and his companions were banned from leaving their hotel without a Soviet escort (he drew the line at having a Russian sleep in the room with him). The Americans could not use their own jeep, because they were not allowed any gasoline for it. They bought gas on the black market, but still couldn't use the jeep without their Russian chauffeur. A couple of Russian officers commandeered it and used it to drive around town picking up girls.[17]

Wilmeth challenged the Russians about the way they were housing the ex-prisoners in prison-like conditions rather than just sending them on their way to freedom. They needn't even go to Odessa, he argued; Eastern Command had plenty of planes and could fly the POWs out to Poltava twenty at a time, making several flights a day. The Soviets told him that would not be possible. There were no airfields at Lublin, or at any of the other POW concentration points. Wilmeth knew from speaking to American pilots at Poltava, as well as from the evidence of his own eyes, that all the towns had airstrips. Anyway, American pilots could land and take off from a field if it was large enough. The Russians flatly denied this: there were no proper airfields and it was not possible to take off from an ordinary field.

In that case, Wilmeth asked, why could the ex-prisoners not be put on trains to Odessa or Poltava as soon as they came into Lublin? Why keep them confined for days and weeks? Because, came the Soviet response, the trains to Odessa were intermittent, and there was no rail connection to Poltava. Colonel Wilmeth visited the Lublin rail station and spoke to the Polish stationmaster. Why yes, there was a train to Odessa every day, the stationmaster said, and there were regular trains to Poltava as well. But the Russians continued to insist that there were not. And anyway, no travel could take place without proper permits, and these could not be obtained instantly.

On February 28, his second day in Lublin, Colonel Wilmeth met Colonel Vlasov, the Soviet head of POW repatriation in Poland, who came all the way from his new headquarters at Praga (by plane, from one nonexistent airfield to another) to take a look at the American interloper.

The meeting took place in the office of the town commandant. It was rather crowded, with all the Soviet officers who had been at the previous meeting attending this one also. Wilmeth quizzed Colonel Vlasov on how many ex-prisoners had so far been evacuated to Odessa. More than three thousand Americans, Vlasov claimed, eight hundred of them having been sent by rail just in the past week. (He was lying; three thousand was more than the entire number of American POWs received at Odessa through-out the whole period;[18] but Wilmeth didn't know that then.) And how many were still unaccounted for in Poland? How many altogether had been liberated from POW camps by the Red Army? Vlasov did not know.

Colonel Wilmeth felt that this was not good enough. It was time to stop pandering to these Soviets, he decided.

"Colonel Vlasov," he said, "I would like you to obtain permission for me to"—he counted off on his fingers—"one, move to Praga to cooperate with your department there; two, have direct communica-tion with the Military Mission in Moscow; three, visit all the POW collecting points at Praga, Kraków, Łódź, and the two yet to be estab-lished, wherever they may be; and four, to visit Odessa."[19]

Vlasov's face darkened as Wilmeth's requests were communicated to him by his interpreter. "Colonel Wilmeth," he replied, "I believe it has already been suggested to you by Captain Purtautov"—this was the bird dog who accompanied the American party everywhere—"that you and your comrades go back to Poltava soon. I endorse that suggestion. You should return there tomorrow, and await the answer to your requests."

"I'm not returning to Poltava," Wilmeth said. "On the contrary, more Americans are coming here. Ten contact teams are currently en route from Great Britain via Tehran. The teams, each with an airplane and a jeep, will go to each of the POW collection points in Poland. The Soviet government will provide billets and food, and the United States government will provide everything else."

As an attempt to bulldoze the Soviets, it was imaginative and bold, but completely ineffectual. It was true that ten small POW contact teams were coming from London, but so far they had yet to be granted entry to the USSR.

Colonel Vlasov was unfazed; he suggested blandly that Colonel Wilmeth might like to go to Moscow to discuss the plan with General Golubev, the Soviet officer in charge of POW affairs. Colonel Wilmeth declined. His patience was almost worn away now.

"Just this month," he said angrily, "the President of the United States and Marshal Stalin both signed an agreement at the Yalta Conference. It contained provisions for the handling of liberated prisoners of war. That agreement, *signed by Marshal Stalin himself,* gives me the right to receive *immediate* information about released Americans and to have *immediate* access to the camps where they are being held." He stared at Vlasov. "I have a copy of the agreement with me. Would you like me to loan it to you? You could read it tonight."

Colonel Vlasov declined the offer. The meeting came to a frigid end.

That had been a week ago now, Wilmeth reflected as he gazed across the rooftops of Lublin, and he had made barely any progress since.

The day after the meeting with Vlasov, 267 American and British POWs were loaded aboard a train and dispatched to Odessa. More continued to drift into town. They were put in the same stinking, ramshackle building. Over the ensuing days, using what limited money he had, Wilmeth purchased soap and toothbrushes for the POWs, as well as lightbulbs, brushes and brooms, and other requisites to make the building more habitable. He also bought picks and shovels so the men could dig latrines.

He tried repeatedly to make contact with the Military Mission in Moscow, requesting more money and reporting the situation, but his messages didn't seem to get through the Soviet system.[20] He asked if he could contact Moscow or Poltava by radio, but the Russians told him there was no radio available. What about the one in the plane he had come in? he asked. It was broken, they told him. The barefacedness of the Soviets' lies was breathtaking.

If it hadn't been for the Polish people, Colonel Wilmeth's mission might have been utterly futile. With each batch of prisoners that came into town, he heard stories of the help that ordinary Poles had given. They had taken the wandering foreigners into their homes, in spite of the risk of trouble from the Russians, and fed them despite the fact that they had so little themselves. In Lublin, the Polish Red Cross provided meals for newly arrived POWs, arranged billets with local families to ease congestion in the official camp block, provided medical facilities and paid hospital bills for the sick, and even helped buy gasoline for Colonel Wilmeth's jeep. To avoid the ruinous official rates for exchanging dollars for rubles and zlotys, and barred by regulations from using the more profitable black market exchange, Wilmeth came to an agreement whereby the US Embassy would reimburse the American Red Cross in Moscow.[21]

By prior agreement with his British counterpart in Moscow, Wilmeth shouldered responsibility for caring for British POWs to the same degree as Americans. He visited French POWs, who were kept in a separate camp, in conditions even more squalid. The burden of responsibility was almost too much to bear. As the days went by, no messages reached Wilmeth from General Deane.

Convinced that the Soviets were blocking communications both ways, Wilmeth decided to get a message to Deane directly. On March 5 he made four copies of a report containing a true account of his experiences in Lublin thus far, put the papers in sealed packets, and gave them to four trusted POWs—two Americans and two British.[22] He put the four men aboard a train to Moscow, with instructions to deliver the packets into the hands of General Deane. Of the four, surely at least one would get through.

On March 7, another batch of POWs was prepared for departure. Fifty-four American and British prisoners were given a rudimentary wash, had their clothes disinfected, and were loaded into a boxcar destined for Odessa.

Among them was Sergeant Richard J. Beadle, who had arrived from Warsaw three days earlier, after his arduous monthlong journey from Stalag III-C.

The boxcar stood in the Lublin marshaling yard all that night and most of the next day before finally being hitched to a train and departing. The Russian commander of the holding camp said that the delay was a punishment for the men's poor discipline during bathing earlier.

A couple of days later, Colonel Wilmeth was informed by Colonel Vlasov that two of his secret Moscow-bound couriers—the American officers—had been caught and detained at Warsaw, where they had been trying to board a plane.[23] Red Air Force guards had also arrested an American ex-POW doctor Wilmeth had sent to a camp near Warsaw to investigate a report that there were hundreds of sick Americans there. Vlasov was furious; Wilmeth had no right to send unauthorized messengers through Soviet territory. Wilmeth insisted that he had every right. Again he offered to let Vlasov read his copy of the Yalta agreement.

Colonel Wilmeth went on with his tasks with a heavy heart, but also with iron in his soul. From this moment on, he would have to fight every step of the way just to be allowed to stay in Lublin, let alone do any good. Meanwhile, two of his secret messengers were still at liberty and might still get the truth to General Deane.

March 9, 1945: Between Lublin and the Ukrainian border

Sergeant Beadle was woken from a fitful doze by the jolting of the boxcar as it came to a halt. Looking out through a gap in the boards, he saw buildings: a rail station and a town beyond. Where they were he had no idea: just another stop on the tortuously slow journey. In the two days since it had been loaded up in Lublin, Beadle reckoned, the train couldn't have covered more than forty or fifty miles.

Near him other men were waking up and looking around, in that slow, painful way of men who are cold to the bone. Some went on sleeping.

Others just stared, hollow-eyed, at nothing. A few were cheerful; just the belief that they were heading for home was enough for them. There were more than fifty men in the car;[24] it was so crowded they could only lie down to sleep in shifts. The Russians had given them some food—black bread, a little luncheon meat, and some sugar and oatmeal—but it had run out some time ago. The boxcar had no source of heat, and it was bitterly cold.

With an effort, Beadle slid back the door and dropped onto the snow beside the track, stamping his feet to try and bring them to life; along the train, made up of a mixture of boxcars, other people were doing the same. Private Ronald Gould followed Beadle out of the car. Gould was English, an infantryman from the Royal East Kent Regiment—traditionally called "The Buffs"—who had also served in the Italian campaign. The Buffs had been fighting at Monte Cassino while the 45th was at Anzio.[25] The two men had met in Lublin and formed one of those instantaneous bonds that spring up among fugitives and refugees; the temporary friendship of lost souls.

They looked up and down the tracks and across at the town beyond the station. Would it be safe to venture out? They had a little cash between them; they could try to buy some food. They knew by now that once this train stopped, it would probably be hours before it got going again. But maybe they shouldn't risk it. If the train did go without them, they'd be screwed.

Growing more and more hungry, Beadle and Gould waited in the boxcar as the hours dragged by. There was no sign of the train going any farther today. Eventually they couldn't stand it any longer. They jumped out, hurried across the tracks, and plunged into the streets around the station, searching for somewhere they might be able to eat. It took a while, but they eventually found a place to buy some food, and then began hurrying back toward the station. Dreadful as it was, the boxcar had become their haven: the only route to home and freedom.

It had gone. The section of track where the train had stood for hour upon endless hour was empty.

Their bad luck was almost beyond belief. If they'd gone into town when they first thought of it, rather than being cautious, they would now be rolling on toward Odessa with their bellies filled.

All was not lost. They had identification papers and a little money. There were other trains they could board, even if they had to wait. Eventually they managed to get aboard a train traveling east. At the Ukrainian border,[26] they were forced to disembark by Russian soldiers. They stepped off the train and into a maze of Soviet bureaucracy. Their identification papers were not adequate; they would need new ones. Given into the care of two Russian official "guides" (armed guards), Beadle and Gould were taken to a town some twenty miles farther east, where the Communist commandant would issue them with the appropriate papers.

At this next town, they acquired three new traveling companions who were in the same situation. Two were British ex–prisoners of war from Lublin who were trying to get to Moscow: a Scottish sergeant called Montgomery and Flying Officer Panniers of the Royal Air Force.[27] The third man was a Canadian civilian. The town commandant gave all five men the papers they required. Then he informed them that they should proceed to Lwów. That meant heading back into Poland—back the way they had come. To compound their confusion and dismay, there was a mix-up, and the five men were taken into the custody of two new guards for the journey to Lwów. Aboard the train it was discovered that their newly issued papers, which had been in the possession of the previous guards, were now lost.

At least it wasn't far to Lwów, and they had a little food: a loaf-and-a-half of black bread and ten grams of sugar (about two teaspoons) between the five of them. The ramshackle little party disembarked at Lwów Station. Their guards told them that they would escort them to the Lwów commandant, who would give them another new set of papers. Beadle and his friends pleaded for food. The guards refused: no food until they had seen the commandant.

As they shambled out under the grand arched entrance of the railroad station and set off down the broad, tree-lined avenue that led to the city center, it seemed to Sergeant Beadle that he would never find his way out of this cursed country. He was doomed to shuttle slowly from one commandant to another, back and forth, collecting more and more useless sets of papers, getting colder and hungrier until he finally died of despair.

Lost in thought and faint with hunger and fatigue, he hardly noticed at first the two men walking toward the little group, apparently on their way to the station. When he realized that they were looking curiously at the prisoners, he studied them closely. They were wrapped up against the cold, but they were dressed unmistakably in American uniform. Proper uniform, not the ragged remnants worn by POWs. One was an Army Air Force officer, a young fellow with an open, friendly face; the other was a sergeant, stocky, dark, and serious-looking.

Beadle halted; so did the two Americans.

"Help," Beadle said, and took a step toward them. "Help us, please."

12.

AMERICAN GENTLEMEN

March 6, 1945: Between Rzeszów and Lwów

At first, it was just flecks of snow that flickered past the cockpit windows of the B-17. But within minutes, the flecks had grown to a thick cascade splattering against the windshield. Visibility dropped dramatically. Captain Robert Trimble glanced at the compass and the other instruments, and eased the control column forward, dropping the bomber gently down to a lower altitude. At around five hundred feet, in the failing light and the snow, he could just about make out the railroad tracks he'd been following for the past ten miles.

Getting to Poltava was going to be harder than he'd anticipated.

The journey that had started in the field near Staszów yesterday morning had begun to get interesting a few minutes after takeoff. Robert had made a rapid turn to get on course for Lwów before the plane's meager supply of fuel was exhausted. It was no use; so much had been used up taxiing the salvaged aircraft to its takeoff field, there wasn't going to be anywhere near enough to make it. When number three engine sputtered and cut out, Robert decided to head for the Soviet airfield at Rzeszów and make an emergency landing. He, Lieutenant Jessee, and Sergeants Picarelli and Matles stayed the night there. The Russians were hospitable, as they invariably were when they didn't feel suspicious of you. Evidently the

Soviet colonel's complaint about Captain Trimble's behavior had not reached Rzeszów. Next morning, unaware of any reason to detain it, the Russians happily refueled the B-17 and allowed it to fly on.

With the tanks full, Robert had hoped to skip Lwów and reach Poltava in one hop. He was anxious to be done with this side mission and return to what he now viewed as his sole purpose in this country—getting American prisoners home.

But the weather had been deteriorating for days, and it was starting to snow as they boarded the plane. This wasn't looking good. But the journey wasn't a long one, and the snow was sparse. Robert's flight plan was indirect; with no proper maps for Lieutenant Jessee to work with, they were reduced to following the railroad tracks, the compass, and Jessee's own knowledge of the lay of the land between Kraków, Lwów, and Poltava. Robert flew at a perilously low altitude, where the dark strand of the railroad showed clearly against the snowy landscape.

For the first few miles out of Rzeszów it went well, but the snow suddenly worsened: the few flakes multiplied rapidly into a vortex, an onslaught of snow that obscured the view, while down below it settled on the tracks, gradually erasing their dark line.

Robert's gut reaction was to drop still lower, and he eased down to two hundred feet—dangerously low even in good weather—and then lower still. His eyes were tearing up with the cold and the strain of looking for the fading tracks. Somewhere ahead, dozens of miles away but rushing toward them at about one hundred and fifty miles per hour, was the city of Lwów. As far as Robert could recall, it had few, if any, buildings higher than three or four stories. But there would be factory smokestacks scattered about. At least there wouldn't be any barrage balloons.

Suddenly a tall smokestack loomed up; not dead ahead, but close enough to give Robert and Picarelli a nasty start. It was no use—they would have to climb. Staying at this altitude was too dangerous, and the tracks could hardly be seen anyway. Robert pulled back on the column and the B-17 rose back up past one thousand feet. From this point on all they had was the Fortress's instruments and their wits. Jessee would have to navigate by dead reckoning, using their compass bearing and speed to calculate their position minute by minute.

The vibration from the distorted propeller shaft in number three engine was getting worse, and the temperature gauge was rising, beginning to overheat. On Robert's order, Picarelli shut it down and feathered the prop. They were now flying on three engines and hope.

When their calculations told them they were nearing Lwów, Robert cautiously began to descend through the storm. The city's streets and buildings emerged vaguely through the snow—just a maze of gray creases, striations, and blobs in the white expanse. Descending farther and straining his eyes, Robert was relieved to see the long northward curve of the railroad track where it ran into the rail station on the western edge of the city. Now he knew where he was. The main airfield of Lwów-Sknilow was close by. He banked the Fortress and began a long turn west-southwest, almost back the way they'd come; there, looming up under the nose, was the expanse of the airfield. Robert had been here before, but only as a passenger with a Russian pilot, never at the controls. He would have to guess where the runway was.

He took a wide curve around the field, judging his approach, then turned and lined up where he reckoned the runway lay, estimating it from a row of telegraph poles with red balls on the wires, which he knew ran across the line of approach. Everything was white, so he trusted to luck and scrubbed off the power. The Fort sank gently down—so reduced in weight, she seemed reluctant to drop the last couple of dozen feet. Straining his eyes between the whiteout and the instruments, Robert drew down the throttles. Flying by feel and experience, he pulled the column back, and felt the satisfying thump of a perfect three-point touchdown. That was good—but now they were rolling at one hundred miles per hour into the whiteout instead of flying; there could be anything in the way—planes, buildings, vehicles. Pushing hard on the brake pedals (one for each of the two main wheels), he fought against the plane's urge to slew sideways on the snow. At last the Fort rolled to a stop, and sat rumbling and vibrating unevenly, like a bad-tempered dog.

There was little point in taxiing away, as they had no idea where they should taxi to, or even where the taxiways were. So, once the three remaining engines were shut down, the three Americans climbed out of the plane, just in time to see a jeep racing across the field toward them, carrying a Russian officer. *Uh-oh*, Robert thought—was this where the consequences of pulling his pistol on the Soviet colonel came back to bite him? If so, how in the world had they known he'd be arriving here now?

The jeep swerved to a halt, and the Russian officer jumped out. He stared, with an expression that looked like a mixture of awe and worry, at the B-17 and the men who had emerged from it. He immediately began talking at them.

"He says there's a cliff," Sergeant Matles translated. "Didn't you know there's a cliff here? he says."

"A cliff?" Robert thought Matles must have misheard—why would an airfield have a cliff?

The Russian beckoned them to follow him. He walked out into the snow beyond the nose of the B-17 and pointed. The Americans looked, and their hearts quailed. There, just a few yards ahead of where the Fort had come to a halt, the ground fell sharply away in a steep bluff.[1] The drop was more than a hundred feet, completely invisible from the line of approach. "*Holy shit*," someone muttered. One pound less pressure on the brakes, one iota more speed on the dial, and they'd have been pancaked down there without ever knowing what had happened.

"No," Robert said in reply to the Russian's repeated query. "I didn't know. I've never flown in here before."

He'd nearly never flown in anywhere ever again. He really would be glad when this mission was over. Salvaging planes was proving to be even more stressful than evading bird dogs and smuggling POWs.

The Russian jeep took the four Americans to the airfield headquarters, where they were treated to vodka and sandwiches by the admiring officers. This side of the Russian character—the warmth and humor, the loud, backslapping conviviality—was a strange contrast to the darker side, and almost, but not quite, made up for it. Once the rit ual hospitality was over, the Americans made their way into the city and checked into Robert's now familiar haunt, the Hotel George.

This visit would be less fraught than his previous one, he expected. It made a pleasant change for Robert having Sergeant Matles to interpret for him, rather than some Soviet bird dog. And he was looking forward to getting a good night's sleep. The beds at the George were the best: warm, comfortable, better than the cold fuselage of a plane, or even the bed back at Poltava that he'd barely had a chance to sleep in, or his billet at Debach. The only bed he'd been in recently that equaled those at the George was the one at the US Embassy in London. And the only one that could better that was the one he'd shared with Eleanor. Whichever house in whichever town, there was nothing to beat that. It seemed such a long time ago now, and a world away.

Robert's thoughts were yanked back to the present by the discovery that he and his comrades were not the only Americans in the hotel. There were nine others, the crew of a B-17 which had crash-landed north of here just over a week ago.

B-17 43-38823, piloted by Second Lieutenant Jack Barnett of the 384th Bomb Group, had taken off from its base in Northamptonshire, England, as part of a force bombing Berlin.[2] The Fortress took multiple flak hits over the target. With two engines dead and leaking fuel, and losing altitude rapidly, Barnett headed for Soviet territory. Coming out of the cloud base at four hundred feet into a snowstorm, the crew located a field suitable for a crash-landing. The damage to both inboard engine nacelles had knocked out the landing gear, so there was no choice but to put the Fort down on her belly.

Barnett and his crew just had time to destroy the bombsight before being picked up by a Red Army unit from the nearby town of Rawa-Ruska, about thirty miles northwest of Lwów. They were accommodated in Soviet officers' quarters, under guard, and fed well. They were also provided with an interpreter. A local woman, she seemed to have no love for the Russians. She confided to the Americans that her parents, who were Canadian, had settled there in 1935; later they were murdered by the Soviets. She believed that most people thereabouts hated the Russians more than they did the Germans.

After two days at Rawa-Ruska, Lieutenant Barnett and his men were taken to Lwów and lodged at the Hotel George. They were advised to keep off the streets at night during the curfew and not to carry sidearms in the hotel. And there they stayed, living in relative comfort, for the next week, waiting for someone to come and pick them up. Suddenly Robert's responsibilities multiplied threefold.

Barnett's B-17, despite the belly landing, was reckoned to be salvageable, which would mean an arduous task lined up for someone from Eastern Command.[3] Someone other than Captain Trimble, Robert hoped, as he listened to the story. He still had a way to go to get the Fortress he already had back to Poltava. But he would take Barnett and his crew—three officers and six sergeants—with him. As always, the Soviets were perfectly happy to allow downed American aircrews to be taken out via Poltava; only ex–prisoners of war were forbidden to go that way.

All thirteen Americans were going to be stuck in Lwów for a while. The snow was setting in, and there'd be no takeoffs for at least a day or two. Also, work would need to be done on that number three engine. With the crew-and-passenger complement tripled, it was all the more important that the plane be mechanically sound.

Robert had barely got used to this new situation when another, rather more sinister, development occurred.

On the face of it, it seemed pleasant enough. The face in question was that of a nice Polish lady who spoke excellent English. She met Captain Trimble and Sergeant Matles in the hotel dining room, and introduced herself as Miss Esa Lowry, a teacher in one of Lwów's schools.[4] She had been requested by the city commandant to go to the hotel and offer whatever help she could to any American servicemen staying there.

"Souvenirs I can obtain," she said. "Or merchandise, or money. Dollars for zlotys or rubles." What she was offering, in effect, was to act as a go-between with the local black market. There was nothing essentially wrong with that—it was the way of life in Poland—but something about this smiling lady made Robert's suspicious hackles rise. Miss Lowry became a fixture at the hotel, a constant presence in the dining room, and took a close interest in the comings and goings of all the Americans. Robert was certain she was in the service of the NKVD.

After a couple of days, Lieutenant Barnett asked for a word with Captain Trimble. His men were becoming increasingly resentful of the way Miss Lowry pried into each man's life and business. She would never let them alone, always trying to make conversation and fish for information. Taking Sergeant Matles and Lieutenant Jessee with him as witnesses, Robert asked Miss Lowry if he could have a quiet talk with her.

He thanked her for everything she had done—or tried to do—to help the Americans, but it had come to his attention that his and Lieutenant Barnett's men did not feel at ease in her presence and could not relax. It would therefore be appreciated if she would kindly leave them alone.

Miss Lowry protested, mentioning again all the services she could provide for the Americans.

"Thank you, but no," Robert said. "Sergeant Matles here is from the United States Military Mission in Moscow; he knows how to handle matters of that kind. He is also competent to deal with the local Soviet authorities."

She protested again, insisting that she could help, but Robert was firm.

"This is a military mission," he said forcefully, and forgetting himself entirely, he added: "Our only interest is in taking Americans home."

If either Sergeant Matles or Lieutenant Jessee noticed this odd remark (as far as they were aware, the mission's sole purpose was to take a salvaged bomber back to Poltava; taking Americans with them was incidental), they didn't comment. Robert himself didn't notice his inadvertent allusion to his off-the-record mission in Poland.[5]

Miss Lowry finally gave up. She left the hotel, and from that day forward, they never saw her again. But if the men imagined that they'd now be free from scrutiny, they were wrong.

Meanwhile, work on the bomber was proceeding at a painfully slow pace. Despite their initial helpfulness, the Russians quickly became

obstructive (presumably the NKVD had spoken to the airfield personnel). It was almost impossible to get transportation out to the airfield,
which was several miles from the city center. Russian mechanics were
doing the repairs to the engine, and Russian guards were protecting it,
but neither were entirely trustworthy, and there was no easy way for
Captain Trimble or Sergeant Picarelli to supervise them. But while the
snow lasted, nobody would be flying anywhere, so it didn't matter a great
deal. Still nothing had been heard of the Staszów colonel; his complaint
had gone straight to Moscow, bypassing the authorities in Poland.

Robert devoted what time he could to looking after his comrades.
Making good his statement to Miss Lowry, he and Sergeant Matles set
out on the afternoon of the 11th of March to buy cigarettes for the men.
The best place to find them would be down near the railroad station, so
they headed out that way.

As they were walking down Chernivetska Street, the broad, straight
avenue that led to the station, Robert noticed a couple of Russian soldiers coming the other way, accompanying a ragged little band of five
men. One of the men was staring at him; he had the gaunt, haunted look
that Robert had learned to recognize.

He couldn't take his eyes off that face; beside him, Sergeant Matles's
attention had also been caught. The gaunt man took a step toward them.
"Help," he said. "Help us, please."

The officer and the sergeant both stopped.
"Who are you?" the officer asked.

The two guards moved to intervene, but the officer gestured to the
sergeant, who spoke sharply to them in Russian, and they backed off.

"Beadle," he said, "T/4 Richard J., 45th Infantry, sir." It wasn't easy
to speak. His throat was dry and sore from the relentless cold and thirst.

"I'm Captain Robert Trimble, Army Air Forces, Eastern Command.
This is First Sergeant John Matles from the Military Mission in Moscow."
With a glance at the Russian soldiers, he asked, "What can we do for you?"

Lieutenant Robert M. Trimble (standing, second from left) and crew pose with their B-24 Liberator *Rum Runner* at Debach, England, on the day of their first combat mission, July 6, 1944. The mission was to bomb a V-1 flying bomb storage site in France. Crew (standing, left to right): Lieutenant Warren Johnson, Trimble, Lieutenant Walter Hvischuk, Lieutenant Raymond Joseph, Sergeant Joe Sarina (squatting, left to right): Sergeant Julio "Chico" Mendez, Sergeant Gale D. Moore, Sergeant Alton R. Stafford, Sergeant Horace Grady Hendricks, Sergeant George Di Ieso.
Courtesy of the Trimble Family

Boeing B-17G Flying Fortresses in formation.
U.S. Air Force

Headquarters of 493rd Bomb Group, Debach, Suffolk, January 1945.
U.S. Air Force

Diplomatic passport no. 2242 issued to Captain Robert M. Trimble, January 22, 1945: photo page.
Courtesy of the Trimble Family

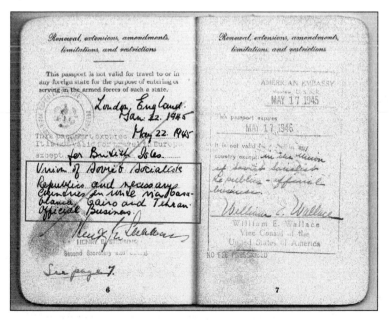

Diplomatic passport no. 2242 issued to Captain Robert M. Trimble, January 22, 1945: page 3, identifying the bearer as "United States Government Official."
Courtesy of the Trimble Family

Diplomatic passport no. 2242 issued to Captain Robert M. Trimble, January 22, 1945: page 6, listing destination as "Union of Soviet Socialist Republics and necessary countries en route."
Courtesy of the Trimble Family

Douglas C-47 Skytrains.
U.S. Air Force

Curtiss C-46 Commando.
U.S. Air Force

The only known photo taken during the Luftwaffe raid on Poltava on the night of June 21–22, 1944.
U.S. Air Force

Left: Colonel Thomas K. Hampton at Poltava, winter 1944–1945.
U.S. Air Force

Right: Colonel Thomas K. Hampton (right) with Major Michael H. Kowal (center)
and Soviet General Perminov.
Michael Wm Kaluta's Collection

Major General Edmund W. Hill (left), an unidentified British officer, and U.S. Ambassador W. Averell Harriman during stopover at Poltava en route to Yalta conference, February 1945.
Michael Wm Kaluta's Collection

Left: Sergeant Arnold Echola (left) and Lieutenant Arnold A. Tillman at Poltava, February 1945.
Lt. Tillman Collection, Courtesy of Texas Military Forces Museum, Camp Mabry: Austin Texas

Right: Captain Robert M. Trimble outside the Operations Office at Poltava, February 1945.
Lt. Tillman Collection, Courtesy of Texas Military Forces Museum, Camp Mabry: Austin Texas

The Tillman short snorter, signed by the officers of Lieutenant A. A. Tillman's crew and "R. M. Trimble, Capt AC" in February 1945. Trimble's signature is immediately above the "ONE" in the center of the bill. At top edge is the signature of Lieutenant Cornelius Daly, navigator, and on the right edge is the legend "Fighting Bastard of the Ukraine" and the date "25 Feb 45." The signature of Tillman himself is on the other side of the bill.

Private Collection of Mike Allard

North American P 51D Mustang undergoing maintenance work at Poltava air base, April 1945.

U.S. Air Force

Red Army interpreters Maiya (seated, right)
and Galia at Poltava, New Year's Day, 1945.
Michael Wm Kaluta's Collection

Intelligence Officer Captain William Fitchen (left) and Meteorologist Major Donald S. Nicholson
with Galia, one of General Kovalev's interpreters.
Michael Wm Kaluta's Collection

Left: First Sergeant John Matles. Photo taken while serving with the U.S. Reparations Mission in Japan, 1945.
Copyright Unknown, Courtesy of Harry S. Truman Library

Right: Major General John R. Deane, head of the U.S. Military Mission to Moscow, in 1944.
U.S. Army

Left: Captain Robert M. Trimble on the road between the American camp and HQ site at Poltava.
Michael Wm Kaluta's Collection

Right: T/4 Rudolph Vergolina.
Courtesy of the Rudy Vergolina Family

Hotel George, Lwów.
Courtesy of the Igor and Irina Kotlobulatov Collection

Aircraft at Poltava, April 11, 1945. C-47 and salvaged B-24 in background. The B-17 Flying Fortress in the foreground is *Maiden USA*, the plane of Lieutenant Myron King, who was at Poltava awaiting court martial at this time.
U.S Air Force

B-24 Liberator *Judith Ann* at Poltava on April 12, 1945. The plane has just taxied in, and the officers present believe it to be carrying Generals Hill and Deane (the photo was officially captioned accordingly). In fact it was carrying a mystery passenger en route from Italy to Moscow.
U.S. Air Force

B-24 Liberator *Judith Ann* at Poltava on April 12, 1945. Taken some time later; the reception committee has departed, and ground crew are attending to the aircraft.
U.S. Air Force

Major General S. K. Kovalev and Major General John R. Deane
at Poltava, April 12, 1945.

U.S. Air Force

Color guard leading the march through the American camp to the memorial service for President
Franklin D. Roosevelt.

U.S. Air Force

Soviet artist Senior Sergeant Sapokar with his portraits of Stalin and Roosevelt.
U.S. Air Force

Memorial service for President Franklin D. Roosevelt, held in the theater at Poltava on April 14, 1945. Newly appointed commanding officer Captain Trimble is seated front left. Front far right is outgoing commanding officer Colonel Thomas K. Hampton.
Michael Wm Kaluta's Collection

Memorial service congregation (detail). Captain Robert M. Trimble seated front left, with Major Michael H. Kowal beside him. Behind Captain Trimble is Captain William Fitchen.
Michael Wm Kaluta's Collection

Captain Robert M. Trimble at Poltava, April 1945.
Michael Wm Kaluta's Collection

Lieutenant William Kaluta and Lieutenant Clotilde Kaluta (née Govoni) serving wedding cake to Captain Robert M. Trimble in the Officers' Club at Poltava, May 20, 1945. Kaluta's shoulder patch is that of the Military Mission to Moscow, a U.S. eagle with "America" in Cyrillic letters.
Michael Wm Kaluta's Collection

Eastern Command officers at Poltava (from left): Major Don Nicholson, Lieutenant Bill Kaluta, Captain Robert Trimble, unknown, Major Mike Kowal.
Michael Wm Kaluta's Collection

Robert and Eleanor Trimble with baby Carol Ann,
shortly after Robert's return to the U.S., summer 1945.
Courtesy of the Trimble Family

Left: Medals awarded to Robert M. Trimble (top row, from left): Distinguished Flying
Cross, Bronze Star, European African Middle Eastern Campaign Medal (awarded 7 times),
World War II Victory Medal, (bottom row, from left): Air Medal (awarded 6 times), Amer-
ican Campaign Medal, French Croix de Guerre with Silver Star, and Fiftieth Anniversary
Russian "Great Patriotic War" commemorative medal.
Courtesy of the Trimble Family

Right: Robert Trimble in 2009.
Courtesy of the Trimble Family

Quickly, Beadle told the story of the last few days. He and his companions were en route from Lublin to Odessa, but had been diverted and lost their papers. They'd spent days in a cold boxcar and had hardly anything to eat. Since boarding the train at the last town, they'd had no food at all; the guards had told them that they could have nothing until they had seen the Lwów commandant and been cleared. He also described some of the experiences he'd had before arriving at Lublin, and the conditions in the camp there.

As Beadle hastily told his story, Captain Trimble's face went from the cheerful, warm expression that was its natural state to a scowl. Sergeant Matles's heavy brows drew down at every word, and his broad, fleshy features turned stony. He spoke again in Russian to the guards, and a dispute broke out. Clearly Captain Trimble and the sergeant carried some official weight, because the guards backed down without putting up much of a fight.

There was a brief consultation between Trimble and Matles, then the sergeant said firmly to Beadle, "You're coming with us. All of you."

The motley little band—American, Scottish, English, and Canadian—set off along the avenue toward the center of town, bracketed by the two Russian soldiers. The guards insisted on maintaining their position of authority, one marching ahead, the other bringing up the rear, as if all seven men were their prisoners.

After a walk that took them through more than a mile of grand, icy streets and snowbound parks, they arrived at Mickiewicz Square, dominated by the elegant block of the Hotel George. It was a grand-looking place, despite the boarded-up shops that occupied most of the ground floor of the building.

To the ex-prisoners' eyes, accustomed to nothing but battlefields, bivouacs, prison-camp barracks, and boxcars, the hotel lobby was almost unbearably opulent. The marble floor, the pillared archways that opened onto the two curving sweeps of the main staircase, the Art Nouveau decor, and the general air of refined Victorian splendor were otherworldly. Between the two arms of the staircase was a short passage leading from the lobby to a glazed double door; above it was the single word, "Jadalnia."

Judging from the sounds and smells drifting through, they guessed that *Jadalnia* was Polish for "Dining Room." Now, there was a thought that was worth standing in line for.

Almost better than that was the bathing. While Sergeant Matles went away to make some phone calls, Captain Trimble arranged rooms for the prisoners, and they all took baths. It was the first real head-to-toe, soap-and-water wash any of them had had in months; they were filthy, some of them lousy too. They lingered, soaping and scrubbing away the dirt and stink of the prison camps, the boxcars, and the endless miles of walking and sleeping rough.

Nothing could be done about their clothing, so once they were clean, the men had no choice but to pull on the same dirty, ragged garments. But they felt a world better than they had before.

O nce the five men were cleaned up, Robert and Sergeant Matles took them to the dining room and let them eat their fill.[6]

They talked over what was to be done. The situation wasn't good. They wouldn't be able to take the ex-POWs with them when they went back to Poltava. The Russian guards were still hanging around, and insisting that the men be taken to the city commandant and placed under his authority. The Soviet authorities Matles had spoken to said the same, as did the Military Mission in Moscow. It was decided that Matles should take the men to the commandant, get them their papers, and then put them immediately on the next train to Odessa.

The men weren't too happy about being put back in the hands of the Russians, but there was nothing anybody could do. The Englishman and the Scotsman seemed especially perturbed. As the men were getting up from the dining table, they approached Robert. "Can we have a quiet word, Captain?"

Robert took them aside.

"We must get to Moscow," Flying Officer Panniers said. "We have sealed papers to deliver to your General Deane at the American Mission."

"Papers?"

"They come from an American officer in Lublin, a Colonel Wilmeth."

The name took Robert by surprise. So Wilmeth really had managed to make it to Lublin, had he? And was sending POWs out with secret messages for Moscow, by golly! Presumably things weren't going well up there. The two men explained that they'd been on their way through the Ukraine when they were sidetracked back to Lwów. It was imperative that they get to Moscow. They'd undertaken to put the sealed packets directly in General Deane's hands. They contained detailed reports on the situation of ex-prisoners in Lublin, which was terrible.

Robert felt more keenly than ever the frustration of being sidetracked into salvage work. Moscow had been wrong to assume good faith on the part of the Soviets. But however much he sympathized, and however urgent the men's errand, they would still have to report to the Soviet commandant in Lwów, along with the others. If they didn't get the right authorization papers, they'd probably get picked up and diverted back again. Odessa was one thing—Russians down the line were accustomed to seeing ex-prisoners and refugees heading that way—but routes into Russia were different. There was a train to Moscow the following day: Captain Trimble would ensure that they were on it.

More phone calls were made, then Sergeant Matles set off with the POWs and the two Russian guards—who still insisted on marching before and behind them as if they were prisoners.

It was a walk of twenty-five blocks to the city commandant's office (Beadle counted them wearily). The commandant issued the men with the required papers, including permits for the two who wanted to go to Moscow. But the other three—the two Americans and the Canadian civilian—must go to the rehabilitation center to await proper processing and evacuation to Odessa. They could not be put immediately on any train.

The little party set out once more,[7] making their way to the rehabilitation center. This turned out to be a large barbwire enclosure, like a concentration camp,[8] on one side of a street, with an office building on the other side. They went into the building, where they found an office presided over by a surly-looking Russian major. When Matles introduced himself and stated his business, the major glanced up from his paperwork, cast an eye disdainfully at the sergeant's stripes on the sleeve of Matles's coat, and pointedly ignored him.

Sergeant Matles squared his shoulders, reined in his temper, and addressed the major again. "I am a representative of the United States Military Mission in Moscow," he said firmly. "I am an aide to General Deane, and acquainted with the ambassador. I would appreciate a little help."[9]

The major looked up. "Go down and see the evacuation officer," he said, and went back to his paperwork.

Matles went downstairs, where he found the captain in charge of evacuating prisoners of war. In contrast to his superior, the captain was all helpfulness, gushing with reassurances that the men would be well looked after. "Warm quarters they shall have, and clean beds in a hotel. We will get them new clothes, a bath, haircut and shave, and of course they will be fed. In one day, perhaps two, they will be on a train to Odessa."

Sergeant Matles relayed all these promises to the men, and asked them if they wanted to stay; or would they prefer to come back to the hotel? Unwilling to put the sergeant and Captain Trimble to any further trouble, and not relishing the walk back to the hotel, the men agreed to take their chances with the Russians.

"Take the phone number," said Matles, writing it down and handing it to Sergeant Beadle. "Call me at the hotel if you have any problems. Or just come straight there."

Taking the two British men with him, Matles set off back to the Hotel George. If he'd had more experience of the Soviet attitude to ex-POWs, he might have taken them all back with him, without bothering to ask their views.

Reporting back to Captain Trimble, Matles learned that there'd been a new and irritating development.

A very friendly woman had appeared that day in the dining room, introducing herself to the Americans as "the one who is to take Miss Esa Lowry's place." Captain Trimble had ordered everybody to just ignore her.

She was not to be engaged in conversation; her questions should not be answered, and her offers of help should not be acknowledged. But he cautioned them not to be obnoxious. "Remember, you're American gentlemen," he said. "Don't forget to act as such."

The next morning, Robert and Sergeant Matles took the two British men to the railroad station, where they gave them a supply of rations and personally saw them onto the train for Moscow. Whether they ever got there, Robert never heard. (Indeed, by the time Robert returned to Poltava, Wilmeth's situation in Lublin had reached a crisis, and it mattered little whether his secret messages got through.)

Now that the business of the POWs had been dealt with, Captain Trimble and his team could get on with the matter of having the bomber's engines fixed up. Or rather, they could if the weather would ease up and the Russians would let them have transportation out to the airfield. Robert's frustration was starting to gnaw at him. The sooner he returned to Poltava, the sooner he could get back in the field and resume helping all those POWs who were still out there.

Robert had noticed how angry Sergeant Matles was at the plight of the POWs, but so far Matles had only seen the better side of it. Sergeant Beadle and his companions were relatively fit and healthy—they had to be, to have come so far on their own initiative. Matles hadn't seen the long-term prisoners: the ones weakened by starvation; the sick; the men hiding out on remote farms, unable to hike through the snows, traumatized by their experiences, too scared of the Russians to seek help from them. Those were the men Robert was in this country to help. He was here to help all of them, but those were the ones that really tugged at his heart.

This didn't look much like a hotel with warm beds and clean rooms, Beadle thought. He shifted uncomfortably on the bare plank bed and looked around at the other people crammed into the noxious little room. He counted thirty, including himself and Gould.

Things were bad, and getting worse.

After Sergeant Matles left, Beadle, Gould, and the Canadian had been taken across the road to the camp, where they'd been made to wait for three hours. Things looked up a little when they were allowed to wash and shave. Then they were marched to a building a block down from the camp. Whatever it was, it wasn't the hotel they'd been promised by the Russian captain. They were put in a bare room with a dozen other people, all French, a mix of ex-POWs and civilians from the Nazi labor camps. There was no heating in the room, and the beds consisted of bare boards. With no blankets, the two Americans spent a cold night. Meals consisted of a meager allowance of soup and black bread and some tea.

On the evening of the second day, some Russian soldiers came in with armfuls of clothing, which they distributed to everybody. It was all Russian-style—rough, uncomfortable, and poorly made. Beadle and Gould were allowed to keep the clothes they had arrived in, but the Frenchmen were stripped and left with nothing but the crude Russian garments. The only good things provided were fur-lined caps. Beadle was thankful for the two good woollen shirts he had on, which were comfortable and provided a little warmth. But not for long. Later, the Russians changed their minds; in the middle of the night they rousted the two men out of bed and made them strip. Beadle's woollen shirts were whisked away, leaving him with nothing but the Russian stuff.

After that, things got worse.

The next morning, sixteen civilians were herded into the room, a mixture of men and women, and even some children, all liberated from labor camps. There was no longer any room to move, let alone lie down and sleep. One of the civilians, a woman, was sick, but no help came. And still there was no word of transportation to Odessa. It began to feel as if they would be stuck in this airless room forever, getting hungrier, and sooner or later falling sick.

Sergeant Beadle and Private Gould decided they'd had enough. Even the stalag hadn't been as bad as this. The building wasn't tightly secured (it was a "rehabilitation center," after all, not a prison), so the two men were able to sneak out past the Russian guards. Finding their bearings, they made their way back to Mickiewicz Square and the Hotel George. They just hoped the Americans, who had been eager to get their plane fixed up and leave, hadn't gone yet. If they had, there would be no option but to try and make it to Odessa on their own.

When they reached the hotel, it looked like it might be too late. There was no sign of the Americans in the lobby or the dining room. Not daring to inquire at the desk, Beadle and Gould sneaked up the stairs, went to the room Captain Trimble had been occupying, and knocked on the door.

The door opened, and to their immense relief, the familiar face of the captain appeared. His eyebrows went up at the sight of the two men in their motley collection of ill fitting Russian garments. He quickly ushered them inside, and summoned Lieutenant Jessee and Sergeant Matles. The three of them listened in growing anger as Beadle related their experiences during the past few days.

Robert instantly came to a decision. Beadle and Gould weren't going to Odessa—they were coming back to Poltava with him, no matter what anybody said.

From now on they were both to forget that they'd ever been in the infantry or in a prison camp: as far as the Soviets were concerned, they were aircrew, like Lieutenant Barnett and his men. If there was trouble when they got to Poltava, then Captain Trimble was prepared to answer for it. He was boiling with anger and willing to defy anybody who got in the way of these two men's liberation.

Sergeant Matles backed him up. He was furious, recalling the way the captain at the so-called rehabilitation center had lied through his smiling teeth about hotels and clean beds. Lieutenant Jessee was of the same mind. He and Matles vowed to make the strongest possible statement to Eastern Command and the Military Mission about the need for a fully equipped, permanent American team stationed in Lwów to deal with ex-POWs.

Robert agreed, but privately knew it would do no good. From what he'd heard of Wilmeth's situation in Lublin, and from his own mission briefings, as well as what he'd seen with his own eyes, he knew that no American team would be allowed to come here: not while Hell still had any heat left in it.

13.

RISING TIDE

"Hey, Yankee!"

The raucous shout echoed across the busy street. Robert, Lieutenant Barnett, and some of the crew, out for a stroll through Lwów for fresh air and exercise, stopped in their tracks and spun around, startled.

"Yankee!" Two wild-looking men in ragged greatcoats were running across the street toward them, waving their arms. They skidded to a halt in front of the American officers, gasping for breath and blurting out that they were former prisoners of war and in Russian hands and boy were they glad to see some Americans.... Robert, glancing past the two men, saw a pair of Russian soldiers hurrying across the street after them, unlimbering their rifles.

The Russians caught up with their charges and tried to intervene. Robert held up a hand, flashed his passport, and ordered them to back off. His ability to deal with Soviets had come on greatly since his first arrival in Poland. They respected the voice of authority, and he was learning how to wield it. It helped that he was becoming a familiar figure around Lwów, and the ordinary Russians believed him to be a man of some importance.[1]

Once the two fugitives had got their breath back, Robert took their names. They were Sergeant Rudolph Vergolina[2] and Jim McNeish, a

Scotsman. They had been on the move for weeks since being liberated, and were overflowing with joy at seeing Americans.

This time Robert didn't even bother with the city commandant. Taking the two men under his wing, he ordered his walking party to about-turn, and walked them back to the hotel. The Russian soldiers tagged along behind, all but forgotten.

Entering the lobby, Vergolina and McNeish experienced the same sense of awe that Beadle and Gould had felt—the warmth and comfort, the exquisite, opulent decor, and the air of Victorian gentility were almost overwhelming. Robert arranged baths and beds for the two men, adding them to his ever-growing tab. It was wonderful to see the joy they took in such simple pleasures as being able to shave and wash with soap and water, and how strange the prospect of sleeping in a real bed seemed to them. When they were cleaned up, they were taken down for dinner, which they ate like animals, scarcely pausing for breath.[3]

Gradually their stories came out. Vergolina did most of the talking. He was a Milwaukee man, and a lively spirit, a fellow of almost irrepressible cheerfulness who seemed to have taken his dreadful experiences in his stride. He was striking to look at, with heavy, pronounced features accentuated by the gauntness from months of near starvation. He'd been a medic in the 2nd Infantry Division, detached to a unit that landed on Omaha Beach on D-Day.[4] Somehow he'd survived the hellfire of the landing and was reunited with his regular platoon, which arrived on D + 1. They were immediately thrown into the ferocious fighting to hold the beachhead. After only a week on French soil, Vergolina was captured when a counterattack by an SS battalion overran his platoon's position.

Like Beadle, he wound up in Stalag III-C. His experience of the Red Army's violent liberation was very different from Beadle's. Herded by the Germans to the rear of the evacuee column, he hadn't been caught in the deluge of Russian mortar and machine-gun fire that fell on the head of the column as it marched out of the camp. He only saw the aftermath later—the dozens of POWs lying dead and wounded in the snow around the gate. Entering the camp, the Russian soldiers went methodically from building to building, shooting the handful of Germans who'd been caught there. A squad also went into a barracks block that had been set aside for the dozens of Russian POWs who had contracted tuberculosis during a recent epidemic. Bursts of submachine-gun fire came from the building, then the squad came out again.[5] Rudy Vergolina, inclined to be positive about everything, thought perhaps it had been a mercy killing, but he had a hard time convincing himself, and the event left him badly shaken.

Lingering in the vicinity of the camp for a week or two, Vergolina and his friends saw many more instances of Russian cruelty: German prisoners executed and civilians murdered. The Red Army was on German soil now, and the bitter enmity between the two peoples caught fire. Seeking shelter in a house near the camp, Vergolina found the entire family dead, all apparently shot by the father to save them from the Russians. Only the family dog was left alive, alone and barking.

Some of the remaining prisoners decided it was time to move on. The Russians were obviously going to do nothing for them, and the front line was still dangerously close by. In groups, the POWs began to drift east, joining the thousands of other wanderers. Sergeant Vergolina eventually found himself in the region near Danzig, where there was still fierce fighting going on to pry the Germans out of the Baltic ports. Somewhere between Danzig and Warsaw, Vergolina met up with Jim McNeish, a Scottish ex-POW.[6] They banded together and headed south, toward Warsaw.

The American and the Scotsman went through a strange odyssey together. They wandered through the ruins of Warsaw, so flattened that Vergolina reckoned you could stand on a stool and see the whole city. Dispossessed people still lingered, sitting despondently around the shells of their former homes. After dark there was still a crude, sad cabaret nightlife going in the cellars of ruined buildings, despite the Russian patrols enforcing the curfew. Even Rudy Vergolina's buoyant spirits were crushed by it, and the two men hurried on. They stayed for a while in a village near Zamość, as the guests of farming folk. Moving on again, they were robbed by bandits, and rode for days on the roof of a boxcar, huddled together for warmth.

Eventually rounded up by Russians and brought to Lwów, they were put in the so-called rehabilitation center. Kept in a different location than Beadle and Gould, they had a less unpleasant experience; they were fed tolerably and allowed out for exercise. But after many days of this, they began to feel that it would never end; the Russians were never going to let them go back to their own people. One day, while out for a walk, they spotted a party of Americans led by a captain. Seizing their chance, they lit out in a bid for freedom.

Robert knew what he had to do. Rudy Vergolina and Jim McNeish joined the motley band that was rapidly growing up around him.

The first stage—simply adopting them—wasn't too difficult. The two Russian guards, less persistent in their duties than some of their comrades, had given up and left. And fortunately, the Polish lady who had been Miss Lowry's replacement had finally given up and left the hotel after two days of being obstinately but politely snubbed by the Americans. That would make it easier to conceal the identities of the new guests, who were quietly adopted into the roster scheduled to leave for Poltava.

That brought the personnel load for the poor beat-up Fortress to seventeen. Robert hoped the damaged crate would be up to it. After more than a week at the airfield, the number three engine was still in pieces on the hangar floor. Eventually, in spite of continual Soviet inconvenience, he and Sergeant Picarelli managed to arrange the necessary repairs, and by March 16—their eleventh day stranded in Lwów—"687" was ready to fly again. The weather had cleared, and the following day was scheduled for departure.

During the last couple of days, while Robert and Sergeant Picarelli were preoccupied with readying the plane, Sergeant Matles found himself dealing with a rising tide of strays and refugees. It seemed word had got out that there were helpful Americans staying at the George. Occasionally civilians claiming to be American nationals turned up, asking for help with contacting the embassy in Moscow. Some had birth certificates and were indeed US-born. Matles did what he could to put them in touch with the embassy.

The trickle became a stream. On the evening before the scheduled departure, Sergeant Matles was in the hotel lobby when five men walked in off the street, all American ex-POWs. They were in an appalling state after three days on the road with no food at all. Matles tried to arrange for them to be given rooms and meals, but the hotel's assistant director put her NKVD-controlled Intourist foot down. She had no rooms, she said, and no food either. Both claims were transparently absurd, and it was obvious from her manner that she was acting against her better instincts. Someone somewhere had been leaning on the hotel. Matles demanded to see the hotel director. When he appeared, Matles tore into him, threatening to call in the US Embassy if food and quarters were not provided for the Americans.

While Matles argued with the director, the assistant director took pity on the bedraggled men; she discreetly led them away and gave them a meal, and arranged accommodation for them. Informing Matles of what she had done, she begged him to make the director approve it. Of course he would; in return, he asked that she take care of any other American personnel who might show up at the hotel after he had gone. She promised she would, and he believed her.

That same evening Robert was approached by a Polish civilian, who offered a sworn statement detailing Soviet atrocities committed against citizens in Lwów. Although he had plenty of reason to believe the man's account, there was absolutely nothing Robert could do. Like Colonel Wilmeth, who at that moment was receiving similar approaches from the Polish underground army in Lublin, he had been briefed to ignore such contacts: if the Soviets learned of the Americans having anything at all to do with anti-Soviet elements in Poland, they would shut down access to the country altogether, and helping the POWs would become impossible.[7]

The next morning, the Poltava-bound team made ready to depart. They had managed to secure an old Model A Ford truck that looked like it had been there since the Depression and had never recovered. Robert, Picarelli, and Jessee went out to the airfield to prep the plane for takeoff, while Sergeant Matles took care of the rest of the party. There was Lieutenant Barnett and his crew, plus Sergeants Beadle and Vergolina, Private Gould, and Gunner McNeish, all disguised as aircrew.

It simply wasn't possible to take any of the recently arrived POWs as well: aside from the B-17's limited capacity, everybody at the hotel knew they were ex-prisoners. Robert and Sergeant Matles had done the next best thing, arranging to have them put immediately on the next train for Odessa, without having to pass through the appalling Soviet camp.

Everyone was loaded up on the truck. Matles was about to climb aboard when he saw a large group of ragged-looking men walking into the hotel. He jumped down again and followed them inside. As he'd guessed, they were all Americans, all ex-POWs, all in dreadful, filthy, emaciated condition. Seven were officers, the rest enlisted men. With word getting out to the bands of strays that help could be found here, the Hotel George was becoming a magnet for lost prisoners. Matles got tea and beer for them, and arranged for them to go immediately to the railroad station and board the Odessa train. Whether they ever got there he had no way of knowing. Meanwhile he had a plane to catch, and he was running late.

At the airfield, the B-17 was warming up, running smoothly, and ready to make one last effort to get the hell out of this country.

It seemed that fate was determined to throw every possible obstacle in their way—as the engines were being run up, it began snowing again. As if that weren't enough of a worry, Robert and Picarelli had noticed that the plane, which had supposedly been under guard the whole time, was missing various little bits and pieces. A fire extinguisher had been removed, along with a headset from the radio compartment, and a discarded hacksaw was found on the floor. They could only hope that nothing vital had been removed or damaged.

Her flak wounds stuffed with rags, her holes patched up with plywood, and overloaded as she was with passengers, B-17 687, the Fort with no name, taxied out into the snow, revved up, and roared down the runway. She lifted off and soared away in a long, slow turn above the snow-swept city, carrying her cargo of Americans and Britons eastward to Poltava and safety.

She'd had a long and strange journey since taking off from Snetterton Heath a month ago, with Lieutenant Tillman at the controls, and there was a long way still to go—but 687 was back firmly in American hands.[8]

That night, Captain Trimble, in consultation with Sergeant Matles and Lieutenant Jessee, sat down to write a report of the salvage mission. So much had happened, it was difficult to recall it all, and hard to judge what to leave out. The Cossacks in the night, the furious Russian colonel glaring over the barrel of the Colt, the takeoff from the tiny sloping field, the blizzard whiting out the windshield . . . and the ragged, pitiful prisoners, desperate for help.

There would be flak to take over the decision to bring the four POWs to Poltava.[9] Their aircrew disguise, which had been sufficient to get them out of Lwów, wouldn't fool the Soviets at Poltava. They were bound to learn of it, and they would be furious.

They did indeed find out, and it was said by one observer that "their consternation knew no bounds."[10] What upset the Russians most was the presence of British POWs among the exfiltrated men. The Soviets were even more suspicious of the British than they were of the Americans. There was a long history, going back more than a century, of competitive espionage between the British and Russian Empires in the battle to control Asia. More recently, in the early days of the Russian Revolution, the British had hatched a plot to assassinate Lenin and overthrow the Bolsheviks.[11] The British were also much more secretive, less willing to share intelligence than the Americans were.[12] Consequently, British personnel were regarded by the Soviets as enemy agents until proven otherwise.[13] The arrival of Ronald Gould and Jim McNeish enraged them. As a result, the diplomatic position of Eastern Command shifted one step closer to a crisis.

Officially, the American authorities sternly disapproved of Captain Trimble's actions, but privately they thought he had done the right thing.

On the morning after their arrival at Poltava, before the Soviets had a chance to react to what had happened, Sergeants Beadle and Vergolina were put aboard a transport flying out to Tehran. Meanwhile, Gould and McNeish were dispatched to the British Embassy in Moscow for clearance. The parting between Rudy Vergolina and Jim McNeish was a sad one; they had endured so much hardship together, and helped each other through. At last they were within reach of the one thing they all yearned for—home.

The next day, a cable was received by Eastern Command from General Booth, commanding officer of Persian Gulf Command. It stated:

```
Ex-prisoners of war arrived Teheran 1730 hours, 18
March 45 plan to depart 1330 hours, 19 March 45.
T/4 Rudolph Vergolina, 36210949 and T/4 Richard
J. Beadle, 34077320. Both are liberated.14
```

Just a few days after leaving snowbound Lwów, Richard Beadle and Rudy Vergolina were in Cairo, experiencing in reverse the journey that Robert Trimble had made more than a month earlier.

While they were blinking in the bright Egyptian sunlight and thinking thoughts of home, Captain Robert M. Trimble was heading back out to the snows of Poland. So long as there were prisoners wandering helpless, his business was not finished. He was about to face his toughest emotional trial yet, as well as his greatest triumph.

14.

FAR FROM HOME

March 23, 1945: Red Army Hospital, Lublin, Poland

The building was warm, the wards were clean, and the seven American ex–prisoners of war were comfortable in bed.[1] The Russian medical staff gave the Americans every care they could, treating them not merely as patients but as honored guests. It was an extraordinary about-face in Soviet treatment of ex-POWs. Colonel Wilmeth was astonished by it.

Wilmeth and his medical colleague Colonel Kingsbury had been puzzled when the Soviet administrator cordially invited them to visit the hospital. And they were positively astounded to see how well the Americans were being treated.[2] It could not have been more different from the conditions in the holding camp in the town. This was positively luxurious; this was how former prisoners of war *should* be treated. In fact, to be perfectly truthful, an objective observer might have thought the VIP treatment a little excessive.

By now, Colonel Wilmeth had too much experience to imagine even for a minute that this marked a change of heart among the Soviets. When he began talking to the men, he immediately discovered the reason for their exceptional treatment. These seven men were survivors of the massacre at Stalag III-C.

Wilmeth and Kingsbury already knew about the incident; these were not the first men from that particular prison camp to have passed through Lublin. Sergeant Richard Beadle and many others who had been there had reported how Soviet infantry and tanks had fired on the column of POWs as the German guards were marching them away.[3] Dozens were killed or wounded. The official story that had come back from the Soviet front line was that the Russians had believed the camp to be a barracks, and that the marching POWs were Hungarian troops in German service. It seemed a plausible claim, but Colonel Wilmeth had grave doubts about it.[4] He knew—and so should have the Red Army—that Hungarian troops were not used by the Germans in Poland. And the men would have been visibly unarmed and obviously not in Wehrmacht uniform.

These seven in the Red Army hospital at Lublin were the surviving wounded. They told Wilmeth their stories. As frontline veterans, they didn't blame the Russians for the massacre; accidents happened all the time in war, they said, although this had been a particularly dumb one.

It had taken weeks for the enormity of the "accident" to be recognized by the Soviets: weeks during which the victims were subjected to the very same neglect as other ex–prisoners of war. But now word had come down from the very top of the Soviet tree that these men were to be treated with honor and every possible care.

If it was intended to be an apology, it went far beyond what was necessary—so far that Colonel Wilmeth was deeply suspicious of the motives behind it. Marshal Astakhov, deputy commander of the Red Army Air Force, had dispatched two airplanes from Moscow to Lublin to transport the seven men to Odessa. (That was nice, but no more than Eastern Command had been desperately trying to arrange for all its POWs for months now.) So as to honor the men properly, each of the two planes was to be crewed entirely by decorated Red Air Force combat veterans, and the two pilots would be holders of the Hero of the Soviet Union award—the Soviet equivalent of the Medal of Honor.

When Colonel Wilmeth was told about these plans, he accepted the gesture graciously on behalf of the United States Army and kept his cynical thoughts to himself. When the men were put aboard the planes the next day, they were loaded with presents, food, and bouquets of flowers. Wilmeth's suspicions were confirmed: the episode had more to do with propaganda than with making amends.

This lavish treatment would be presented to the world as an example of how the Soviet Union honored and cared for her allies' liberated prisoners. The Soviet government and its tame press would contrast this treatment sharply and unflatteringly with the abominable suffering that Russian ex-POWs were allegedly subjected to by American and British forces in Western Europe. This claim was propagated constantly by the Soviets, despite the evidence provided by Washington, the US Embassy, and SHAEF headquarters showing that it was false.

Colonel Wilmeth had had this propaganda line thrown in his face just a couple of weeks ago, during his last meeting with Colonel Vlasov.[5] Once again the meeting had turned quickly into an indignant confrontation.

Vlasov had begun by presenting Wilmeth with a list of numbers of ex-prisoners that had been shipped to Odessa from various collecting points in Poland. Wilmeth knew the figures were incomplete and inaccurate, and asked for better ones. Only Moscow had accurate figures, he was told. Why Moscow would have more information than the authority on the ground in Poland wasn't explained. It was impossible for Wilmeth to check the figures because he'd still been unable to contact General Deane in Moscow. He'd tried to send a message through the Polish commercial telegraph system, but was barred from using it (it had no connection to Moscow, they told him, even though he knew it did).

Having delivered his useless data, Colonel Vlasov delivered what he hoped was a body blow. As of the next day, March 13, Lublin was to be closed as a POW collecting point. There were no more ex-prisoners expected to arrive; all had been evacuated. Colonel Wilmeth's work was done, and he could therefore go back to Moscow. His permit had expired.

Wilmeth wasn't impressed. "Could you put that in writing?" he asked.

Vlasov, tight-lipped, refused. Wilmeth had learned that the way to deflect Soviet intimidation was to ask to have a claim put in writing, signed. None of them dared put anything on paper without approval from above, so even if they were telling the truth (which was rare), they ended up looking like they were lying.[6]

"I've heard that our American contact teams have finally arrived at Poltava," Wilmeth said. "Why are they not being allowed into Poland?" Vlasov said nothing. "Two weeks ago," Wilmeth went on relentlessly, "I was promised a truckload of supplies from the local Red Army depot. Where is it?" No answer. "Can you obtain permission for American planes to fly supplies into Poland?"

Colonel Vlasov said that it could not be done.

"*Somebody* has to bring in supplies," Wilmeth said angrily, "since you and your comrades seem to be utterly incapable of doing anything for the POWs."

Again he listed the ways in which the Soviet Union was failing to honor practically every principle Comrade Stalin had signed up to at Yalta; again he offered to let Colonel Vlasov have his copy of the agreement and see for himself.

Wilmeth's imperturbable placidity finally gave way. "It's a damn shame," he said, "that people who parade themselves as our friends act in every way *other* than friendly. I'm sick of it. *Sick*."[7]

Colonel Vlasov's temper broke as well. "I can tell you," he hissed furiously, "that Soviet ex–prisoners of war are receiving *far worse* treatment from the Americans than any American prisoners are receiving from the Soviet Union. They are being abused, and your government refuses to repatriate them to the USSR."

Wilmeth had heard this line being put out by Radio Moscow. It was a constant tune that they sang whenever Stalin wanted to score a propaganda point against the USA. Given Stalin's stated view of Soviet soldiers who surrendered, Wilmeth very much doubted the sincerity of these concerns—even if the allegations they were based on had been true.

"Do you know how many Soviet POW contact personnel there are in the European theater right now?" he asked Vlasov. "*Two hundred*. And they are permitted to go *anywhere they want to* behind American lines, at all times. And what do we have here?" He pointed to himself. "Two officers, myself and Colonel Kingsbury, confined to Lublin."

Not for much longer, Vlasov reminded him. His permit had expired.

Wilmeth asked him to put this in writing and send it as a message to General Deane in Moscow. Colonel Wilmeth would await General Deane's instructions. In the meantime, he would remain in Lublin.

Feeling that he ought to try to repair the diplomatic breach he had opened up, Colonel Wilmeth invited Colonel Vlasov to dine with him that evening. To his surprise, Vlasov accepted immediately. The fact that he did so without any consultation with his superior officer—unthinkable in the regular Red Army—finally convinced Wilmeth that Vlasov was NKVD.[8]

Indeed, as the days passed and he learned more about the ongoing Sovietization of Poland, and as he built up a picture of the experiences POWs were having in the journey from the stalags and oflags to the Soviet holding camps, Colonel Wilmeth was coming to suspect that the entire POW repatriation authority was being run by the NKVD.

The attempts to force him to leave Lublin intensified. He was told that a "big scandal" would result if he did not leave for Moscow, and he might not make it safely there if he did go.[9] His messages to General Deane were manipulated or falsified to give the impression that all was well, and that no further help was needed for POWs in Lublin because there were none there.[10] False orders, allegedly from Deane, instructing him to return to Moscow, were given to him. He ignored them.

Meanwhile, the argument over Wilmeth's situation at Lublin was going to the very top. Not only did General Deane want Wilmeth to stay; he was busily trying to get permission to go to Lublin himself and see what was happening. He had off-the-record sources of intelligence and knew very well that things were bad.[11] Consulting with Ambassador Averell Harriman, he requested that President Roosevelt take the matter up with Stalin directly.[12]

On March 17, Roosevelt cabled Stalin.[13] He asked why American aircraft were not being allowed to fly supplies into Poland, why they were not being permitted to evacuate sick POWs by air, and why the contact officers currently in Poland were being blocked from assisting their fellow Americans. "I have information that I consider positive and reliable," he wrote, "that there are a very considerable number of sick and injured Americans in hospitals in Poland," and he added that there were many ex-POWs who were still "at large in small groups." He asked that General Deane be allowed to travel to Lublin at once. "Frankly," the President added, "I cannot understand your reluctance to permit American officers . . . to assist their own people in this matter."

Five days later, on March 22, Stalin replied.[14] He stated that Roosevelt's information was "not exact." There were no American ex-prisoners of war in Poland now, aside from seventeen who were sick (including the seven in hospital at Lublin). These men were about to be flown to Odessa. Stalin added that he personally had no objection at all to General Deane visiting Poland, or any other American officers. But his hard-pressed army commanders would not welcome the extra burden of having to look after noncombatant foreign officers, especially when there were German agents at large who might harm or abduct American officers. (A curious echo of the warning that Captain Trimble had been given by his OSS contacts about the "German agents" ruse that the Soviets might use as a way to murder inconvenient Americans.) "Our commanders pay with their lives," Stalin went on, "for the state of matters at the front and in the immediate rear, and I do not consider it possible to limit their rights in any degree." He conveniently overlooked the fact that the areas of Poland in question were now dozens or even hundreds of miles from the front line. Stalin concluded by gravely reminding the US president that Russian POWs currently in American camps were subjected to "unlawful inconveniences" and even beatings. Marshal Stalin's concern for these men, whom he'd previously decreed to be "criminal deserters" and "traitors" who ought to be shot, was remarkable.

Hearing of Stalin's reply, US Ambassador Averell Harriman was outraged: "Stalin's statement," he wrote to the President, "that the Red Army command cannot be bothered with a dozen American officers in Poland to look after the welfare of our liberated prisoners is preposterous when we think of what the American people have done in supplying the Red Army with vehicles and food." He added darkly: "When the story of the treatment accorded our liberated prisoners by the Russians leaks out I cannot help but feel that there will be great and lasting resentment on the part of the American people."[15]

As the month of March wore away, so did Colonel Wilmeth's will to continue. But his resolve did not. He had built up a reliable little network of agents—some of them ex-POWs living in Polish homes, others from among the Polish underground—who passed him information. When the Russians told him that no more American or British POWs were expected to come into Lublin, he knew the truth of it: Soviet guards had been posted on the roads into town, directing POWs to go elsewhere. The same was happening in other Polish cities—Kraków, Łódź, and Warsaw. And as rumors of the way POWs were treated spread across the country, fewer and fewer were willing to try to enter the towns anyway.[16]

In the many interviews he conducted with ex-prisoners, Wilmeth learned that there was a pattern to their experiences.[17] With some exceptions, liberated American POWs were usually treated well, if rather offhandedly, by the frontline Soviet troops. The same was not true for captured Germans and liberated Russians. There were frequent murders. One group of American ex-POWs told of being given twenty-five German prisoners as a "gift" by their Soviet liberators, to kill as they saw fit: shoot them, hang them, chop them to bits, the Russians suggested, and they were disappointed when the Americans declined.[18] The truly abusive treatment of liberated American and British POWs usually began, as far as Wilmeth was able to make out, when they came to the rear areas, which were controlled by the NKVD and its operatives within the Red Army. Men like Colonel Vlasov.

If only the POWs could be brought to Odessa, they would be safe. Latest information was that the arrangements there were working out well.[19] The facilities originally set up by the Russians had been typically awful,[20] but the American contact officer, Major Hall, had worked to help improve them. There were now repatriation teams from America, Britain, France, and Belgium, all working efficiently with the Russians to process the ex-prisoners and put them aboard the British troopships that would take them to their home countries. (There was a simple and chilling reason for Russian cooperation at Odessa. The ships arrived filled with Russian ex-POWs who were handed over to the Soviets.[21] The fate of about half of these men would be incarceration in the gulags or even death; many were executed in warehouses near the docks.[22])

For Colonel Wilmeth, gathering the British and American POWs and getting them from Poland to Odessa was the hard part. Toward the end of the month, unable to make progress, constantly reminded by the Soviets that his presence was unwelcome, he finally gave up. There was nothing more he could do. He made arrangements to leave Lublin and return to Poltava.

His mission was indebted to the tune of $36,000 to the Polish Red Cross. He left them his unused surplus medical supplies, worth about $500. The Red Cross reckoned that their value on the black market would easily pay off the debt.[23]

Colonel Wilmeth and his party were flown out of Lublin on March 28. Their mission was not finished. Wilmeth knew there were still ex-POWs out there, of all nationalities, who didn't dare come into the towns. They needed assistance, guidance, reassurance. Somebody needed to be out there, helping to bring them to safety.

Somebody was. One man was out there alone; one man whose sole purpose was to get Americans home. And not just Americans: all stray people from the free world were his concern.

Late March 1945: Northwest of Lublin

What he remembered most vividly was the distant sound of the freight trains on the Pennsylvania Railroad.

Side by side, father and son, they would sit under the trees on the bank of the Juniata River, or wade out off the rocks, their fishing lines running into the broad, slow water. Robert loved those fishing trips, in that golden time before his father went away and everything was poisoned and turned to darkness.

There was a sound that haunted that valley. A long series of booming reports, like distant cannon-fire, rolling up the river, echoing through the mists that hung over the forested slopes. Slow as a ticking clock . . . *boom* . . . *boom* . . . *boom* . . . continuing for a minute or more. To a young boy, it was ominous, frightening. His father smiled at him and explained that it was the sound of a long freight train setting out from the Enola rail yard. As each car's coupling locked in place with the pull of the engine, it would make that sound, which would reverberate for miles up the river valley.

The Enola Yard, a vast nexus of sidings and junctions, stood on the side of the Susquehanna River across from Harrisburg, right next-door to Camp Hill. When he was a boy, the railroad entered Robert Trimble's soul. It was always there in the background, on those weekend trips with his father. In the winter they hunted deer and would live out in the wilds for days at a time among the snows that lay on the pines and the red spruces. It was a beautiful place, fresh as the morning of the world, the valley ridges cutting across the land as if the tines of a vast rake had been dragged through this country when it was young and hadn't yet hardened.

And from time to time came that *boom* . . . *boom* . . . *boom* . . . as one of the great half-mile trains with its hundred or more cars started up the valley toward Pittsburgh, or south for Baltimore.

It echoed in his memory now, marking out the rhythm of his steps as he walked along the railroad through the wilds of Poland.[24]

Robert had been back a few days now, having replenished his stock of cash and rations at Poltava, and caught a flight back to Lwów, ostensibly still on salvage and aircrew recovery business, but in reality slipping out of the bird dogs' scenting range and heading deep into the country.

The agents' messages—moving by word of mouth now through the network of POWs and informants that Wilmeth had helped link up, as well as via the embassy—still reached Robert at the hotels in Lwów or Kraków or Lublin, or even at the homesteads out in the country, or wherever the mission happened to take him.

There were more messages, more calls for help than a single man could cope with, and they came not only from American POWs but from people of other nations, all kinds of people who had been set loose from the Nazi camps and abandoned. Although Robert wasn't conscious of it, the stress of his mission, layered on top of what he had gone through during his combat tour, was beginning to wear away at him. He was approaching that point where fractures start to appear in a person's inner being.

A message had reached him the previous day: a rendezvous with a band of POWs, concentrated in an area northwest of Lublin. It was close to a railroad route, so getting them to a station and aboard a train shouldn't be too difficult. He could even follow the tracks to the meeting point. And so he set out on what now seemed almost like a routine mission. What he saw that day would haunt him the rest of his life. He didn't like to think about it; didn't even like to acknowledge that it was there in his memory. Only with patient persuasion could he be drawn to talk about it.

It was a beautiful day, bright and clear, seeming to promise the first approach of spring. Out here, away from the towns and roads, there was peace. And there was a familiarity too—the slopes covered in bare birches and green pines dusted with snow, casting long winter shadows across the crackling ice floes that dotted the slow-moving Vistula River. It could almost be the Susquehanna, and this railroad could almost be the line that snaked up the Juniata valley toward Pittsburgh and Cleveland.

But there were differences. It was eighty years since war had last visited Pennsylvania. In the valley of the Vistula, although there was peace this minute, war had been here very recently. This very spot had been on the front line as little as two months ago, the Vistula forming the boundary between the opposing forces of the Wehrmacht and the Red Army. That changed with the beginning of the Soviets' Vistula-Oder Offensive in January. The traces were still to be seen: pieces of broken gear and weapons poking through snowy hummocks; wrecked buildings, an occasional burned-out vehicle, and trees splintered by shellfire.

In this area there were at least three abandoned Nazi concentration camps, satellites of the main death camp of Majdanek in Lublin.[25] And this river, farther upstream, passed by an even more notorious camp: it was into the waters of the Vistula that the SS had dumped the ashes from the ovens at Auschwitz-Birkenau.

But to Robert, lost in his own thoughts, that was all far away.

He paced steadily, walking between the rails, where the snow was thinnest, the ties firm and familiar under his boots. Robert Trimble was far from home, but at times like this, alone in the wilds, he could almost imagine he was back there. The smell of the winter pines was in his nostrils, and the mournful squalling of crows in the far distance. His mind was in the past, in the head of the adolescent boy he'd been, when he still had a father and his closest pals were his fellow Boy Scouts.

Camping out in the woods was a favorite pastime, but there were jaunts farther afield. In 1933, the Scout troop bought a dilapidated old Bell Telephone truck, and their scoutmaster drove them up to Chicago to visit the World's Fair ("A Century of Progress!"). For Robert, the best part was sleeping under the stars at Niagara Falls on the way home. But the favorite times were with his dad: fishing, learning to hunt deer. His father was devoted to young Robert—until one day, with no explanation, he left and never came back. It was like having a limb blown off by a sudden bomb blast. The scarring ran deep into Robert's soul, leaving a place that was hardened, closed off.

But he still loved to hunt and fish, still loved the wild country.

It took a war to bring him happiness again. In the fall of 1943, he was posted to Fort Worth Army Airfield in Texas, to begin transition training on the B-24 Liberator bomber. He'd become a skilled pilot, and this was his introduction to the shoulder-winged, twin-tailed behemoths he would eventually fly in combat. They were built nearby at the Consolidated Vultee factory, and during the course of the war, Fort Worth was the training base for thousands of pilots. When Second Lieutenant Robert M. Trimble arrived, he and his buddies were given accommodations by a local oilman who had a huge ranch near the airfield.

The men's wives came to live with them. For Robert and Eleanor it was their perfect honeymoon—a Shangri-La for two kids from blue-collar Camp Hill. Robert taught her to fish on the ranch's lake and hunt in the woods. One evening they walked down by the lake. "I could imagine us staying here forever," Eleanor said. "Couldn't you?"

"Well, I'd like to," Robert said. "Everything I want is here. Hunting, fishing . . ." He corrected himself: "*You*, hunting, fishing . . ."

She scolded him, and they laughed. He could still see in her the teenage schoolgirl, radiant from basketball practice, coming into the shop where he'd worked Saturdays as a soda jerk. "Cat got your tongue?" she taunted him as he bashfully served ice-cream sodas to her and her best friend. She was pretty, but there was more than just a teenage fancy in their attraction; they were drawn to each other, two children scarred by their fathers.

With the Texas sundown coloring the waters of the lake, he took her in his arms. "The war could change our lives forever," he said. He let the words hang in the air; the unspoken question was whether it would change their lives for better or worse. So far, it had brought them this idyll, but it could so easily bring them unthinkable grief. . . .

Robert was so deep in his memories, he wasn't sure at first what it was that yanked him back to the present. The cawing of crows, the cold air burning his cheeks, the thump of his boots on the railroad ties . . . everything was the same. Everything except the peculiar whatever-it-was that was scattered along by the tracks about a quarter mile ahead. From a distance it looked like a knocked-over cordwood stack. Not an uncommon sight: most of the Polish locomotives burned wood, which was why they were so underpowered and slow. But it didn't look right: the billets were much too long for firewood—about the length of a man.

As Robert drew closer, his steps slowed. The crows he'd been hearing for the past mile or so were fluttering and circling overhead, and he understood what the objects were. For a moment, preposterously, he thought they might be railroad workers on a nap break.

There were dozens of bodies, scores of them, maybe a couple of hundred, lying heaped or in rows next to the tracks. As he approached, his feet carrying him onward in spite of the feeling of foreboding settling on his heart, he noticed that some were actually lying on the tracks. Not just on them, he realized—*tied* to them. They had been mutilated, decapitated or cut in half by the wheels of a train.

Moving carefully, and fighting down the urge to vomit, Robert stepped among the corpses. The crows hopped away or went flapping up into the air, squawking. Other than the ones tied to the track, the bodies were mostly laid in rows, as if they'd been lined up and shot in batches. How long ago it had happened, he couldn't say. The bodies were frozen. They could have lain here for days. Not much longer than that, or they'd have been covered in snow. Their faces were edged with frost, but seemed almost alive, spared the bloating and discoloring of decomposition. They looked disconcertingly as if they might wake if they were disturbed.

Most of them were in German uniform; others were in tattered remnants of what appeared to be Red Army clothing. The latter were in an emaciated state and were obviously Russian prisoners of war. What had occurred here was a mystery, but some possibilities suggested themselves. Most likely a consignment of captured Germans and liberated

Russian POWs had come down from the front line all herded together, probably by train. American ex-prisoners had reported this kind of mixing of captured enemy soldiers and liberated prisoners. If that was the case, then up to this point the Russian POWs had been lucky; at this stage in the war, the Red Army was so desperate for troops, the standard procedure was to march liberated Russians straight to marshaling centers, regardless of what state of emaciation and sickness they were in, kit them out, and ship them straight to the front line.[26]

As for what had triggered this massacre, that was slightly more of a mystery. Soviet troops on the Eastern Front were no strangers to atrocities. And there were known incidents of them murdering their countrymen who had been POWs. The culture inspired by Stalin's decrees was long-lasting. Even POWs who had escaped the camps and fought with partisans against the Germans weren't immune to suspicion and retribution from the Red Army.[27]

But there was a ritualism about this—a profoundly cruel deliberation—that was different. The train carrying these men must have reached this point, and something occurred—some dispute, some incident that triggered the kind of emotional chain reaction that prefaces an atrocity. One of the former Nazi death camps was nearby—the railroad was a branch line that went right past it—so perhaps that had something to do with it. Maybe there was alcohol involved. Something had fueled the hate that these people felt for one another. Robert studied their frozen faces. Could these Germans actually be Russians in Nazi uniform? It was possible. It would explain the extremity of the murders.[28]

Robert sank down on his haunches, weak with grief and disgust. What kind of a world was this? He thought of the sights he'd seen at Auschwitz, and of the Soviets' callous neglect and abuse of their allies' liberated prisoners, and the woman outside the hotel in Lwów at the mercy of the jeering soldiers, and of baby Kasia, dead under a mound of rocks on the roadside. How could this be a world worth fighting for? How could it be a world that men and women could bring new life into? How could a man ever go back to his home taking sights like this with him? How could there ever *be* a home again?

As his gaze roamed over the dead faces, he noticed that one of the Russians was no more than a boy. Seventeen at most. About the same age as Robert, the innocent Eagle Scout from Camp Hill, had been when his heart and life were broken by his father's departure. For this poor boy, life had ended violently, in unspeakably terrifying circumstances. Where was his home? Had he left it willingly, like Robert, eager to fight for his country? Or had he yearned to go back there, back to his mother? Robert felt a connection to him. He couldn't bear to leave him where he lay, where his murderers had discarded him, among the bodies of their enemies.

Acting on an impulse that he could hardly explain, Robert dropped to his knees and started to move the rigid corpse. He would bury the body, let the boy have some dignity in death.

He carried the remains away from the tracks, to a spot where a patch of sunlight came through the bare trees. It was a dreadful task; the Russian boy was one of those who'd been tied to the track and cut in two. Robert tried to dig a shallow grave, but the ground was frozen solid; all he could do was scrape a trench in the snow. Covering the boy's face with a spare shirt, he piled snow and rocks over the remains. It was the best he could do. He mumbled a halting prayer. Drained, bowed over beside the wretched grave, he fell into a kind of swooning sleep.

A slamming door, a shout, and Robert was jerked awake, listening anxiously to the silent house.

Nothing. Not even the sound of his mother crying. Not anymore. Her grief had hardened into a grim resolve, and she went about life as if it were a battle. Now that there was no man in the house, she had ordered Robert to start bringing in a wage by working after school and on weekends.

Robert himself had gone through the same emotional journey. His father's betrayal had been inexplicable, a sudden total severance from the man who had taught him, loved him. Robert had adored and idolized his dad. But Fred Trimble had wanted a better life for himself. On the tails of the Great Depression, he hitched up with the secretary he'd been having an affair with and headed for California. He never looked back, never called.

At first Robert had cried like a boy bereaved. But he was a boy on the verge of manhood, and soon the crying had to stop. The anger remained, though, the anger and the soul-deep scars that he would keep for the rest of his life.

He went to work on the Pennsylvania Railroad. The freight trains that had been the background to his existence in Camp Hill, their boom and rumble echoing through his hunting and fishing trips, became his daily life. Underneath he nurtured a longing to fly. He became fascinated by airplanes and yearned to be able to go up in one. Maybe there was an unconscious urge to escape the bonds of hurt and responsibility that confined him. With war on the horizon, he got his chance: in July 1941, after a failed attempt to volunteer for the Royal Canadian Air Force, he joined the US Army and began working his way toward the Air Corps. At first they wouldn't take him for pilot training, because he wasn't college-educated, but the desire was strong in him, and he gradually wore them down.

But through it all, it was the railroads that ran in his veins. He could never escape their pull, and whenever he fished on the Juniata, still there would come the distant *boom . . . boom . . . boom . . .*

He woke with a start, and found himself slumped in the snow beside the makeshift grave. How long had he slept? He glanced around groggily. It couldn't have been more than a few minutes. The patch of sunlight had barely moved.

Robert looked at the dark rows of corpses beside the railroad tracks.

Having offered a prayer for the boy, he whispered another for all of the dead, for all the suffering people everywhere.

. . . And in the silence of contemplation, he realized what it was that had woken him: the familiar sound of a train in the distance, coming closer. He listened intently.

It might be just a civilian train. More likely, it would be a military transport or supply train. It might even be carrying prisoners of war from the front. Robert could guess what his fate might be if the Soviets knew that he had witnessed the aftermath of this atrocity.

He jumped to his feet, grabbed the pack containing his supply of rations and medical kit, and took off at a run up the slope, heading deep into the trees.

Once he was well out of sight of the railroad, he veered back toward his original direction. He had a rendezvous to make. People needed him—people stranded far from home. Robert Trimble was the only hope they had now. He wasn't about to let them down, no matter what the journey cost him. His own way home lay alongside theirs.

15.

ISABELLE

Late March 1945: Lwów, Poland

A young woman walked along the road leading through the northwestern suburbs of Lwów. As she passed into the city, she kept her eyes cast down at the cobbles, avoiding the gaze of the citizens and of the Russian soldiers who stood about, loafing on corners or guarding the entrances to buildings.

Walking close to the tram lines, where the snow and ice had been cleared, she passed through almost as if she were invisible. During her time in the labor camps she had developed the important skill of not attracting attention to herself. But here, exposed on the street, it was more difficult. And she wasn't used to the city environment—the imposing town houses, the lingering grandeur of the old Galician era, and the crowds of people. The camps had been crowded, but not like this, and she had since grown used to the isolation of her little group of fellow refugees.

Her clothes were threadbare and inadequate in the freezing weather. But there were many people on the streets who didn't look much different. The locals and the soldiers were wrapped up warmly, but there were people about who appeared to be refugees of one kind or another.

It was a chilling place to be, if you knew the recent history of this

region the way this young woman did. Beneath the city's faded ele-
gance, Lwów was a place where death and madness had taken root. The
traces of it were everywhere. The splintered stonework from gunfire
and shrapnel was the least of it. The young woman's route took her past
the Janowska camp, where the Nazis had exterminated the Jews from
the Lwów ghetto. It was now being used by the Soviets as a prison camp.[1]
She hurried by, keeping her gaze averted from the sentries outside the
gates. Coming into the city center, she passed by the Brygidki prison. A
strange-looking place, its façade resembled a row of rather squat man-
sions, and its walls were blackened by fire. It oozed menace. In the days
before Barbarossa, in 1941, when eastern Poland was a Soviet dominion,
Brygidki had been an NKVD prison. When the Germans launched
their war against the USSR in June 1941, there were thousands of political prisoners in Brygidki and other Soviet jails in Lwów, most of them
Ukrainians. The NKVD, panicking as the German forces raced across
Poland toward them, executed the prisoners in one horrific onslaught
that went on for a week, then set fire to the prison.[2]

The Germans entered the city to find it littered with bodies. The
response of the SS was to add to the slaughter. The Jews of the city
instantly became the scapegoats for the Bolsheviks' massacre. Rumors
were put about that they had aided in the killing; in fact, they had been
among the victims. Local Ukrainians and the SS began roaming the city,
searching for Jews. Those who weren't murdered on the spot were herded
to Brygidki, where the bodies of the massacre victims were buried in a
vast pit in the prison yard. The Jews were forced to do the work of burial.
German soldiers, wearing gas masks to stave off the stench of the rotting
corpses, fired intermittently at them, and their bodies were thrown into
the pit. The German officer in command took off his gas mask long
enough to bellow at the laboring, dying Jews. "The whole world is bleeding because of you!" he ranted. "Look at what you've done!"[3]

Nearly four years had passed since that day, but the city was still
palpably haunted by it.

Keeping her eyes on the icy cobbles, and following the directions she had memorized, the young woman turned right beyond Brygidki and found her way to the grand avenue leading to Mickiewicz Square. At the end, she paused and looked up at the imposing façade of the Hotel George. This was the place, the rumors went, where freedom could be found. There was a man here—an American, they said—who could help the lost and stranded to get home.

The young woman's heart beat faster as she steeled herself to enter the intimidating doorway. She was sure to be seized and thrown out before she'd even crossed the threshold. Possibly even handed over to the Russians. But she had no choice. She had promised her friends, her comrades, her countrywomen, that she would try.

The lobby of the George was a rather grand affair, but pleasant. The lofty, molded ceiling and the white marble floor tiles were bright with light from the glazed entranceway. On either side were a couple of sofas and a few small tables and chairs. At one of them sat an American officer, engrossed in studying some papers while a cup of coffee cooled in front of him.

He'd had a hard couple of days out in the wilds and was looking forward to a night in his bed. The hotel staff and the Russian officers who frequented the place had grown used to the presence of Captain Robert Trimble during the past couple of months. He gave out that he was on aircraft salvage business, and nobody but the NKVD had any reason to doubt it. Often he would be away for days and nights at a time (nobody knew where he went exactly, despite some of them trying quite hard to find out), but he always returned to the George sooner or later.

Occasionally he had been known to bring other people with him—Americans usually, sometimes British, most of them ragged ex-prisoners. More often, though, he arrived alone, and people came to him, the daring ones, having heard that the ticket out of this country was in his power to give. Some seemed to believe that he had powers that were almost magical. But that was just wishful thinking; hope was a scarce commodity in this land, and what little there was had to be seized with both hands.

While he drank his coffee, Robert was picking through the messages that had come in for him while he'd been away. The most important were the handful that had come in from the agents out in the field. But there was also information on downed US planes and aircrew. That was still part of his job, and still his official reason for being in Poland.

The NKVD were close to him this minute, as they invariably were to any foreigner in Poland on official business. Robert was aware of at least one bird dog sitting at the next table. By now, he could virtually smell a bird dog without even needing to see them. They rarely made much effort to be discreet, and out on the streets it was usually quite easy to shake off the officer escorts. It was the civilian informers who were the dangerous ones.

Robert looked up from his papers to see a young woman standing in front of him. She had approached so unobtrusively he hadn't noticed her. She was dressed in ragged, dirty clothes, and her face was thinned out by hunger. Her glance swept across his uniform and insignia. "*Vous êtes américain?*" she said hesitantly.

Before Robert could reply, a Russian officer who had been standing over by the desk came across and addressed her sharply in his own language. The mantra was so familiar, Robert understood it perfectly. "What is your business here?" the Russian demanded. "Where are your papers?"

The young woman stared at the officer, either not understanding him or just struck dumb with terror.

Taking her hesitation for guilt, the Russian seized her by the arm. Snapping an order at her, he tried to drag her away. She struggled and cried out.

Robert had no idea what was going on, but he wasn't about to sit by and do nothing while a young woman was manhandled by some NKVD bully. He was on his feet in an instant. He laid a hand on the Russian officer's arm. "Leave her. She wants to talk to me."

The Russian stared at him. "She has no papers," he said in English. "She is under arrest and must be questioned."

"I'm a representative of the United States government," Robert said, reaching into his pocket for his passport, "acting on behalf of the embassy in Moscow. I am entitled to speak to this lady."

The Russian reluctantly let go of the woman's arm. He scrutinized the passport suspiciously, then handed it back, mollified. Robert had learned long ago (as had Sergeant Matles in Lwów and Colonel Wilmeth in Lublin) that mentioning governments, diplomatic entitlement, and the magic word "Moscow" almost invariably had this effect. Russian officers—especially those in the lower ranks of the NKVD, who were paranoid as a matter of professional course—were terrified of any power that stood above them, and especially worried by anything that came out of Moscow.

Glaring at the young woman, the officer withdrew, grumbling a threat that he would look into Captain Trimble's claim and would come back if it didn't check out.

Robert sat down and invited the young woman to join him. The bird dog at the next table edged closer to be sure he could overhear their conversation.

The young woman said something to Robert in French. He didn't understand a word. "*Vous ne parlez pas français?*" she said.

"I'm sorry," he said. "No, I don't. I wish I did, Miss, er . . . ?"

"Isabelle," she said. "I am named Isabelle. You are *américain?*"

"That's what it says in the passport," he said, putting it back in his pocket. "Are you okay?"

She shook her head. "*J'suis loin de la France . . .* ah, *je veux dire*: a long way from France, me."

Robert smiled. "So I can see. And I guess you're not here on vacation."

"Thank you to . . . to stand up for me to the Russian," she said, struggling to find the words. "I have hoped to find the *américain* at this hotel—you are he?" Before Robert could stop her, she blurted out: "You help me to France? I am lost, I escape—you can help?"

At the next table, the bird dog was leaning so close he was almost falling off his chair. Robert shook his head firmly. "I'm sorry, miss, I can't help you." At the same time, he tore a strip off a piece of paper and scribbled on it. He stood up, clearly indicating that the meeting was over. "I think you've mistaken me for somebody else. Now, I have other business to attend to. Please excuse me." He took her hand and shook it vigorously between both of his. "I wish you good luck. Good day." Then he sat back down and busied himself with his papers, taking no more notice of her.

For a moment, she stood there, shocked and dismayed. From the corner of his eye, Robert saw her back away, then turn suddenly and push through the main door. It slammed shut behind her. Conscious of the curious gazes directed at him, he heaved a sigh, while behind him he sensed the bird dog subside in disappointment.

O ut in the street, Isabelle felt like sitting down on the sidewalk and crying. All that she had survived, all that she had endured, only to have the tiny scrap of hope crushed. Had she got the wrong man? But surely not—the way he had sent the Russian officer about his business, this must be the American the rumors whispered about.

Isabelle wondered if she would ever see her homeland again. Three years ago, she had been a free woman—or as free as you could be in a Nazi-occupied country. She had kept her head down, minded her own business.

Then came the labor conscription. At first the Germans tried to tempt young French people with promises of pay, but few people wanted to go hundreds of miles to a foreign country to work for the occupying power. So the Nazis switched to their natural way of doing things: coercion. In September 1942 the puppet Vichy government passed the law that established the Service du Travail Obligatoire—compulsory labor service. All men aged between eighteen and fifty and all women between twenty-one and thirty-five were eligible, and began being conscripted to do "*tous travaux que le gouvernement jugera utile dans l'intérêt supérieur de la Nation.*"[4] Needless to say, the "nation" in question was the Third Reich, not France. Failure to register for the STO was punishable by up to five years in prison.[5] Many rebelled, and as the conscription expanded, ever greater numbers of young French people went into hiding and joined the Resistance.

By February 1943, more than 160,000 French civilians had been swept up in the STO.[6] Isabelle was one of them. They were put on trains and sent to Germany, where they joined the great teeming hordes of other foreign workers—mostly Poles, Ukrainians, and Russians. The majority labored in German factories, but Isabelle was among the thousands put to work on the farms of Germany and Poland.

They were not technically slaves—they were paid, on a scale according to race. The French received (in theory, but usually not in practice) the same wages as German workers, while the Russians earned the least. But in every other respect it was enslavement. The workers were herded into camps which were run on the same model as all the Reich's prisons. By 1944 there were more than five million foreign workers in the Reich's factories, mines, and farms, together with prisoners of war. As the war dragged on, they were joined by concentration camp inmates, who really were slaves and suffered worst of all. Altogether, forced laborers made up about a quarter of Germany's entire workforce.[7]

As was the way of things, the women in each category suffered more than the men. There were rapes of female workers by their overseers and commandants.[8] Isabelle was one of the victims. It was only an issue for the Nazi authorities if the woman was an Eastern worker—a Pole or a Russian. The punishment for German personnel indulging in sexual relations with Eastern workers, regardless of whether it was consensual or involved bribery or rape, was to be sent to a labor education camp. The woman would be sent to a concentration camp. From the earliest days of the forced labor program, brothels for the use of male workers were set up in the camps. To prevent the crime of miscegenation, the prostitutes were drafted from among the female workers of the appropriate race.[9]

It was a living nightmare, but worse was yet to come for the forced laborers.

As the war dragged on and the Reich shrank, food became scarce. Starving laborers began to rebel, taking to robbery to feed themselves. In dozens and in scores, they were put to death. At this very moment, while Isabelle stood dejected outside the Hotel George, rebellious forced laborers all over Germany—in Dortmund, Düsseldorf, Münster, every big city—were being executed en masse.[10] Others died in the homicidal mania that was running loose in the towns and villages of Germany in the closing months of the war. It was an altogether wilder kind of madness than the industrialized murder of the Nazi regime; everywhere, the Gestapo and SS murdered their charges, sometimes in retribution, sometimes to instill terror, and often, it seemed, just acting on their own sociopathic hate and bloodlust.

Isabelle knew what these people were capable of. On the Eastern Front, as the Red Army closed in, SS units were killing foreign workers who tried to avoid being driven along with the retreat. Not far from where Isabelle herself had been incarcerated, a group of her own compatriots were killed for attempting to escape. At Oppeln in Silesia,[11] between Kraków and Wrocław, French laborers trying to hide in a cellar were driven out by Germans with flamethrowers, herded together in a farmyard, and shot.[12] They were a few among many. Most were force-marched westward, along with the POWs and the concentration camp inmates, but hundreds, thousands, escaped the roundup and went into hiding.

Among them was Isabelle. With a small group of friends, she had managed to drop out of the march one night when the Germans moved on suddenly to get away from a Soviet advance. The women headed east and hid themselves in the Polish countryside, not far from where they had been enslaved. Like most other liberated prisoners, they feared and avoided the Soviet forces. Isabelle's little party of Frenchwomen made contact with other groups, and soon there was a network of them, all women, scattered across the countryside near Lwów, hiding out in barracks in the former camps or sheltered in abandoned farm buildings.

One question went back and forth between them, without an answer: *How can we get away from here and get back to France?* They were trapped. But then they heard the rumor about the American officer who helped people get to Odessa. He was hard to find, they said, let alone to contact. Sometimes he'd be in one city, sometimes in another. And he was only interested in prisoners of war, particularly Americans. Would he be willing to help French civilian workers?

It was worth a try. Isabelle, who spoke some English, was elected to seek him out. He was known to spend time in Lwów. That was where she should go. Terrified of being rounded up by the Russians and sent to one of their holding camps, she had set out to walk into the city.

And now, that slender hope had come to nothing. Standing on the sidewalk outside the hotel, Isabelle wondered how she could go back and tell the other women that the American wouldn't help them.

As she walked away, she became aware that there was a scrap of paper balled up in her clenched fist. Isabelle recalled the American's hands enfolding hers and the hearty shake. She unscrewed the paper and turned it over. There was a number written on it. A hotel room number. Presumably his. But why? A familiar cold sensation gripped her. Was there going to be a price to pay for securing his help? With a flash of anger, she asked herself whether there were any men at all in the world who would do something for a woman without such payment. Was there no man who would do a person good without taking his price?

As evening drew in, Robert went up to his room and started getting ready for bed. For the rest of his life he would remember how blissful this bed at the Hotel George felt when he came in from a mission out in the countryside. He pitied the poor people who were living out there constantly, waiting for the opportunity to escape, or for some-body to help them.

He thought about the young Frenchwoman and hoped she would make use of the room number he had slipped to her. (Or *hoped* he'd slipped to her; he wasn't at all sure he'd done the move right.) It wasn't safe for anyone, let alone a young girl, to be alone on the streets after dark. Thinking back to that first night in this hotel, and the woman being tortured and murdered, still gave him the creeping horrors. Even if you were a man and were armed, breaking the curfew could get you shot. The Russians seemed to believe that German spies came out in swarms after dark, like cockroaches.[13] It wasn't at all uncommon to hear gunshots in the night, and to find bodies on the streets in the morning.[14]

Just as Robert was about to get undressed, there was a soft knock on the door. He opened it, and with a thrill of relief he recognized the raggedly dressed young Frenchwoman. So he hadn't fumbled the hand-shake trick!

"Come in," he said warmly, throwing the door wide.

Isabelle came in, bringing the unmistakable odor of the farmyard into the room with her. For a woman who was hoping to be helped, she didn't look very friendly. She stood and stared coldly at Robert as he closed the door.

He went to take a step toward her, and she held up a hand. "Wait," she said haughtily. "I want a bath, please."

"Okay," he said. "That's easy to arrange." Bathing was usually the first thing ex-prisoners wanted when he brought them here; that and food. They didn't usually demand it in such frosty terms, though. "Whatever you want. I've got a towel and soap here. The bathroom is down the hall. I'll have to come with you to—"

"No," Isabelle said, snatching the towel and soap from his hands. "Please, let me to bathe first, before you are with me."

He stared at her a moment, brain ticking over, then it clicked. "Whoa, whoa," he said. "It's nothing like that! Is that what you thought?"

He looked at her face, at the trace of fear behind the hostility, and was appalled. He'd heard the stories; he knew as well as anyone the kind of things that had gone on in those camps. "You're safe now," he said. "Nothing to be afraid of. Listen, the bathroom is down the hall; I have to come with you to make sure nobody stops you in the hallway. Come on."

He led her, still suspicious, down the hall to the communal bathroom. "In there," he said. "Lock the door. I'll wait for you, Miss, er . . . ?"

"Isabelle," she reminded him, her expression softening. "Call me Isabelle."

After she had bathed, Robert went downstairs and brought back some food. She ate ravenously. Between mouthfuls she told him fragments of her story—the conscription in France, the journey to Poland, the forced labor. The atmosphere of fear and abuse in the camps had intensified as the years went by. Just this past year Isabelle had been raped more than once by the slave drivers who ran the camp. She described how at last she and her compatriots had managed to escape the march west, only to find themselves stranded in Soviet territory.

Robert told her again that she was safe now. "I'll take you to the station and put you on the Odessa train. You'll be home in no time."

She looked at him, studying his face. "I have heard that the Americans have liberated France," she said. "But you—why do you do this, for nothing?" After what she had been through, the idea of a man helping a person without expecting something in return was mystifying. She had apologized for her suspicions of him, but still she didn't understand.

Neither did Robert, entirely. It would be many years before he would be able to look back on all this and begin to figure it out. He had seen too much death, and it was as if he was trying to fight back; as if helping people, doing good, could somehow push back against the tide of violence, cruelty, and callousness that was threatening to engulf the world. He couldn't articulate it to Isabelle—or even to himself; all he knew at the time was that his missions helped to stave off the nightmare of what he had been through.

"Anyhow," he said. "We'll go to the station in the morning and get you on a train. You'll be in Odessa in a couple days. There'll be a British ship to take you home, and—"[15]

"*Ah, non,*" she interrupted, almost panicking. "*Non! Toutes mes amies—il faut qu'elles m'accompagnent.*" She stopped and gathered herself. "Excuse me. My friends . . . I will not be without them. It . . . they must too, go with me."

"Sure," said Robert, unfazed. Refugees were almost never alone. They always came in pairs or groups. "How many of you are there?" In his head he started working out ticket costs and a plan for getting them to the train station without attracting attention.

"Four hundred," said Isabelle carefully.

Robert blinked. "Four . . . er, I think you mean *forty.*" Forty was a lot to manage at once, but he'd handled larger numbers. He went back to his mental arithmetic.

There was a pencil lying on the table; Isabelle picked it up and wrote on a piece of paper: *4 0 0.*

"I can count," she said. "Four hundred."

The number swam in front of Robert's eyes. It wasn't possible to get that many out in one go. No way in the world. Nobody sane would even attempt it. Four hundred Frenchwomen, marching through Lwów? They'd be arrested before they got within a mile of the station. They'd have to be split into groups; but that could take days. He tried to puzzle it out. Say ten groups of forty . . . but there was only one train a day. In the meantime he had other calls on him, other people needing help. Maybe eight groups of fifty, or five groups of eighty . . . but no, it wasn't feasible, not without abandoning the stray POWs who needed him.

He saw her watching him anxiously. "Oh, don't worry," he said. "We'll think of something. Do you have any papers? Identification?"

She shook her head.

"Okay, well, I guess we'd better sleep on it." He looked regretfully at the quilt and the soft pillows that had been calling to him for the past couple days. "I guess you'd better have the bed," he sighed.

That night he lay awake on the hard floor in his parka, trying to work out a solution. He couldn't bring four hundred women into Lwów, and he couldn't split them into groups. There had to be another way.

And then the solution dawned on him. *Couldn't bring them into Lwów* . . . That was the answer, right there: he didn't need to bring them in. The idea was absurd, it was dangerous. But it was a plan. He was going to need a whole train.

16.

BAIT AND SWITCH

Isabelle walked out of Lwów in higher spirits than when she had entered it.

Earlier that morning, while the Hotel George was shaking itself awake, Robert had gone downstairs and scared up some breakfast. While they ate, he explained his plan. If he couldn't bring the women to the train, he reasoned, he would have to bring the train to the women. All they needed to do was be in the right place at the right time. It was simple enough in concept, but might be hell's own job to put into action. It was going to take some days to set up.

After she had eaten her fill and understood the plan, Isabelle crept down the back stairs, slipped out through a side entrance, and headed back the way she had come the previous day. In her pocket was some cash Robert had given her to buy some better clothes, so she'd look less like a refugee. She would have to return to Lwów before all this was over, and couldn't take the risk of being detained by the Russians.

Out beyond the city, Isabelle turned off the main road and began the long walk back to the shelter she shared with her friends. Would they be willing to trust this friendly American? Isabelle believed they could. But whether they could rely on him to get them to freedom was another matter. There were many hazards and pitfalls along the way.

The train station was almost deserted when Robert arrived. It was still early morning, and not many passenger trains came and went from Lwów. His footsteps echoed in the cavernous ticket hall; like the Hotel George and many other buildings in Lwów, the station was a relic of the Austro-Hungarian Empire, when the city was called Lemberg and was capital of the kingdom of Galicia. It was built with palatial pretensions: all domes and stucco outside, all pillars and molded plasterwork inside.

Robert had become a familiar sight to the ticket sellers. The man behind the glass screen this morning was Józef. "*Dzień dobry, kapitanie,*" he called as Robert approached.

"Good morning to you too." Robert was glad it was Józef today; he spoke decent English. They chatted awhile, and Robert bought a ticket, in case there were any NKVD people watching; under cover of paying, he slipped some extra bills under the glass, and murmured: "We need to talk. Meet me at noon in the Pokój Węgierski. There'll be a good lunch and a bottle of the best."

The Pokój Węgierski—Hungarian Room—was a restaurant near the Hotel George: decent, but not fancy. Józef hesitated in surprise, but then nodded and palmed the bills.

As Robert left the station, he glanced about; there were a few soldiers around who watched incuriously as he passed, but nobody who looked like they might be trailing him. It was hard to tell; the NKVD's official bird dogs were army officers, and as easy to spot as a whore in church. But you could never be sure about informers infiltrated among the local population. They could be anyone, from nice middle-class ladies like Esa Lowry to folks who looked like refugees. But although he'd only been in the game a short while, Robert had learned to sense when he was being watched. Either that or he'd simply caught the Russian disease of paranoia. Either way, he wasn't feeling under scrutiny this minute.

By noon, when he sat down to wait for József in the Hungarian Room, his confidence was ebbing. Every other patron seemed like a potential spy, and his worry that József would be followed, or just wouldn't show up, grew and grew. What if the Russians apprehended the ticket seller, interrogated him? Worse—what if they made an informer of him? It wasn't at all beyond the NKVD to threaten people's families, and Poles were found dead on the streets regularly.

When he saw the familiar face at the restaurant door, Robert's anxieties subsided a little. József came in, sat at the table, and gratefully accepted the meal and bottle of wine that Robert had ordered for him.

The next part was going to be tricky. Tentatively, without going into too much detail, Robert began to outline the situation he was in. He needed transportation to Odessa for four hundred people, and he had an idea in his head about how it might be achieved.

József listened to the proposition in silence, with a deepening frown. When Robert was done, the ticket seller shook his head. He couldn't do it by himself. He would need to involve his superiors, and some other railroad employees—engineers and brakemen. Robert understood; he explained that he'd worked as a railroad brakeman before the war, back in America. He knew how the system worked and understood how the stunt could be pulled. József promised to speak to his superiors and to his friends who worked on the trains. They were all Poles like him; local men who had been living here the last time the NKVD ran the city. They had no love for the Soviets.

It would take a few days to organize, József said. That was fine, Robert told him; it would take a few days for his Frenchwomen to get themselves together. And in the meantime he had other business to deal with, other strays needing his help.

Next morning, Robert stopped by the rail station. He needed tickets for some men he was channeling to Odessa, so he took the opportunity to check in with József. He felt uneasy—the sensation of being watched—but couldn't spot anyone tailing him. It must be simple paranoia.

The ticket seller had consulted his bosses, and they were willing to help. But they insisted that the American pay the money for the tickets up front, before they would allow the necessary arrangements to be made.

That was fine with Robert. But he couldn't just extract the cash and hand it over in public view. He would have to come back. After a further brief consultation with Józef, he walked away. As he crossed the station concourse, heading for the men's room, he still had that eerie sensation of being watched, but although he had noticed several people scattered about the concourse and the rooms adjoining it, he didn't register the one pair of eyes that followed him carefully.

In the men's room, Robert locked himself in a stall and began unbuttoning his layers of clothing, burrowing down to his special undergarment—the much-loathed, incommodious money vest. It had become slightly less uncomfortable lately, as his stock of cash was depleted. He extracted a block of dollar bills and began counting them out. The bills were brand-new, and each one had to be peeled away from the block. When he'd counted out a good number, he stuffed them in his pants pocket. From another compartment in the vest he drew out his stock of Russian rubles. He'd already checked them back at the hotel and knew he had plenty for the tickets. He folded the bills up in bundles and put them in the pockets of his parka.

It was quite a sum. But how much it was actually worth to the United States government depended on how you translated it. The money situation in Soviet territory was totally crazy.[1] According to the official exchange rate dictated by the Russians, which their banks and the US Military Mission were obliged to honor, this parcel of tickets was going to cost north of a thousand dollars. But it seemed less painful if you looked at it through the local black market exchange rate. In Poland, US dollars were like gold. At black market rates, the total bill for the four hundred tickets would be about forty bucks.

Robert peeled off the last few bills and put them in his parka pocket. Altogether he'd allowed enough for twenty extra tickets on top of the four hundred. He was concerned in case more women had joined Isabelle's crowd in the meantime. Best be prepared. It would be a crying shame if any of those girls got left behind.

A few minutes later, Robert walked back out of the men's room carrying his parka over his arm. Józef was sitting on a bench in the concourse. Robert sat beside him, and they chatted for a while about their homes and families, taking out their wallets and showing each other their photos. Eventually Robert stood up, said goodbye, and walked out of the station building. He strode off toward Chernivetska Street, apparently unaware that he had left his parka behind on the bench; even outside, with just his flying jacket between him and the biting breeze, he still seemed not to notice.

He also failed to notice the figure that left the station building a few moments after him, following him up the long avenue toward the city center.

Back in the station concourse, Józef scooped up the parka and hurried across to the ticket office. Inside, checking that nobody was looking in through the glass, he rifled through the pockets, extracted the bundles of cash, and tossed them into the safe. He slammed the door shut, heaved a sigh of relief, and went back to work.

When Robert pushed open the door of the little eatery, he found Isabelle already waiting for him. His heart lurched a little when he realized that she wasn't alone: three other young women were sitting with her. It was a foolish risk, coming into the city so many at a time. Isabelle introduced him to her companions, all young French girls like herself. All the women, she said, had wanted to see with their own eyes the American who was going to save them, but only these three had dared come into town. They gazed adoringly at him, and he experienced a moment of masculine frailty, grinning back like a teenager.

Isabelle, who had lost none of her earnest demeanor, brought the conversation back to business. Robert went over the details of the arrangements he had made. Isabelle and her friends knew the country-side for miles around Lwów far better than he did. At every mention of a place and time, they nodded; they knew where it was, and knew how best to get there. They suggested refinements to the plan. Four hundred was a lot of women to maneuver around the countryside, but they quickly worked it all out.

The only thing that beat them was how they were going to eat. It would be three days to Odessa, even if there were no holdups. Robert took out the wad of dollar bills from his pants pocket and passed it sur-reptitiously to Isabelle. They could get a whole heap of rubles for that many dollars, and buy food for everyone en route. Along with the money, he handed over the wad of tickets he'd quietly pocketed while chatting to Józef.

When they got up to leave, the women's eyes were aglow with excitement. They looked at Robert as if he were a combination of Gala-had and Cary Grant; it was an effort to maintain his officer-like bearing while they smothered his face with kisses. Amid this cloud of bliss, Robert's sensible side was just thankful that he hadn't been followed—this little scene would have made any bird dog suspicious.

While her friends treated him like a hero, Isabelle gazed seriously at him: the same appraising look she'd given him on that first evening at the hotel. "*Demain,*" she murmured, "*nous verrons bien.* Tomorrow we shall see." Then suddenly she smiled, reached up to him, and kissed him softly on both cheeks. "*Adieu,*" she said. And then, chivvying her friends ahead of her, she was gone, the door swinging shut behind them.

It was the last he ever saw of any of them.

Józef was brewing coffee in the back office when he was startled by a violent rapping of knuckles on the ticket window.

Muttering a curse against impatient travelers, he ambled through. At first he wasn't at all surprised by the sight of a Soviet officer, backed by two armed soldiers. Russians were hardly an uncommon sight in the station, and the officers could often be imperious. But this one did look particularly stern. To a Pole who had lived through the Soviet rule and the Nazi regime, the sight of an irate man in uniform with urgent business was worrying. There was a fourth man with them—a nondescript civilian in workman's clothes. Józef didn't know it, but he was the very man who had followed Captain Trimble out of the station earlier that morning.

This looked bad; Józef had visions of the Brygidki prison, and of himself lying dead in some backstreet.

The officer ordered him to open the door. He obeyed instantly, and all four men came into the office. "Where is the coat the American officer left here?" the Russian officer snapped. Józef indicated the parka, still hanging on the chair where he had left it. The officer seized it and searched it, turning out all the pockets, feeling inside the sleeves and the lining, under the fur collar.

Nothing. The officer directed a short burst of angry Russian at the civilian informer, who shrugged and muttered something about having seen what he had seen and come as quickly as he could. No, he didn't know where the American had gone. He only had one pair of legs.

Throwing down the coat, the officer turned to the terrified Józef and uttered the words every Pole most dreaded to hear: "You are coming with us."

T he word spread from farm to farm, from village to remote homestead— wherever the Frenchwomen had found refuge, the news came. Deliverance was at hand.

In ones and twos, in small groups and large bands, the women gathered their few belongings and, saying farewell to the kind Polish families who had sheltered them, took to the roads in the fading light of dusk. They passed unseen across fields, through isolated copses and along country lanes.

Arriving first at the woodland rendezvous, Isabelle and her friends watched their countrywomen congregate, chattering excitedly in low-ered voices. There were greetings and snatches of song and laughter.

Would it all be worthwhile? Would the American honor his word? Those few who had met him were confident he would, and others just had faith that their fortunes must change. But they all knew that the American's word and his honor might not be enough. There was also skill and cunning to reckon up, not to mention luck. The NKVD was a dangerous opponent.

The women settled down to wait through the long, cold night.

R obert woke with a sense of dread. *I'm crazy*, he thought, wondering, not for the first time, what he'd got himself into. How had he ever imagined he could pull off a stunt like this? Four hundred women? Crazy, completely insane.

He went over the plan again and again in his mind. Was there any-thing he could have done differently? Countless things, probably, but he couldn't think of them, other than to tell Isabelle *No* right at the start. Well, that had been out of the question. Beneath the anxiety, Robert was conscious of a sense of joy at the thought of setting all those women free. The same feeling he had about all his missions, but this was an extra-large slice of it.

When he looked at it cold, he knew he'd done the best he could in the time available—much like all his activities since coming to this country. If it wasn't enough—why, he'd told them all along that he was an airman and a soldier, not a spy. He'd said those very words to Colo-nel Hampton, back at Poltava on the day he arrived, when they sprung their big surprise on him. (Had that really been less than two months ago?)

Robert went down to the dining room for breakfast. He was deter-mined to resist the urge to go out to the train station. There was no need. He'd set his plan in motion; it was out of his hands now. He absolutely didn't need to go there, no matter how much his curiosity urged him to.

He kept this up for about an hour. Then he put on his hat and jacket (regretting the parka he'd sacrificed the day before) and set out on foot for the station. He had to know whether any problems had arisen, or if there was any news of the outcome.

When he was still making his way along the station avenue, he began to get a sense that something wasn't right. Drawing closer, he noticed that there seemed to be a few more Russian soldiers in front of the station than was normal. They also looked more alert than usual. Robert was already feeling the sinking weight in his stomach when he walked into the station concourse and saw even more soldiers—there must have been a full platoon of them—guarding the ticket office, the waiting room, the dining hall, and the platform entrances, detaining people and questioning them.

Before he'd even had a chance to take in the scene, Robert was confronted by a Soviet captain. He reeked of NKVD and seemed to recognize Robert on sight.

"You are Captain Robert Trimble, of the American Eastern Command from Poltava?" he said in English.

Fighting down the sick sensation, Robert acknowledged that he was and produced his passport. While the Russian studied it, Robert glanced at the ticket office; there was a different face behind the glass, no sign of Józef. Gathering up his indignation, Robert demanded to know the meaning of this inconvenience. "I am an authorized representative of the United States Military Mission and Eastern Command. You have no right to—"

"I have every right," the Russian captain interrupted, "to detain and question foreign persons who are suspected of giving aid to possible anti-Soviet spies in the territories governed by the forces of the Soviet Union. I have evidence that you are assisting four hundred such persons to leave Poland, without submitting them to the relevant authorities for screening."

Now Robert knew for certain that they had got to Józef. This possibility had been discussed, and they had agreed that Józef should not attempt to resist interrogation. He should admit to the number of tickets and the arrangements for payment, but claim ignorance of anything else. Robert could only pray that the Russians hadn't taken the interrogation further, because the thought of Józef resisting torture was as bad as the thought of him spilling the whole plan.

The captain had no power to arrest Robert, but he detained him at the station while his men conducted their searches. The one thing that gave Robert hope was the fact that they seemed to expect the passengers to arrive here. They must have a low opinion of his intelligence. Sometimes it was good to be thought a fool.

Hour followed hour. Robert heard the familiar railroad sounds echoing through the halls—arrivals, departures, freight cars being shunted in the huge marshaling yard next to the station. It was impossible to tell which of them was the incoming train from Przemyśl, bound for Odessa. He knew the Soviet captain had men up on the platforms, detaining and boarding every train in the hope of finding illicit passengers in it. If the Russian was smart, he'd detain every train for the next twenty-four hours, or send them all out filled with NKVD guards.

Robert looked at his watch, and wondered how Isabelle was.

Freedom held its breath . . .

Outside the city, once it had shaken itself clear of the suburbs, the main rail line cut across the vast, gently rolling farmlands and flat marshes, taking a great sweep eastward before turning southeast toward the Ukraine and Odessa. About ten miles out from Lwów, it passed through a mile-long stretch of woodland. Shallow banks of scrub grass and bushes rose on either side of the track, and met a dense tree line. Hidden among the pines on the slope above the tracks, shivering in the bitter cold, was Isabelle.

She and her friends had been hiding, keeping their anxious vigil, all through the freezing night, waiting for deliverance or disaster. Isabelle hadn't conceived the plan, but she shared the weight of responsibility. She had believed she could trust Robert and had led her countrywomen to believe they could too. If the rendezvous failed, or if it led to incarceration in a Soviet camp for all of them, she would bear part of the blame.

Morning had come and worn away; midday had passed, and yet there was no sign of the train. If it didn't come, or if it was filled with Russians, or if any one of a hundred mishaps occurred, all the women could look forward to was more imprisonment, more suffering, quite possibly death. Isabelle, her heart sinking, dug into the dwindling reserves of hope that had kept her going through the past two years. The train *had* to come; it must.

Isabelle believed in Robert. He was a good man; perhaps even a hero. But in this world, there were limits to what good men could do.

Isabelle's faith was wavering, hope slipping from her fingers, when she heard the faint whistle in the distance. She tensed. There was no mistaking it: the sound of an approaching train.

Would it be the right one; would it be expecting the signal? Would there be agents of the NKVD on board? Those creatures were everywhere. This moment would show whether her American was a hero after all. Isabelle's heart beat faster. When she saw the steam above the trees beyond the distant bend in the track, she rose from her hiding place and ran down the slope. Slipping on the ice, stumbling over the stones, she clambered onto the rail bed and stood up in the center of the tracks. She raised the sign she had made: a sheet of board bearing a single hopeful word scratched in charcoal: "France."

The locomotive thundered toward her, shaking the ground under her feet. Holding her sign in the air, Isabelle waited for freedom . . . or death.

In the cab, the engineer peered ahead through the rushing smoke and steam. Suddenly he spotted the tiny figure; he swore and yelled a warning to the fireman. The brakes slammed on, the wheels locked, shrieking on the rails, scrubbing off speed as the train bore down on the tiny figure of the woman. Isabelle closed her eyes and prayed. The locomotive slid and shuddered, throwing forward a huge billow of steam that embraced her, blanking her from sight.

As the train came to a halt, the engineer, fearing the worst, jumped down from the cab and ran through the fog to the front of the engine. As he got there, the steam cleared. There was the young woman. She was still standing, her face pale, close enough to reach out and touch the engine in front of her.

They stared at each other.

The engineer came to his senses first, and shouted at her in Polish: "Well, come on, woman!" he said. "Don't just stand there—we're late!" Whipping off his cap, he waved it in the air. Isabelle snapped out of her stupor. At that moment, cheers broke out from every direction: dozens upon dozens of women emerged from their hiding places among the trees and came hurrying down the slope toward the train. With a cry of *"Allons! Allons en France!"* Isabelle flung her sign aside and joined the other women swarming along the trackside and clambering in through the car doors.

The American had proven himself. They were on their way to freedom.

The Soviet captain glared at Robert as he walked away. He had no further excuse to detain him. When five hours had come and gone, it was obvious that nobody was coming to board a train, let alone four hundred people. "Maybe they saw you and your men and changed their minds," Robert suggested. The captain knew he'd missed something, but there was nothing he could do. He might even have been wondering if this whole charade was an elaborate bluff to distract the NKVD from something more important going on elsewhere.

Robert bade the captain a polite farewell and walked out into the cold sunshine, heading back along the well-worn route toward the city center, tired but triumphant.

I t was time to go.

Robert had packed, and was ready to leave. Tucking the empty money vest into the top of his kit bag, Robert turned and looked at himself in the mirror, straightening his tie.

He was leaving Lwów. Several days had passed since the departure of Isabelle, and his money and store of rations were about used up. What was more, he was being recalled. It seemed his aggravation of the Soviet authorities in Poland had built to the point where Moscow had taken notice. Whether it was bunking in Polish homes rather than official Soviet barracks, holding off senior officers with a pistol, smuggling POWs, or bamboozling suspicious NKVD captains, sooner or later something had to give.

But he'd be back, he told himself. There was a mission in this country still unfinished. He figured he'd exfiltrated as many as a thousand people out of Poland since the middle of February, but there were still a lot of strays out there: Americans, British, French, and all the nationalities of the Allied nations. The numbers were getting fewer, but the cases were all the more desperate. Those that remained tended to be the ones least able to care for themselves: the sick and the starved. They were likely to be a major challenge for one man on his own. But there had to be hope. Maybe he'd have to return with another salvage team as cover.

Isabelle and her compatriots had reached Odessa safely. This morning the news had reached him at the hotel, having found its way back along the chain of railroad workers to Lwów: "Liberation of France successful," said the cryptic note. He'd known it would be okay; once people were on the train for Odessa, they were likely to be let alone.

Robert put on his parka, thankful to have it back. He'd been to the station the day before to collect it. Józef had been there, back at work in his usual window, a little paler than he'd been before, but still in one piece. As well as his parka, Robert got from him an account of how the rendezvous had worked out.

A jeep with a Russian driver had been provided to take Robert out to the airfield. He tossed his kit bag and pack in the back, climbed in, and the jeep sped off across Mickiewicz Square and up the grand avenue. The Soviets for once were falling over themselves to be helpful, so long as it meant he was leaving the country. Or maybe they just wanted to be sure he'd go.

The C-47 took off, and as it circled around to head east, Robert looked out the window. The city was emerging from its winter shell. The snows were thawing slowly, and out in the countryside streaks of green were showing through the white. A fanciful person might have taken it as a symbol of warmth and hope for the future.

In fact, the opposite would have been truer. The Russian bear was stirring from its winter lethargy, and was about to tighten its claws around its possessions. The Soviets had decided that the time had come to curtail American movement once and for all. Their patience with American interference in their territory had come to an end. As Robert looked down from the C-47 climbing over Lwów, he had no idea that he was seeing the city for the last time. His mission was over, and he was about to be launched on a course that would thrust him right to the sharp end of US-Soviet relations and push the United States and the Soviet Union to the brink of war.

17.

BLOOD SACRIFICE

Poltava, Ukraine

The storm had been gathering slowly, over many weeks and months, but when the lightning fell on Poltava it did so with shocking suddenness. Soviet mistrust of American activities in Poland had swollen to a dangerous level.

Captain Robert M. Trimble and Colonel James D. Wilmeth both rode the skirts of the storm into Poltava, landing just before it broke. Both officers had helped to stir up the tempest. Now, as it swept across Eastern Command, both would find themselves maneuvered into positions where they would have to help their comrades weather it. For Captain Trimble the part he would be forced to play would reveal to him the sickening duplicity and dishonor of politics on the grand scale.

On the 28th of March, Major General S. K. Kovalev, commanding officer of the Poltava Air Base, on instructions from Moscow, issued an order forbidding all flights by American aircraft.[1] All transports belonging to Eastern Command and Air Transport Command were grounded. Salvaged bombers waiting to be ferried back to their units were barred from leaving. More than a dozen rescued combat crews from the Eighth and Fifteenth Air Forces—more than one hundred and eighty men—were stranded. The Soviets even refused clearance for the evacuation of six wounded airmen whose injuries were too severe for Eastern Command's little hospital to treat properly.

In Poland, ongoing salvage work on downed American aircraft was brought to an immediate halt. The salvage teams were detained by the NKVD, and the planes they had been working on, together with their transports, were sealed.[2] From now on, the local Soviets said, all force-landed American aircraft would be regarded as trophies of war and would be repaired and flown out by the Red Army Air Force.

Tensions escalated.

On March 30, General Aleksei I. Antonov, Red Army chief of staff, wrote an indignant letter to General Deane, in which he set forth a list of actions by individual American personnel that had "violated the order established by the Command of the Red Army." Apparently oblivious to the irony, Antonov upbraided the Americans for having breached the code of good behavior that was expected between allies and having perpetrated a "rude violation of the elementary rights of our friendly mutual relationship."[3]

Antonov didn't mention the unauthorized exfiltration of ex–prisoners of war, because he didn't know about it; no Soviet officials did (although a few NKVD bird dogs on the ground in Poland clearly suspected that Captain Trimble had been up to something nefarious under cover of aircrew rescue). But Antonov did complain stridently about the behavior of Colonel Wilmeth, who had insisted on staying in Lublin beyond the agreed date of March 11, for no good reason that the Russians could see (or were willing to recognize).

But Wilmeth's misdemeanors were minor compared with the actions of three otherwise obscure individuals. Two were American bomber pilots, and the third was a Russian engineer. Each one had perpetrated deeds which proved in Stalin's eyes that the Americans were engaging in espionage and giving secret aid to anti-Soviet Polish partisans.[4]

The first of these men was Lieutenant Myron King, one of the dozens of B-17 pilots who made forced landings in Poland in early 1945.[5] On February 3, Lieutenant King's Fortress, *Maiden USA*, was damaged in a raid on Germany, and he had to make an emergency landing at a Soviet airfield near Warsaw.[6] After a two-day stopover, King was ordered by the Russians to fly on to another Soviet base, escorted by a Soviet plane. During the flight, the B-17 crew discovered that a young Polish man had stowed away. They thought little of it, believing him to be an official interpreter working for the Soviets. Unable to pronounce his Polish name, they called him "Jack Smith." He was suffering from the cold, so they allowed him to put on some spare American flight clothes. Jack Smith confided to the Americans that he had an uncle in London, and begged them to let him come with them when they flew back to England.

When the two planes landed at Szczuczyn Airfield, the presence of Jack Smith was quickly discovered by the Soviets. He wasn't an interpreter. The fact that he was dressed as an American airman caused instant suspicion. It appeared to the Russians that Lieutenant King was attempting to assist a disguised Polish saboteur to escape the country.[7] The B-17 was seized and the crew was detained. The Russians kept the Americans in effective custody (although not actually under arrest) for seven weeks, transferring them from Szczuczyn in Poland to Lida in Belarus. Eventually, on the understanding that charges would be brought against Lieutenant King by the American authorities, the crew were cleared to fly on to Poltava, where they arrived on March 18. It was only when other suspicious incidents occurred that the Russians started believing that King's actions were all part of a covert American plot.

One of those incidents was Captain Trimble's arrival at Poltava on March 17 (the day before King) carrying four POWs disguised as American airmen. But that was a small affair—a mere irritant—compared with others that struck the Russians as deeply suspect.

On March 22, a B-24 Liberator piloted by Lieutenant Donald Bridge of the 459th Bomb Group, based in Italy, made an emergency landing at the airfield at Mielec, Poland.[8] The bomber had run low on fuel during a raid, but was otherwise undamaged. This caused the Soviets to be immediately suspicious, and they barred Lieutenant Bridge from taking off once the plane had been refueled. After two days, Bridge decided that he wasn't going to wait around for Soviet approval. Claiming that they were just going to check on their personal belongings, he and his crew went out to their aircraft and started it up. Avoiding Russian attempts to block them, they took off and flew back to their base in Italy.

The very same day that Lieutenant Bridge landed in Poland, another American B-24 took off from the Soviet base at Kecskemét in Hungary, where it had been under repair, bound for its home base in Italy. On board was a stowaway, a Captain Morris Shenderoff, who was one of the Soviet aircraft engineers at Kecskemét.[9] Morris Shenderoff was American by birth and citizenship, but also part Russian. Born in Cleveland, Ohio, as a teenager he was taken back to the mother country by his Russian parents. The family decided to stay in the Soviet Union. Although young Morris Shenderoff wanted to go home to America, the Soviets took away his US passport.

When war broke out, Shenderoff, who had become a mechanic, was drafted into the Red Army. After a series of appalling experiences on the Eastern Front, he was severely wounded and transferred to the Air Force. He ended up working as an engineer at the base at Kecskemét. The NKVD were suspicious of him, especially when he made friends with the crew of an American B-24 that was under repair. He told the Americans his story, and the pilot, Lieutenant Charles Raleigh, agreed to fly him out. Shenderoff boarded the B-24 in his capacity as engineer, and the crew took off, telling the Soviets that it was a routine test flight.[10] As soon as they were airborne, they set a course and flew to Italy.

When the bomber landed at Bari in Italy, Shenderoff identified himself to the American authorities and pleaded for asylum, claiming what he believed were his rights as a US citizen. He was taken into custody, interrogated, and detained while a decision was made about what to do with him. The Soviets, furious about his defection, began making strident demands for his return.

General Antonov informed General Deane that all these Americans' actions had caused "extreme perplexity" to Red Army Air Force personnel. Indeed, Captain Melamedov, the officer at Mielec who had allowed Lieutenant Bridge's plane to land was "so put out" that "on the very same day he shot himself."[11] Antonov laid all these crimes at the door of General Deane and demanded that he do something about them. While the Soviets waited for a response, all movements of American aircraft and personnel in Soviet territory were barred.

Tensions escalated further. At Poltava, General Kovalev started laying down plans for dealing with Eastern Command in the event of a sudden escalation to war between the United States and the USSR.[12] All he had at his disposal was a technical battalion, an engineering battalion, and a unit of SMERSH, the Red Army's counterintelligence branch. Each unit was briefed accordingly. If hostilities broke out, the American camp would be surrounded, all American planes and munitions would be seized, and American radio communications would be shut down. Any US personnel caught outside the camp would be detained at special facilities in the city of Poltava.

The Americans knew nothing of these plans, but they were acutely aware of the atmosphere of tension and imminent breakdown. Eastern Command began working round the clock to secure its classified documents, and it was noticed that the adjutant had begun wearing his pistol on duty.[13]

Presented with a choice of a diplomatic—maybe even military—face-off or a conciliation, the United States didn't hesitate: it chose conciliation. The war wasn't won yet, and the West might need Soviet help to defeat Japan. The generals and the politicians involved cited sensible reasons for the diplomatic path they took, but in truth the Americans had simply been wrong-footed by the sheer brazen self-righteousness of the Russians. From this moment on, all American pressure on the Russians over the evacuation of ex–prisoners of war came to an end. The day before the Soviet order that grounded American aircraft, Ambassador Harriman had still been up in arms, writing to Foreign Minister Molotov "setting forth our complaints regarding the treatment of our prisoners of war liberated by the Red Army."[14] That wouldn't happen again.

Official POW contact, such as it was, now passed to the British, who were allowed to send a team into Poland, on terms similar to those endured by Colonel Wilmeth. Having regarded the British as the more suspect of its allies, the Soviet Union now seemed to be coming around to the view that the United States was the one to watch. It was as if the Russians were realizing that the openhandedness of the Americans, with supplies, intelligence, and general cooperation, might be some kind of ruse.

Lord Halifax, the British ambassador in Washington, advised the US secretary of state that Anthony Eden, the British foreign secretary, was "of the opinion that it would be better for the present not to renew the attempt to secure permission for contact officers to enter Poland." Eden was convinced that "the Soviet Government suspects that the contact officers would, under cover of dealings with prisoners of war, proceed to contact Polish leaders, and, in fact to convert themselves into the proposed Observation Mission."[15] The Observation Mission was a scheme by the British and American governments to place observers in Soviet-occupied Poland to monitor and report on conditions there. Nothing could have been more guaranteed to provoke Soviet anger.

And so the British and the Americans both began acceding to Soviet demands. At Russia's insistence, court-martial proceedings were initiated against Lieutenants Donald Bridge and Myron King. In Italy, there were deliberations over whether Morris Shenderoff ought to be sent back to Russia.

Flexing their muscles, the Soviets escalated their demands still further. They insisted on the removal of senior Eastern Command officers whom they didn't like. The first to go was the commanding officer, Colonel Hampton. He had aggravated the Russians by commenting negatively on their behavior in Poland, by attempting to expedite Wilmeth's journey to Lublin, by being combative in his dealings with his Soviet opposite number, and by generally standing up for what he saw as the rights of Americans.

The Military Mission in Moscow acquiesced, and on April 10, Colonel Hampton was officially notified that he was being relieved of his command ("without prejudice") and reassigned to USSTAF headquarters in Paris.[16] As of April 11, operations officer Major Michael Kowal would assume command. The Soviets were notified accordingly.

They weren't satisfied. Lieutenant General Nikolai V. Slavin of the Red Army General Staff, the Soviet liaison officer for the American Military Mission, wrote to General Hill to protest, and General Hill immediately cabled Colonel Hampton: "Have just received a letter from Slavin which states that Major Kowal has shown himself to be inamiable and frequently hostile ... and was a source of deterioration of relationship."[17] The retention of Major Kowal at Poltava, Slavin said, was "absolutely undesirable." Having held the command for less than a day, Kowal was relieved of it and notified that he too was being reassigned to USSTAF HQ.

That left Eastern Command with a power vacuum. They had several majors at Poltava, but none of them were flyers. The AAF, like air forces everywhere, had a regulation that the officer in command of an air base must be a rated pilot. It happened that the ranking pilot at Poltava right now was none other than Captain Robert M. Trimble.

On April 12, bewildered and reluctant, Robert became the CO of Eastern Command. General Hill asked USSTAF to send a more experienced officer, but it never happened.[18] Into the lap of Robert M. Trimble, the humble captain who'd already had far more than he'd bargained for since leaving England, fell the task of repairing the diplomatic damage that his actions had helped to cause. If the Soviets were conscious of the irony of appointing the one man who had done more than any other to defy Soviet control in Poland, they never showed it.

As it turned out, Robert's first day in command was also very nearly his last.

From different directions, fourteen hundred miles apart, two B-24 Liberators were heading toward Poltava. Both carried passengers who were important, but in very different ways. Both planes were scheduled to stop at Poltava for refueling before heading on again. One of them was destined to almost cause a diplomatic incident.

The American and Russian commands at Poltava had been notified of the arrival of the two planes. One was coming from Moscow; aboard were General Deane and General Hill, who were en route to the United States. The other was coming from Bari in Italy en route to Moscow, carrying a passenger whose identity was not disclosed.

Somehow, perhaps due to the shift of command, perhaps due to the strained relations between Americans and Soviets, and certainly due in part to the secrecy surrounding the Moscow-bound plane, wires were crossed, and nobody quite knew which of the two planes was coming in at which time. Eastern Command's officers were under the mistaken impression that the aircraft from Italy, heading for Moscow on a "special Soviet mission," was a B-17.[19]

It was near lunchtime when the tower received word that a B-24 Liberator, call-sign 6E, serial 771, was approaching the field. Personnel who had been on standby were alerted. A ground crew and a refueling crew headed out to the hardstandings. The word spread that this was the Deane and Hill flight. Thoroughly accustomed to greeting planeloads of VIPs during the Yalta Conference, a reception committee of Russian and American officers hopped into jeeps and zoomed away down the road to the field. Among the party was brand-new commanding officer Captain Trimble. Robert wasn't at all accustomed to VIPs. Colonel Hampton, doing all he could to ease the transition, was accompanying him, and would take the strain of the occasion.

The heavens had decided to rain on Robert's first day. The snows had thawed, and Poltava was being steadily soaked by spattering showers. In the open jeeps the officers pulled their collars up and their hats down, and waited for the plane to arrive.

Robert wondered what was happening in Poland while he was greeting generals. How many Americans were still hiding out or rotting in Soviet holding camps? The grounding of American aircraft, still in force after two weeks, irritated and worried everyone, but to Robert it was profoundly frustrating and disturbing. He wondered where Isabelle was now, or little Kasia's mother. Beadle, Vergolina, Gould, McNeish—he knew they had reached freedom. Then there were all those gaunt men, the hundreds whose names he couldn't recall (if he had ever known them) but whose faces lived in his memory, who had been put aboard the Odessa trains.

Had they made it? It was reported that Odessa was the one place where the Soviets were honoring their duty, but only because they were exchanging batches of Western ex-POWs for batches of their own.[20] The fates of those repatriated Russians didn't even bear thinking about.

"Here she comes," said an officer sitting next to him, who was scanning the horizon. "Top brass, three o'clock level."

The familiar silhouette of a B-24 was curving in to land. It touched down and taxied toward the hardstanding where the ground crews and reception committee were waiting. The officers got in line. To Robert and a few of the other airmen, something didn't look right about the aircraft. Normally a Moscow VIP like Deane would fly in *Becky*, Ambassador Harriman's passenger-converted Liberator. But the plane that was taxiing in front of the rain-soaked lineup was a combat B-24 with unit markings on her tail fins, a shark's mouth decorating her nose, and the name *Judith Ann* written on her fuselage. And unless those were just the empty cooling barrels protruding from the gun positions, she also appeared to be fully armed.

Judith Ann rolled to a stop. The little parade of officers saluted and waved, a little uncertainly, and waited for the visitors to disembark and exchange polite greetings. The official photographer snapped a picture. The officers waited . . . and waited. Figures could be seen in the waist gun window, but nobody got out.

Robert, with no experience of the proper protocol, thought perhaps the generals were waiting for him to come and greet them. Whatever it was, as commanding officer he'd better investigate. He glanced at Colonel Hampton, who nodded.

At that moment, another jeep came racing across the field and drew up on the hardstanding. A group of Russian officers, looking like they meant serious business and all very conspicuously wearing pistols outside their greatcoats, jumped out and stood between *Judith Ann* and the reception committee.[21] Robert walked toward the plane, but his way was barred by one of the Russians.

"Instructions from General Kovalev," said the Russian officer. "No American personnel are to approach this airplane. It is engaged in a special Soviet mission. Refueling only is permitted. Please instruct your fuel men to begin their work. All other personnel are required to leave, please."

This must be the plane from Italy en route to Moscow. But why would a combat B-24 from a group down in Italy be engaged in special missions for the Soviets? Given all the US combat aircraft that had been salvaged and stolen by them, the arrival of this one now was deeply suspicious.

"This is an American AAF aircraft," said Robert. "All American aircraft at this base are the responsibility of Eastern Command. I'm going to inspect it."

He went to pass the Russian officer, who barred his way again.

Robert, his hackles rising, tried again. "As of today, I am the commanding officer here. All US aircraft landing at this base are subject to my clearance. I demand to know the full schedule and purpose of this aircraft."

He glanced at the pistols on the Russians' belts, and at the cold stares they were directing toward him. He was acutely conscious of the tension that had set Poltava on pins during the past two weeks, and even more conscious that he might be about to whip the tension into a crisis, but there was something going on here that stank. Bracing himself, he pushed past the Russian officer, ducked under the tail of the aircraft, and pulled open the access door.

Expecting the plane to be full of Russians, he was surprised to find himself staring at a group of startled American officers, including two immaculate Military Police captains. They sat on makeshift seats, and sandwiched between them was a disheveled, anxious-looking man wearing what appeared to be the uniform of a Soviet officer. His wrists were handcuffed. There were two other officers in the crowded waist section of the plane, a major and a colonel. Suddenly Robert felt very outranked.

"I'm Captain Robert Trimble, officer commanding Eastern Command. What is the purpose and schedule of this flight?" The officers glanced at one another and raised a skeptical eyebrow at his claim to be the CO, but said nothing. "This aircraft is not to proceed without my clearance. I'm not about to grant clearance to an aircraft that I believe to be suspicious."

"This is an approved flight to Moscow," said the colonel. Despite his American uniform, he had traces of Russian in his accent. "It has been authorized in advance by the Military Mission, Eastern Command, and the Soviet authorities."

Robert looked at the handcuffed man again, and at last he understood—Italy, Moscow, a Russian officer . . . This must be the man the rumors had spoken of—the Russian captain who claimed to be American, who'd got himself flown from Hungary to Italy in a bid to escape. Shenderoff, Captain Shenderoff. So they'd decided to hand the poor guy over to the Russians, had they? Not if Robert Trimble could do anything about it. The Soviets weren't the only ones who could be obstinate.

"It hasn't been authorized by me," he said. He stepped past the colonel and squeezed along the narrow walkway through the bomb bay, heading for the front of the plane. (He'd forgotten how tight it was getting from one end of a Lib to the other.) In the radio compartment behind the cockpit, he took a headset from the operator and ignored the stares of the pilots.

"Tower, this is Trimble; I've got a B-24 here with no schedule and what looks like a Russian political prisoner on board. First, I want you to make clear to the Russians that this flight is not clear for takeoff unless they fully disclose its purpose . . ."

"Sir—"

"Second, get Moscow on the horn immediately, relay the situation, and put them through to me."

"Sir, is that B-24 number 49771, with er, lemme see . . . a shark mouth paint job, yellow cowls, and checkerboard tail with black diamond?"[22]

"That's the one."

"Sir, the Soviets have already cleared this flight, and we've had authorization from Moscow, no questions to be asked. We have to clear it."

Robert stood with the headset against his ear, wondering what to do next. Did he dare defy Moscow? In the silence that followed, he heard a hubbub of voices from the back of the plane, speaking Russian. General Kovalev himself had arrived on the scene and was loudly demanding to know what was going on.

Kovalev was a small man with Asian eyes and a bald head, an exquisite manner and a permanent retinue of pretty female interpreters. He adored parties and, during the heyday of Eastern Command, had been an enthusiastic participant in officers' club dances—drinking, dancing, and laughing the night away.[23]

He wasn't laughing now. General Kovalev believed himself to be a man at the leading edge of a country about to go to war with its principal ally, and he was liable to explode at the slightest provocation. Nonetheless, he had been ordered by Marshal Stalin to dial down the antagonism in his handling of the Americans.[24] His heavy jaw was set, and he glared at this young captain who had dared to interfere with a secret Soviet mission ordered by Moscow.

"What is happening here?" he asked.

Again, but with less conviction, Robert stated his refusal to clear the flight. Kovalev took in the situation and understood immediately. "Captain, I see what you are attempting to do, but your actions are ill-advised. If you leave this airplane now, this incident will not be reported." Robert noticed Colonel Hampton at the doorway, gesturing at him to come out. He glanced at the handcuffed prisoner. "I assure you," said Kovalev, "this man will receive justice. Now please leave."

Robert was reminded of the Soviet officer at Rostov, assuring him that the stowaway boy would "get his wish." He could still hear the gunshot.

There was nothing he could do. He was outranked and outnumbered ten times over. Obeying Hampton's urgent beckoning, he disembarked from the plane, defeated and ashamed. The door was slammed shut, and Captain Shenderoff's fate was sealed.

The reason for Kovalev's sudden appearance became clear when a second B-24 was seen taxiing in from the runway. This was *Becky*, the VIP transport from Moscow. The plane drew up on the hardstanding next to *Judith Ann* and halted. Here at last were the brass.

Still in a daze, Captain Trimble helped Colonel Hampton greet the generals. It was hard to tell Deane and Hill apart physically: similar height, similar build, dressed in identical raincoats. Blunt-featured, Major General Edmund W. Hill looked more like a cop than a general. His roots were in the pioneering spirit of the early aviators; he'd served in the infantry in World War I and later became an airman, with an amateur passion for airship and balloon piloting (his 1928 sporting license was signed by Orville Wright himself).[25] Now he was the go-to man for contact with the OSS. Major General John R. Deane, on the other hand, looked exactly like the smooth military politician he was. As Robert was introduced to them by Colonel Hampton, it didn't occur to him that gathered here were the only three men in Russia—Hampton, Hill, and Deane—who had known all about his covert mission.

They were in an upbeat mood, and Hampton pulled out all the stops to warm Hill and Deane's welcome. They noticed the B-24 parked nearby, but made no comment. Although General Deane knew exactly who was aboard, even down to the composition of the crew, he didn't acknowledge it.[26]

The generals and the reception committee drove back to the headquarters site, leaving the ground crews to check and fuel up the two aircraft. The official photographer lingered for a while, taking pictures. He had no idea what had gone on with the two planes and had missed the actual arrival of the generals.[27] Soon he too departed the scene. Sealed inside *Judith Ann*, the crew, the passengers, and their prisoner waited.

An hour after she had arrived, *Judith Ann*'s engines roared into life again, and she taxied out and took off toward Moscow. On arrival, Captain Morris Shenderoff was handed over to a Major Storbanov of the Red Army. Lieutenant Colonel Stepanovich, the American with a slight Russian accent, was careful to obtain a receipt for the handover.[28]

At that point, Morris Shenderoff, who had been born in Cleveland, and whose only desire had been to escape the country of his ancestors and return to the land of his birth, disappeared. Nobody, from General Deane down to Captain Trimble, ever learned for certain what happened to him. But a rumor later reached Poltava that he was shot within minutes of leaving the plane.[29]

The Soviets had taken one of the scalps they had demanded. There would be more before this was all over.

18.

SPARE THE CONQUERED, CONFRONT THE PROUD

April 14, 1945: Poltava

The President was dead.

On the grim stone road outside their barracks, in the shadow of the old bombed ruins, the officers and men of Eastern Command mustered, immaculate in their dress uniforms. They formed up four abreast in a long column that filled the road. At its head was a color guard of three men bearing the flag of the United States, the first time in Eastern Command's existence that the Stars and Stripes had been flown at Poltava.[1] The colors had been brought out of storage, and this parade had been mustered, to mark the passing of President Franklin D. Roosevelt.

The news had reached Poltava the previous morning via British radio.[2] The Americans, already demoralized and resentful toward the Russians, were cast into an angry depression. They had lost their officers, and now they had lost their leader. Like the ousting of Colonel Hampton and Major Kowal, Roosevelt's death was the fault of Stalin, they believed.[3] The Soviet dictator was too frightened to leave his own country, so the sick president had been forced to travel all the way to Yalta for the Big Three conference, and the stress had been his final undoing.

General Kovalev made a gesture that helped heal the division; upon hearing the news, he immediately marshaled his officers and marched them to the American camp, where they paid their respects and offered their condolences. The Americans were surprised and touched to learn that the Russians too were upset by the death of Roosevelt. They had thought of him as Russia's friend, a man who would bring peace to the world. They knew nothing of Truman, and it worried them.[4]

Today, as Eastern Command paraded their colors and marched through the camp to the theater, where a memorial service was to be held, Poltava's Red Army officers joined them, in a rare show of unity. With all the combat crews who were stranded at the base by the grounding of flights, the little theater was packed, with dozens of men sitting in the aisle. The colors were set either side of the stage, which was draped with the Stars and Stripes. Poignantly, on the right of the stage was a portrait of the President that had been painted by a Soviet artist some months ago, with a matching head of Stalin on the opposite side.[5]

Seated in the front row were Eastern Command's senior officers. Nervously, Captain Robert Trimble rose from his seat and mounted the stage. In the silence, he began his address. "Today the United States has lost a great leader," he declared, and glanced down at Colonel Hampton, seated solemn-faced among the Soviet officers, and at Major Kowal, sitting with his fellow Americans. "And Eastern Command too has lost a leader."[6] Most of the men and women who heard him speak had only learned yesterday that he had been made commanding officer; some of them barely even knew who he was. It was a curious and almost chilling echo of the succession of President Truman.[7]

Robert retained no memory of what else he said in his address, but it didn't matter; in his opening lines he had said what really mattered to the Americans gathered in the theater. The leaders they knew and trusted were gone, and the future was uncertain. Like Captain Trimble, all they could do was push ahead and do their best, and not give up.

The day after the memorial service, the new commander and his officers held a conference with General Kovalev and his staff.

It seemed such an absurd situation. Robert had subordinates who outranked him—his executive officer was a major—and he was facing a Russian opposite number who was a general. But he gritted his teeth and did his best.

Despite the fact that he ranked lower than the men he was dealing with, there were still moments when he had to swallow his pride. Notwithstanding the brief show of Russian-American unity at the memorial service, relations were still tense, hovering on the brink of open conflict. In Soviet eyes, the Americans were in the wrong; they had behaved in suspicious ways in Poland and were still on a kind of probation. The ban on American flights and movements was still in force after more than two weeks.

During his stopover a few days ago, immediately after the incident over Shenderoff, General Hill had taken Robert aside and told him that he must do everything he possibly could to appease and cooperate with the Soviets.[8] This meeting was the first step. It had been convened expressly for the purpose of asking General Kovalev if there was anything the Americans could do to improve relations.

Knowing the Soviets as he did, and with his firsthand knowledge of what they had done (and were still doing) in Poland raw and vivid in his memory, to Robert every word he spoke at that conference felt like an affront to his own morals and a blow to his self-esteem. He could feel himself becoming a part of the machine.

General Kovalev responded diplomatically. He had always been content in his relations with the Americans, he claimed. He understood their anxieties, which were no doubt caused by their inability to get their stranded combat crews home. Kovalev inquired kindly whether the Americans wished to take part in the upcoming May Day celebrations.

And he suggested that if Captain Trimble should have any problems at all in running his command, he should come right away and talk them over. "Anything that you cannot settle by yourself," the general said, "I am certain that you and I can handle easily together."

It was an olive branch, in a way, but it was an olive branch offered to a young and inexperienced officer whom General Kovalev clearly believed he could push around and patronize. The words were kindly spoken, but the power remained in Soviet hands, and Eastern Command's airplanes were still grounded until further notice. Over the weeks that followed, Captain Trimble would prove to be a little less easy to mollify than Kovalev had anticipated, but for now Robert held his temper in check and kept relations running smoothly.

Or at least, fairly smoothly. Robert kept his mouth shut about the POWs he believed were still stuck in Poland, but he quizzed Kovalev about the American salvage personnel who were trapped there by the flying ban. They must have long since run out of rations, and Robert had doubts about whether the Soviets would feed or take care of them properly. After a pointed inquiry to Kovalev about resuming salvage work, Robert received a message from Moscow ordering him to desist.[9] Eastern Command's role in salvage was at an end, he was told; the Russians would be conducting salvage of US aircraft from now on.

This was preposterous. As Robert and his chief engineering officer knew, the Russians didn't have the skills to repair and fly an aircraft like the B-17 properly. There was also the Soviets' history of stealing American aircraft. However, the Russians seemed intent on acting in good faith, and did repair some planes, fly them back to Poltava, and hand them over. Robert's expectations were confirmed when a B-17 flew in with all four of its engines overheating and smoking like volcanoes. The Russian crew hadn't known how to operate the cooling flaps built into the engine cowls. The Russian mechanics also had a habit of filching bits and pieces from salvaged planes, and they stole tools from Eastern Command's stores.[10]

In protest, Captain Trimble began refusing to accept any aircraft turned in by the Soviets in substandard condition. Another order came from Moscow: "Desire that you accept any American planes turned over to you from Soviets without raising question of missing parts with local Soviet command."[11] Robert replied that any aircraft repaired by the Soviets would need a complete overhaul by American mechanics. He also requested that Eastern Command be relieved of any responsibility for the safety and performance of Soviet-salvaged planes when they were sent back to their units.[12] Hill authorized him to do the necessary remedial work on the planes, and to report any problems to him rather than to Kovalev.

What really got under the skin of the Americans at Poltava was the demoralizing sense of being trapped and ignored. There were still sick men in the hospital, needing evacuation to Tehran, and dozens of combat crewmen waiting to go back to their units. There was no mail delivery. And there was a simmering anger that the politicians, diplomats, and generals were giving way to the Soviets far too much.

The Russians, for their part, still felt that the Americans had not yet been punished enough for their airmen's misbehavior in Poland. There were heads that still must roll.

Morris Shenderoff was not the only sacrifice the American Military Mission gave to the Soviets, but he was the only blood sacrifice. As April wore away and the Russians maintained their blockade on American flights in Soviet territory, two more AAF officers were punished.[13] Near the end of the month, Lieutenant Donald Bridge, the pilot who had flown his B-24 from Mielec without Soviet clearance (allegedly causing a Russian officer to commit suicide in shame), was court-martialed at Fifteenth Air Force headquarters in Italy. He was found guilty and fined $600, and his record was besmirched. Meanwhile, Lieutenant Myron King, who had allegedly tried to smuggle the Pole "Jack Smith" to England, was being held at Poltava. He was awaiting transport to Moscow, where he was to be court-martialed in the US Embassy.

Acting as judge advocate at King's court-martial would be none other than Lieutenant Colonel James D. Wilmeth, also stranded at Poltava by the flying ban. The defense was being organized by his comrade from the Lublin trip, Lieutenant Colonel Kingsbury. Lieutenant King's defense counsel (who happened to be the only trained lawyer involved in the proceedings) was Second Lieutenant Leon Dolin, a B-17 pilot who had force-landed in Poland and who had been brought in from Lublin by Colonel Wilmeth.[14]

The accused and the legal team were scheduled to fly from Poltava to Moscow on April 18, on a Russian-crewed, American-owned C-47. When Captain Trimble heard who the pilot was going to be, he immediately refused clearance. It was Lieutenant Roklikov, the crazed incompetent who had busted up a C-47 and nearly killed Robert's salvage team with his bungled landing and takeoff at Staszów. Repeated attempts to have him removed from duty had come to nothing. Now Robert tried again. He sent a message to General Kovalev: "It is not within my jurisdiction to allow any American aircraft here to be flown by Lt Roklikov."[15]

Another meeting was called, and Robert experienced in full the Soviet ability to flatly deny reality.[16] General Kovalev brushed away Robert's expert eyewitness account of the pilot's escapade at Staszów and insisted that Roklikov was an excellent pilot. "If I had an airplane of my own," the general said blithely, "I would happily let him take it up and land it however he chose."

This time Robert was determined not to be bowed. He refused to clear the flight. There was a stalemate, and it was Kovalev who was forced to give a little. Would it help if he were to personally guarantee the safety of Colonel Wilmeth and the other passengers? Robert said that it would not. The flight could not be cleared. But sensing that Kovalev would never yield, and feeling the pressure from Moscow to get the King case settled, Robert had to be content with Kovalev's personal guarantee. Getting a Soviet officer to stake his honor on such a promise was quite an achievement.

Colonel Wilmeth and his party left Poltava that day, and made it to Moscow in one piece. They were taken directly to the embassy. Wilmeth had left this place over two months ago on his hopeful mission to help the prisoners of war in Poland. Having been treated shamefully by the Soviets there, he was returning in the role of their puppet prosecutor against a fellow American officer. As far as he could see, there was barely any case at all against the young lieutenant.[17] But he was under orders to ransack the rulebook and cobble together whatever charges he could.

The charade began on April 25 and ran for two days, in an atmosphere of unease and ill will. Lieutenant King was found guilty and, like Lieutenant Bridge, was fined $600, with a permanent black mark on his record.[18] The officers of the jury, ashamed of what they had taken part in, all signed a request for clemency, which they forwarded to General Deane, currently in Washington. Deane, effectively acting on behalf of the Soviets, denied the request. The purpose of this trial was not justice; it was diplomacy.

Diplomacy was satisfied. The sacrifices were sufficient, and the Americans had been humbled. The day after the verdict, General Kovalev officially lifted the ban on American flights in and out of Poltava. On that day, Captain Robert Trimble, sensing the return of peace to his command, cabled Moscow: "On twenty eighth day of Soviet grounding . . . local test hops for combat and transportation aircraft allowed. . . . One B-17 and one P-51 scheduled to depart for Italy tomorrow with Soviets quite cooperative."[19]

Knowing what this peace had cost, Robert was disgusted. He felt ashamed of himself and, for the first time in his life, ashamed of his country. It was only chance that had prevented Robert himself from being part of the court-martial. His name had been on the list of potential court members, and only his appointment as CO had saved him.[20] The mood throughout Eastern Command was low. The officers and men felt that they had been let down by their superiors. The Soviets had been appeased when they should have been stood up to.

Lieutenant Myron King returned to Poltava that same day. He had been flown out of Moscow in a rush, in case the Soviets made a stink about the leniency of his sentence.[21] Captain Trimble took advantage of the lifting of the flying ban and ensured that King and his crew got on a flight the very next day to Tehran (their B-17, *Maiden USA*, had already been ferried back to England).[22] When General Kovalev—learning of their departure after the event—complained, Robert advised him to take the matter up with Moscow.[23]

In his few quiet moments, when he was able to give thought to his own situation, Robert wondered what might have happened to him if he'd been caught in any of his prisoner-exfiltration missions. If this was what they would do to men who'd given the kind of trivial offense that King and Bridge had, what would the Soviets have done to him? Well, he knew the answer to that already—they'd most likely have killed him off quietly, somewhere out in the wilds, and blamed the partisans and terrorists. Would the US generals in Moscow have stood up for him and held them to account? He doubted it. To do so would have been to admit their complicity. That was why there were no written orders and no trail leading from his activities back to them.

What Robert couldn't reconcile was the contradiction. On one hand there was the moral urge, the sense of loyalty and brotherhood that had made his superiors bring him here and send him out to rescue his compatriots; on the other was their willingness to sacrifice innocent people to the Soviets now—not just these three officers but the men and women left behind in Poland. Robert didn't understand politics, and maybe never would.

Everything was coming to an end.

At 1900 hours Poltava time on May 7, 1945, the BBC, broadcasting from London, announced that the war in Europe was over. They were a tad premature, as the final surrender would not be signed until the following day. Nonetheless, the pent-up emotions among the

Americans at Poltava, and the natural joy at the end of the conflict, produced an explosion of celebration.[24] They danced and sang in the streets, firing their weapons in the air.

Russian soldiers watched the display with surprise and puzzlement. When told the reason, they refused to believe it; the end of the war had not been announced by Moscow, so it could not be true. The next day, there was still no word from the Kremlin. Finally, in the early hours of May 9, the word came through: the Great Patriotic War was officially over—the Germans were beaten. The Russian contingent at Poltava erupted in a display of jubilation even greater than their American counterparts'. Later that day, a joint parade was held in the city. Once again Eastern Command marched in pride behind the colors of the United States. Soon, they believed, their job would be done and they would be able to pack up and go home.

Everything was coming to an end. Everything except the ghosts and the memories that would linger for decades among the men and women who had served.

A reception was held at the US Embassy in Moscow to celebrate Victory in Europe, and as CO of Eastern Command, Captain Robert Trimble was invited.

He arrived in Moscow filled with a mixture of anticipation and trepidation. Robert would be mingling with the very topmost of the top brass, and he had mixed feelings about them, and the contradiction that he would never be able to reconcile. It was they who had foreseen the cruelty of Soviet conduct in Poland and had conceived the humane covert mission that had brought him to Russia. They had, in effect, risked all for the sake of American servicemen. That made them noble and honorable, didn't it? He couldn't have done what he had in Poland if they hadn't put the means in his hands and provided him with cover. But when it came to the final diplomatic horse-trading, those same men had sold their own officers, and the entire nation of Poland, to the Soviets. Or

their masters in London and Washington had, and they had helped enact
the bargain.

What would happen to Józef now, or that delightful lady who
ran the Hotel George, or the Kratke family on their farm at Staszów?
Would the young girl's brother, Tadeusz, ever be able to return home?
Would the citizens ever be safe after dark on the streets of Lwów?

Robert took a cab from the airport and was driven to the US
Embassy. It stood on Novinskiy Boulevard, one of the grand thorough-
fares encircling the heart of the Russian capital. The embassy was even
bigger and more impressive than the one in London, a glorious, palatial
building in honey-colored stone and white stucco.[25] Remembering what
had happened to him the last time he entered an American embassy,
Robert felt a little uneasy. And the idea of lavish parties when there
were so many people suffering made him uncomfortable. Perhaps he
could at least talk to someone in power, and get them to put pressure on
the Russians to alleviate the situation at Poltava. Morale was still low,
with the Soviets still being awkward about American flights. And mail
was still not getting through.

He was greeted by a young attaché from the Military Mission, who
escorted him to the ballroom. The place was brimming over with gold
braid and satin gowns. Senior officers of the armies, air forces, and
navies of the three allies mingled with civilians of the diplomatic corps,
nibbling canapés and guzzling wine, and gossiping at the tops of their
voices under the crystal chandeliers.

As he was escorted around the room and introduced to people,
Robert was warned sotto voce by his companion that half the Russian
women present were employed by the NKVD. There really was no
escaping them—from the streets of Lwów to the heart of the diplomatic mission, the Soviets got their spies and informers everywhere. In
a culture so obsessed with spying, it was hardly surprising that you
ended up with the kind of mean-spirited paranoia that treated ex–
prisoners of war like potential partisans, and men like King, Bridge,
and Shenderoff like terrorists.

The attaché steered Robert toward a little group of very senior-looking people. He recognized General Deane. Standing beside him was a thin man with a cheerfully gaunt face, as if someone had given Abe Lincoln a shave and told him a really good joke.

Deane drew Robert into the group. "Averell," he said to the thin man, "this is Captain Trimble, our excellent new commanding officer at Poltava."

So this was Ambassador Harriman. He offered his hand. "Delighted to meet you, Captain. So you're the interim commander I've heard about?"

Robert balked a little at "interim," but pressed on. "Sir, I was very excited to receive your invitation. I hope we can find time to talk about a few matters. There are some problems still at—"

General Deane tensed beside him, but Harriman was already talking over Robert. "Captain, it's been great meeting you, and I hear you're doing a superb job. I have a lot of ground to cover this evening, so you'll forgive me if I circulate. Enjoy yourself, and take care!"

Robert was introduced to more people, and General Deane chatted with him a little, carefully steering the conversation away from shop talk. After a while Robert found himself alone again with the attaché.

"Are the brass always this offhand with their soldiers?" he asked.

The attaché laughed. "Oh, always. I hardly ever know what's going on—until my superiors want something, and then I can't do it fast enough for them."

"My command at Poltava is being undermined by the Soviets, and my people are depressed. I've asked for help, but all I get is instructions to do whatever the Russians want."

The attaché drew Robert to one side, away from some Russians who were standing within hearing distance. "Well, we are guests in their country. Over the past year we've had constant complaints from the Soviet authorities about American misbehavior at Poltava—road accidents, GIs exploiting the black market, local women being harassed.[26] You name it, we've been accused of it, and some of the claims are true."

Robert didn't need to be told—handling such complaints was part of his daily round as CO. "As guests," the attaché went on, "we have the obligation to behave impeccably. If we hope to maintain good relations with the USSR, we have to do what they want."

During his evening in Moscow, Robert came to the conclusion—as if he'd needed any prompting—that he wasn't cut out for politics.

There were other things too that were outside his area of competence. A little later, as he was wondering whether it was okay to up and leave the party, he was approached by a glamorous lady with movie-star looks—the most beautiful woman he'd seen since the queen of Iran. She didn't bother introducing herself, and already seemed to know who he was. "Do you smoke, Captain?" she asked. He admitted that he liked an occasional cigar. She took his arm in hers and guided him out to a balcony.

In the chill air and a haze of perfume and cigarette smoke, she plied him with conversation and questions. She was fascinated by his experiences as a pilot and very keen to learn about the condition of American flyers who had been forced down in enemy territory and how they were rescued.

Robert sighed. He had been here before, just a few days ago. On the evening after the VE Day celebrations, there had been a show put on at Poltava's theater and a party afterward. Robert had met a pretty Ukrainian performer who called herself Lydia. He wasn't proud of what had followed. Having taken on board far more booze than was good for him, and with his innate susceptibility to female charm, he allowed himself to be persuaded to go back with her into the city to meet her parents; strangely, they turned out to be an old couple who didn't seem to know Lydia any more than they knew Robert. More vodka was drunk. Lydia took him up to her room.

Breathing perfume and alcohol over each other, they ended up on the bed. Gazing hungrily into his eyes, Lydia slid her hand along Robert's thigh . . . and asked him about his parents. And his schooling, and his religion. In a pie-eyed stupor, Robert wondered what was going on.

Lydia, continuing the seduction with her eyes and hands, questioned him intimately about his mission in the USSR.

When he returned to the base next morning with a hangover that would split tree trunks, all he could recall was Lydia's questioning, together with a vague memory of passing out. He didn't believe he'd answered her questions (not coherently, anyway) but couldn't swear to it.

The drink hadn't flowed nearly as freely at the embassy reception, and when the beautiful lady stumbled and asked Robert to put his arm around her to steady her, he instantly recalled Lydia. "Captain, you're so handsome," the lady breathed, looking up at him with Rita Hayworth eyes. She really was unbelievably beautiful. But he wasn't plastered this time, and knew perfectly well that all she was interested in was the information locked up inside his head.

With profound reluctance, and fighting against every masculine urge, Robert made an excuse, disengaged himself gently from the lady's hold, and retreated back inside the building.

It had been a narrow escape. He was just a small-town boy at the mercy of these professionals. He had no training in espionage, and missing home and Eleanor the way he did, he lacked the strength to resist this kind of seduction for long.

In the taxi on the way to his hotel, he thought over the evening he'd had and wondered how long he could keep up this business of politics and leadership. Was it all just a game to these people? The soldiers and civilians on the front line—were they just pieces to be played for and sacrificed in the winning of power?

The next morning, he went back to the embassy, hoping to secure a meeting with Ambassador Harriman or General Deane. He felt he couldn't go back to Poltava empty-handed; just a personal message that the gods in Moscow were thinking of their people and doing all they could to look after their interests would suffice. Neither Harriman nor Deane was available. Instead Robert was given a tour of the embassy. The facilities for the staff were amazing. In the rec center there were senior officials enjoying a rousing game of indoor tennis. Some folks in the diplomatic corps, he realized, had had themselves a pretty nice war.

Poland had been sacrificed. The government in exile had been cut off over the Katyn dispute and supplanted by a Soviet puppet. And now Russia wanted a slice of Polish territory.[27] Lwów, with its mix of Poles and Ukrainians, had become a gaming chip. Stalin had demanded it on the grounds that it was part of the historic territory of medieval Russia. In time it would be granted to him, renamed Lviv, and a thick strip of eastern Poland would be torn off with it, becoming part of Ukraine.

Robert Trimble couldn't stomach it. He really wasn't cut out for politics. Or so he believed. He wasn't to know that this was how politics felt to many of those who lived their lives inside it.

Looking back on this era, Winston Churchill would reflect sadly, "I have always been astonished, having seen the end of these two wars, how difficult it is to make people understand the Roman wisdom, 'Spare the conquered and confront the proud.' . . . The modern practice has too often been, 'punish the defeated and grovel to the strong.' "[28]

General Deane disliked the way he was forced to bow to the Russians, just as much as Captain Trimble did, especially over the evacuation of American prisoners of war.[29] So did Ambassador Harriman. Even speaking as a pragmatic politician, General Deane would come to regret the appeasement of the Soviet Union by America. "Whenever we did take a firm stand," he would recall, "our relations took a turn for the better." He came to the same conclusion that both Captain Trimble and Colonel Wilmeth had discovered during their time at the sharp end in Poland: "Soviet officials are much happier, more amenable, and less suspicious when an adversary drives a hard bargain than when he succumbs easily to Soviet demands."[30]

Back in 1941, Adolf Hitler had made a grave error about the United States; looking at their democracy, their personal liberties, and their decadent jazz culture, he had concluded that Americans were weak. He heard the soft voice, and failed to notice the big stick. Germany had paid a heavy price for that mistake. Now it seemed that Stalin might be thinking the same way. He saw the generosity and openness of America—the Lend-Lease supplies, the ready sharing of intelligence, the soft-footed diplomacy—and believed that this was a nation that could be bullied.

But as the war drew to a close and the Iron Curtain began to fall, the British and the Americans were playing a delicate, dangerous game. As Churchill would reflect, "Appeasement from weakness and fear is alike futile and fatal. Appeasement from strength is magnanimous and noble and might be the surest and perhaps the only path to world peace."[31]

What Robert Trimble lacked that Deane, Harriman, Churchill, and Roosevelt all had was the ability to reconcile morals and politics. Or maybe he just lacked the experience. The small-town boy, the ordinary American who had become a decorated combat veteran, the combat veteran who had become a secret agent and diplomat, was too low down the ladder to have a clear view of the landscape. He believed that he was no longer doing any good. The stress and the anger were growing, and the cracks were beginning to show.

19.

THE LONG WAY HOME

June 23, 1945: Poltava Air Base

It was Eastern Command's last day. The war in Europe was well and truly over, and their job was done.

Four transport planes, warming up and idling, stood on the steel-mat taxiway, fluttering the grass with their propeller wash. Nearby a small group of officers stood ready to board. During the past week, daily flights of C-46 Commandos had been moving out supplies, equipment, and personnel, and now all that remained was this core group. The few dozen enlisted men had boarded the last two C-46s, and the officers were waiting to embark in the two C-47s.

Their leaders were conducting a final look-see around the base, and taking their time over it. Finally a jeep came speeding from the direction of the headquarters site and pulled up near the planes. In it were Captain Trimble and Brigadier General Ritchie, chief of staff from the Military Mission in Moscow, who had come down the day before to oversee the final checks.

The closing down had been stretched over more than a month, fraught with constant bureaucratic delays. The postal service had been shut down prematurely, nobody had had any mail for weeks, and everyone was on edge. Eastern Command's vast stores—built up for a big command hosting huge numbers of shuttle bombing crews—had to be inventoried and shipped out. Thousands of tons of surplus supplies were handed over to the Soviets on Lend-Lease.[1] They nitpicked every item, claiming things were in poor condition, so as to reduce the recorded value. Even machine guns that had never been removed from their sealed packaging were claimed to be "dirty." Candy bars and packs of cigarettes were stolen in their thousands, and ended up being sold by urchins on the streets of Poltava.

It wasn't a period that Robert Trimble would look back on with any fondness. The strain of keeping the place running and being diplomatic with the Soviets, constantly reining in his annoyance and impatience, added to the stresses that were slowly pulling him apart inside.

He'd made some good friends, and there were happy memories along with the bad and the sad. In April, at the height of the flying ban, when tensions were high, Bill Kaluta, a young Corps of Engineers lieutenant, had married his girlfriend, Lieutenant Clotilde Govoni, a nurse in the base hospital. Kaluta was a lively soul, a beautiful accordion player, and a Poltava veteran who'd been with Eastern Command since its early days.[2] For a day, everyone's spirits were lifted. As commanding officer, Robert acted as substitute father of the bride. The ceremony took place in the city hall, with a congregation of Russians and Americans. Outside, an audience of bemused Ukrainian citizens looked on as the happy swarm of uniforms filed in and out, laughing, joking, and distributing candy to the local children. When called on to kiss the bride, Robert gave Clotilde a quite unfatherly smackeroo on the lips that left her giggling. That one day of laughter and goodwill between Russians and Americans was a bright spot in those dark weeks.

Kaluta was waiting now, as the jeep pulled up beside the idling planes. Robert would be taking one C-47 to Moscow, en route to USSTAF headquarters in Paris, while Kaluta was going with the other C-47 via Cairo. He had charge of all Eastern Command's records, which the Soviets would have given a lot to get their hands on. The packages of documents, which were to be destroyed if necessary, were leaving Russia by the shortest route, and avoiding Moscow. A story went around that the last item of American property to be taken care of had been a previously undiscovered cache of secret weapons and equipment belonging to the OSS, found by General Ritchie in a warehouse. It was apparently a relic of the aborted OSS/NKVD cooperation. To prevent it falling into Soviet hands, Ritchie had the gear loaded aboard a truck in the dead of night, then personally drove it to a nearby lake and dumped it all in.[3]

The officers said their farewells and boarded their planes. After General Ritchie had gone aboard, Robert stepped up into the doorway of the C-47 and glanced back. A midsummer sun shone down on the ruined buildings and the barracks blocks and glittered on the steel-mat runways. It was all very different from the first view he'd had; the mellow warmth a world away from the lacerating cold that had hit him on that February day. Robert marveled at how little time had elapsed since he'd arrived, primed with false promises of an easy racket that would see him through the rest of the war. He'd never believed that he could accomplish the task that he'd been sent into Poland for, but he'd done his best. Hundreds of men and women had been brought from perdition to safety.

It was all off the record, and the only recognition was indirect and muted. In May, in a letter to General Carl A. Spaatz, commander of USSTAF, General Hill had requested promotion for Captain Trimble to the rank of major, exempting him from the normal requirement of twelve months in current rank. Hill came as close as he could to acknowledging Robert's extraordinary service in Poland: "I consider that the exceptional nature of Captain Trimble's duties during the past three months warrant waiver of the current requirement."[4] Robert's performance, both as a flight commander with the 493rd Bomb Group and as CO of Eastern Command, had been rated Superior, but his service as assistant operations officer—the cover for his secret work in Poland which could never be openly spoken about—was rated Excellent.

In all his endeavors he had done better than anyone could have expected, not least himself. "This has been one of the most difficult periods since the organization of the command," wrote General Hill. "Captain Trimble has displayed outstanding diplomacy, energy and devotion to duty under the most trying conditions."

Later that same month, General Deane joined his voice to General Hill's, also calling for promotion and also referring obliquely to "the exceptional nature of Captain Trimble's duties and performance."[5]

Captain Trimble himself was never told exactly what his generals had said about him. As far as he knew, he'd done all right, but no better. Oh well, it was all by and done with now. He ducked inside the plane and slammed the door.

The wheels of the last C-47 came unstuck from Poltava's runway. The last contact was broken. America had been here, and now it was gone. The tiny, fragile island of Western liberty was inundated by the Red waters that had encircled it.

Captain Trimble paid a high price for what he'd achieved. He'd seen and experienced things that were beyond the ken of an air-combat veteran. The dead haunted him. But worse than that was the feeling of betrayal—the way, in his eyes, America had bowed the knee to Stalin and sold out Poland in a fool's bargain.

With Poltava receding, Robert believed he was leaving it all behind—the fear, the frustration, the sickening truths about the conduct of war—but he wasn't. He took it all with him, locked up inside. The war had exacted a price, and he wasn't done paying yet.

The C-47 called at Moscow, where there was bureaucratic business to deal with and General Ritchie resumed his post at the embassy. Robert's promotion to major had never materialized, and Ritchie—who'd become a friend during their brief acquaintance—promised to look into it and back him up. But nothing came of it. Robert, who was hardly thinking straight at all these days, was left to wonder if he'd made some kind of misstep during his time as CO. The memory of "Lydia" and that awful drunken night came back to him, turning his skin cold; but he wasn't aware that anyone had ever known about it. He'd certainly not been reprimanded for it.

Most likely, the promotion never came simply because there was no longer any role for him. With the war ending, Eastern Command dissolved, and demobilization on the horizon, there was no call for dynamic new majors. There was another possible reason too, which suggested itself during another stopover on the way home.

From Moscow, the C-47 flew to Berlin and Frankfurt. For the first time, Robert stood within the homeland of the enemy, the soil upon which he'd dropped so many tons of bombs. The place was utterly devastated—as bad as anything he'd seen in Russia or Poland—and the proud, bellicose people of the Reich were reduced to beggary. It wasn't something he wanted to contemplate, and he couldn't get out of there fast enough.

He took the controls at Frankfurt and flew the next leg himself. In Paris, for the first time in months, it felt like he was reentering the free world. Here was a city barely touched by battle or bombs, where the West was in force. Having been part of a tiny minority in a semi-hostile country, he found it strange to see British and American GIs everywhere, lounging in sidewalk cafés, strolling openly arm in arm with local girls. At long last, *home* started to seem like a real thing—a place that had an actual, solid existence.

In Paris Robert received a surprise invitation. A farewell party was being held for General Carl A. Spaatz, who was stepping down as commander of USSTAF and heading off to the Pacific to take command of the air forces there.[6] Robert took a ride out to the headquarters at St. Germain-en-Laye, a former royal retreat to the west of Paris. The place was dominated by the vast château, which until a year ago had been the headquarters of the German Army. Once more Robert found himself in elevated company; on this occasion he was the only captain in an exclusive party of generals. They were the commanding officers of the constituent arms of USSTAF, a club in which Captain Robert Trimble was still notionally a member. He was even more out of his depth than he had been at the Moscow party.

Toward the end of the evening, General Spaatz approached Robert and shook his hand. Like many of the generals Robert had known, he was a surprisingly kindly-looking fellow in his mid-fifties, with the impression that there was steel underneath the soft features. Spaatz had heard good reports of the young captain's work in Russia. In the course of small talk they discovered that they were both southeast Pennsylvania boys. Spaatz had grown up in Boyertown, a small burg about sixty miles from Camp Hill, son of a local newspaperman and politician who'd had a seat in the Pennsylvania Assembly at Harrisburg.[7]

"We used to play ball against Boyertown in the American Legion,"[8] Robert said, caught up in memories of boyhood and not thinking what he was saying. "We always beat the dickens out of 'em!"

The general spluttered indignantly: "What the hell are you talking about?"

Robert reddened and started to backtrack, but Spaatz laughed and brushed the insult to his hometown aside. "Join me for a cigar, Captain?" he suggested. "I'd like a quiet talk with you."

They stepped out onto a balcony with a view over St. Germain in the summer evening twilight. Spaatz, done with small talk, got straight to business. "I'm heading out to the Pacific in a couple of days," he said. "I just lost one of my aides, and I need a good man to replace him." He looked at Robert through a wreath of cigar smoke. "That man could be you. I've heard good things about you." It was a stunning offer. Robert didn't know what to say or think. "If you accept," Spaatz added, "you'll certainly get that promotion your superiors have been pestering me for."

The Pacific, as aide to a general—that could be quite a racket. On the other hand, Robert had learned the hard way to be wary of handsome-sounding offers. Going by past experience, he'd be tempted into accepting this appointment and in a month's time find himself sneaking through a Burmese jungle with a money vest stuffed with yen and his guts churning.

Seeing Robert's hesitation, Spaatz told him more. There was a covert operation on the table, but like nothing Robert could have imagined. They were planning a new phase in the air campaign against the Japanese, like nothing the world had ever seen. A top secret project was in training that would deliver a knockout blow. A special B-29 bombardment group had been formed, and there was a chance that Captain— sorry, *Major* Robert M. Trimble could be one of its pilots.

Robert had no idea what that meant, and no idea how to react. More air combat? Wasn't that what he'd gone to Russia to avoid? And more secrecy, and being around generals, with all the politics that involved. And who knew where it could lead—maybe another act that would tarnish the image of the United States in his eyes. He'd had enough destruction, enough war, and was heartsick of politics.

General Spaatz gazed at him with his mournful eyes glittering—a sort of somnolent keenness. "What do you say?"

There was a tiny part of Robert—the remains of the urge that had made him want to go to war in the first place, the boy adventurer who still hadn't been entirely erased—that was tempted. He thought it over for a good half minute before shaking his head.

"Thank you, sir, but no. I've got a wife back home I haven't seen in over a year, and an eight-month-old baby girl I haven't even met. I've given all the service I can, sir. I've had enough war. I just want to go home."

Spaatz looked hard at him. "I see," he said. "Well, Captain, I guess we'll just have to find somebody else." He gave Robert his hand and shook firmly. "Take care," he said. And with that, he walked away. It would be some time before Robert learned that he'd turned down the chance of being one of the pilots that dropped the A-bomb on Japan.[9]

For now, he was heading home, and nothing was going to get in his way.

————————

Sitting forward in his seat, Robert stared with an eerie intensity at the Pennsylvania landscape flitting past the glass. The train's bogies clattered under him in the old familiar way, every flickering tie, every bridge, every crossing bringing him closer to home.

Five days had passed since leaving Paris, five days that couldn't go by quickly enough. London—the place where the strange adventure had begun—was his first familiar stopping point. Then another circuitous route—Northern Ireland, Iceland, Greenland, and eventually his own native soil. Washington. Baltimore. And now he was back in the land that had made him, the place he knew like no other. It had that disturbing alienness of a known place when you come back to it after years away. It was fitting that it was the Pennsylvania Railroad that was bringing him home. He'd worked and traveled these rails for three years before going into the Army, and every junction and landmark was an old acquaintance.

But there were new memories overlying it all now. He'd looked at the tracks leading out of Baltimore and seen those boxcars pulling sluggishly out of Lwów, filled with haggard, hopeful men and women; heard the hurrying footsteps in the station halls and remembered the NKVD officer and his men waiting for Isabelle and her friends to arrive; and always in his mind he saw the rails running in under the archway at Birkenau, and the mutilated bodies laid like cordwood by the tracks northwest of Lublin.

He'd left something of himself in all those places, something he would never get back. Where were all those people now, the ones who'd survived the horrors? Had they found their way home? Did they carry the same baggage with them as he did? The same damage sealed up inside? And if they had come home, did the landscape look as strange to them as his home country did to him?

Robert leaned forward as the train pulled out of York; tapped his fingernails on the window ledge as it sped up the Susquehanna Valley. His breathing became short and his heart started to thump as the locomotive slowed into the outskirts of his hometown. It was hard to believe that that was Lemoyne going by the window this moment; if he stood up he ought to be able to see Hummel Avenue. By the time the train thundered out onto the Susquehanna Bridge, he was on his feet and his hands were trembling. Before he knew it, he was glimpsing the red brick and the barn roof of Harrisburg Station, and the train was sliding in under the arch and jolting to a halt.

Hauling his kit bag, he squeezed out the door, joining the exodus of GIs, sailors, and civilians crowding onto the platform. Scanning the sea of people, he saw a familiar face, and walked that way. It was her. He hurried his steps; his feet seemed to vanish from under him, as if he were floating through the crowd; then his kit bag fell to the floor and she was in his arms. "Robert! Oh, Robert!" Eleanor squealed. "Robert!" He felt her tears soaking his face, and inhaled the scent of her—the scent he'd all but forgotten, that carried him back to that evening beside the lake at Fort Worth, the homes they'd shared along the way, and to the times before that, when they were both just innocent kids, before there was a war.

He clung to Eleanor, for how long he didn't know, like a drowning man holding on to a lifeboat. Then he held her at arm's length and looked into her face, the beautiful features pinched and pink with tears, but smiling, telling him breathlessly over and over how much she had missed him. (Only later, looking back, did he realize that his own eyes had remained dry.)

There was another presence there, sitting patiently on a bench beside them, watching curiously as her mommy embraced the strange man.

"Carol Ann," Eleanor said, lifting her up, "this is your daddy."

Robert stared dumbly at the tiny face. Another infant face swam up in his memory—pallid, chilled in the forest snow. He shook away the image and reached out toward his daughter. She reared back, lashing out with her tiny hand, and bopped him on the nose, then screwed up her face and screamed. "Sweetheart!" said Eleanor, mortified. "This is your daddy! Daddy's come home!"

Robert smiled, but his heart ached, wounded by the rebuff. Coming home wasn't going to be as easy as he'd hoped.

He was on home soil, but Robert wasn't out of the Army yet. He might still be hauled back into the machine, and there was even the remote possibility that he could be thrown into the fight again. The war in the Pacific looked like it might be dragging on a long while yet. He could end up flying a combat tour against Japan after all, with or without General Spaatz's special mission.

And it now occurred to him that he wouldn't mind that at all.

He hadn't left the war behind—he'd brought it all with him, every last piece of it, and it infested his home. He'd been back a couple of weeks, and he just couldn't settle. He was nervous, agitated, and under the surface, like a land mine, was a latent anger that could be triggered by the lightest touch.

Home wasn't home at all. It was as much an alien place as the Ukraine had been. Carol Ann no longer screamed at the sight of him, but she reached for Eleanor, not for him. And ashamed as he was to think it, Eleanor herself irritated him. He didn't like to be around her. She didn't understand; she didn't know what he'd seen, never could know or even imagine, and he couldn't communicate it to her. Robert spent as much time as he could alone, fishing in the timeless peace of the Susquehanna.

While he waited for the military to decide what to do with him, he gave thought to civilian life. Eleanor wanted him to settle back to work on the railroad, but he longed to keep flying. He began secretly scanning the ads for civilian piloting jobs. In his idle moments he developed an obsessive bond with his Army Colt; the same one he'd used to fend off the Russian colonel at Staszów. He kept it in a dresser drawer in the bedroom, but was constantly taking it out and cleaning it.

Every day he strove to keep the memories at bay. But they came back to him in his nightmares, and even in his waking life. The sudden burst of a flak shell close by, the zip of splinters through metal, the stomach-knotting tension of riding through a storm of explosions, steadily bearing down on the target, Forts either side falling apart and dropping to earth. The stacked bodies, frozen rigid, bursting out of the shed and lying in the slushy snow. The infant, starved and chilled to death, huddled inside his coat. The gunshot in the street below his window, and the woman's struggle suddenly ceasing. And then there were the things that made the anger begin to boil. The cold, bland smugness of the Soviet officers, and the humbled compliance of the American generals and diplomats, sipping champagne and playing tennis while Poland was turned into Stalin's front yard, infested with secret police and murderers.

Eleanor was frightened and confused. She could see the change in Robert, but couldn't understand it. He was detached and moody all the time. The prospect of his homecoming had been a light in the darkness, sustaining her through all those lonely months while she struggled to keep a home together for him to come back to. But all he had brought was disillusion and fear. There was no rekindling of their romance—just sullen silence, irritability, and long absences. He shut her out, turned away from her, and she didn't know why. And he kept handling that awful pistol.

One Friday evening he returned home after a week away on a military exercise. Eleanor gathered her courage to confront him. Looking at his face, she hardly dared speak. She asked him what was the matter. He denied that anything was the matter. In that case, she asked, why was he behaving like this all the time?

It was like sticking a finger in a raw wound. He exploded with anger, and swore at her. "You wouldn't understand it, not any damn part of it. Or anybody that stayed home and never saw the things we saw over there. How can you expect me to come home and pretend none of it ever happened?"

His eyes blazed, and she quailed; but she kept her courage. "That's just it," she said. "I *don't* understand. I don't know. So how can you blame me for it? Pretend *what* never happened?"

"You really want to know? All right, I'll tell you. Nobody here has any idea what war is like. It's bloody and senseless and inhuman. They tell you it's the Germans, but it's everyone—the Russians, and even us. People starve to death and nobody does a damn thing; they torture, they murder, they rape. I've seen people put to death, cut in half, I . . . I held a—a little baby in my arms and she—she died." His voice started breaking up. "And those damned politicians in Moscow, they sold everyone out—the Poles, even their own people. They crawled to Stalin, that murdering, lying son of a bitch—they fired good officers just because they . . . just for trying to help our men . . . for telling the truth about . . . about . . ."

Speechless with emotion, he put his hands over his face and sobbed. Eleanor, horrified, her heart breaking, reached out to comfort him, but he threw her off.

"We haven't got the right!" he yelled at her. "We haven't got the right to be all happy and loving and pretend the world's all wonderful."

He pushed past her, and before she could call his name he had slammed out the door, run down the steps and out to the street. She heard the car start and pull away.

Eleanor sat down, stunned and shaking, and burst into tears, crying her heart out. It felt like everything was falling to pieces around her, and she didn't know what to do. She was absolutely bewildered. She'd known that war must be awful, but . . . but how could Robert have seen those things he described? He'd been in Russia as a pilot, hadn't he?

What he'd said made her go cold inside. No wonder he was so broken up. But how could it be her fault? She gave up what hope she had retained that the gentle, loving husband she had waved off to war would ever come home to her.

Eleanor was in the house alone with Carol Ann the day the telegram arrived from Washington. Even now it gave her a start, so conditioned had she become over the past year to fear the arrival of a War

Department telegram. It was addressed to Robert. He was away on military business, so she opened it. It was a short, simple message commanding Captain Trimble to report to Army Air Forces headquarters.

Thinking it must be urgent, she called Robert up. Their dialogs with each other had become strained to the snapping point, so she simply read the telegram to him.

Robert didn't know what to make of it. He'd never heard of the senior officer who'd sent it, and there was no hint of what it was about. He arrived home that night and went straight upstairs to start packing. He'd need to stay overnight in Washington so he'd be fresh for a morning meeting.

He seemed brighter than usual when he left the house, and he parted from Eleanor with a semblance of affection. It had occurred to him that he might be about to get some recognition at last for what he'd done. Maybe somebody—Spaatz, Deane, Ritchie—had made a case on his behalf. Of course they could never openly refer to his secret work, but all those powerful men could pull something out of the bag to acknowledge that his efforts were recognized and appreciated by the people at the top. It wouldn't heal anything, but it might help.

Walking out of the hotel into the bright sunshine the next morning, he felt like smiling for the first time in weeks. He took a cab out to the Pentagon. The building was still almost brand-new, and its scale was breathtaking. He found his way to the AAF Department and reported to the front desk. A clerk collected him and escorted him to the office of the general who had sent the telegram.

As soon as he entered the office, he got the feeling that the meeting might not be what he'd hoped for. The general, who had the air of a bureaucrat who'd never been within a hundred miles of a combat zone, was frigidly unfriendly.

The general picked a file up off his desk. "I have a document here. A report on various incidents that occurred in the USSR during the tenure of Eastern Command. I understand you were commanding officer there for a time." He said it in a manner implying that they must have been desperately short of better candidates.

Robert set his jaw. "Yes, sir, I was."

"It seems that you were responsible for several actions which antagonized the Soviet authorities. Refusing to authorize flights for a certain Russian pilot, and demanding that he be suspended from duty; declining to allow your personnel to participate in the Russians' VE Day parade; repeatedly objecting to Soviet flight restrictions which had been enacted to prevent unauthorized activities by US personnel in Soviet-controlled forward areas—"[10]

"Sir, that isn't so," Robert interrupted. "Eastern Command took part fully in all the VE Day celebrations."[11] (As none knew better than he, cringing at the memory of that drunken night.) "And the Russian pilot was a dangerous incompetent."

The general glared at him and went on as if he hadn't spoken: ". . . activities in which you, Captain Trimble, had been one of the perpetrators. Activities which included smuggling British and American prisoners of war to Poltava disguised as AAF aircrew. And, as if that weren't enough, drawing your sidearm and threatening a senior Soviet officer with it. Do you deny *that*?"

Robert said nothing.

"And what do you have to say about *this* . . . ?" The general pulled a document out of the file and handed it to him.

Robert recognized it immediately, and felt sick. It was one of the dozens of routine situation reports he'd written or signed off on as commanding officer. It dated from the time when he was feeling at his lowest about being forced to bow to Soviet demands—the time of the court-martial of King and the delivery of Shenderoff to Moscow for execution. He'd written in large letters in the margin, *Shame on America*.

"What is the meaning of this, Captain? I'm astonished at such a lack of patriotism in an American officer in a position of command. It's disgraceful."

That did it. "Were you over there, sir? Were you ever actually *in* the war?"

The general glared at him. "What does that have to do with it?"

"It has everything to do with it. How dare you question my patriotism? Or anybody's who was there. You saw nothing of what we went through. You have no idea what we gave. We all served our country, and we had to watch politicians like you trade away its honor to a dictator."

"Watch your tone, Captain."

"I'll watch my tone when I'm ready to! Now, you can tell whoever gave you those documents—"

"I said *watch it*, Captain. Show some decorum, or your days in the Army Air Forces are numbered."

"They already are. I already put in for my discharge."

The general fumed silently for a few moments, then hissed: "Captain, you're dismissed. Get out of my office."

Mustering all the dignity he could, Robert saluted, turned about, and walked out the door.

The house was silent. Nobody was home. Robert paused a moment in the hallway, listening, but didn't call out. All he heard was the pounding inside his head.

The journey back from Washington had been a blur. He'd gone straight from the Pentagon back to his hotel and then caught the first train to Harrisburg. Walking into Union Station, he'd got the same weird, dislocating sensation as when he'd first seen it on his return to the States last month—the building looked so much like the rail stations in Lwów and Kraków, he could almost feel the ice under his boots again and the air of tension. It was bizarre to see swarms of GIs and sailors in place of the knots of refugees and Red Army guards.

All the way home, his head had pounded with indignant anger, confusion, and despair. How could it have come to this? After everything he'd been through, all he'd given of himself, to be scorned like that, told he was unpatriotic; to have longed so deeply to come home, only to find that the war tormented him more here than it had when he was in the thick of it. He seemed to have no home, and soon he would have no marriage.

Robert went up the stairs two at a time and strode into the bedroom. He went straight to the dresser and yanked open the drawer where he kept the Colt. He dug through the stacks of underwear, but the pistol wasn't there. Blind with anger, he pulled the drawer right out and upturned it over the bed; then the second drawer. Still there was no pistol.

"Is this what you're looking for?"

He spun round. Eleanor stood in the doorway. The Colt was in her hand.

Robert froze. She held the pistol reluctantly, as if it were a venomous animal, but her finger was on the trigger, and even from here he could see that the safety was off. "You were looking for this?" she repeated, gesturing awkwardly at him with the heavy pistol, and his heart lurched. "Well, you can go ahead and use it—right after I'm done with it. I'm following you to the end."

He stood motionless, going cold with fear as she railed at him. "I don't know what happened to you in the war, of course I don't, but I know it had to be awful. You suffered, but so did I, Robert. *I* suffered too. My heart almost broke when you went away, and every time the mailman called, I was scared half to death. I was *so* proud of you. I saved every clipping from the paper, about your medals. You were my hero." She waved the pistol dangerously. "You were so unhappy when you were young, when your father left. But you *know* I understand that—my father *and* my mother let me down, and they're gone now, and Howard too." Eleanor fought against her tears, struggling to get her feelings out before it was all over. "I so longed for you to come home, but now it's like I don't know you at all. And now it looks like you're getting ready to leave me." She gestured wildly with the pistol. "But if you're going, I'm going first . . ." Eleanor raised the Colt, and her knuckles whitened.

Robert found his voice. "No! Eleanor... put the gun down. I'm begging you. Put it down. Please, Eleanor, I love you..."

Eleanor just stared at him, her eyes red with tears. The pistol barrel was shaking, but she didn't lower it. He took a step toward her. Something was breaking down inside him, a barrier of thorns that had grown around his insides, and the truth about what really, ultimately mattered in his life dawned on him. "Eleanor, you're scaring me. Don't do this. . . . I can't live without you. I love you."

They stared at each other. Slowly, the barrel of the Colt lowered, and slipped out of Eleanor's fingers, falling with a thud on the carpet. Robert dropped to his knees and threw his arms around her, and sobbed. The tears that had refused to come when he embraced her at the station flooded out of him, the emotion that had seemed dead during the weeks that followed shook him to his core. He cried, and her arms went around him, pressing his head against her belly. "Don't ever leave me," he said. "You're more important than anything to me."

Eleanor stroked his hair, her heart close to bursting. The words she said stayed with them both as long as they lived. "I'll never leave you, Robert, as long as you never leave me."

Slowly, Robert's breathing subsided, and a peace began to settle on him. He felt a gentle tug on his sleeve, and opened his eyes, focusing through the tears. Carol Ann had crawled into the room, drawn by the noise, and was looking up at him uncertainly, her mouth open. Robert reached out toward her tentatively, smiling. She hesitated, then grasped his finger and smiled back.

He had come home at last.

EPILOGUE: NOT WITHOUT HONOR

He awoke to birdsong. For a while his mind was lost in a mist, and he had no idea where he was. He recalled lying on the ground, with a fierce sun on his back, and a painful flame igniting in his skull. He believed he'd been in the garden, tending to some plants, when a haze came over him, and then he was burning up. They told him later it was dehydration and low blood pressure, and too long gardening in the sun. He recalled being lifted and carried, and then blackness . . . and now birdsong.

It was around noon when he opened his eyes. He was in a hospital room. The sound he'd thought was birdsong was the soft bleeping of machinery. He found his eyeglasses on the stand beside the bed, and his dirty gardening clothes folded nearby. Pulling the tube from his arm, he got out of bed and pulled on the clammy garments. Then he shuffled out into the corridor, following the glow of daylight to the front desk.

"Where am I?" he asked.

They told him he was in the infirmary of the Willow Valley Manor retirement community. He relaxed. The Manor was his home; he had an apartment in the complex, living there alone now. He was growing accustomed to the solitude, but it was hard. They told him to go back to bed. He refused, and when a nurse came to assist him, he brushed her aside. "Leave me be," he said gruffly. "Go find some sick people to tend to."

He headed off down the hallway. He was getting the hell out of there and going home, but he had a call to pay first. He knew the infirmary well; how odd that he hadn't recognized it. He took the familiar turn, stopped at the familiar door, and opened it.

She was asleep. He padded across to his regular chair and sat down beside the bed. Taking her hand in his, he murmured softly, "It's me." Eleanor's eyes opened and gazed dully at him for a few moments, then she smiled, and he forgot about the aches that had dogged him all the way from his own bed.

Eleanor would not be long in the world now; she had been in the infirmary for six months, and was fading week by week. After all those long decades together, it was hard being without her. He'd kept her by him for as long as he could, until the round-the-clock care became too much for his own deteriorating health. All that was keeping him going now was sheer stubborn toughness.

Their hands lay together, and he talked softly to her, reminding her of the world outside and the lives they'd lived together, even though she could no longer understand. "You saved my life, Eleanor," he said. "Three times, by my count. First time when we were nothing but kids. And again when you let me go to Russia instead of another combat tour. And the third time . . ." He squeezed her hand, and she smiled again.

He sat there an hour, and soon she was sound asleep again, her breathing accompanied by the soft chirping and sighing of the machines. He laid her hand down, stood up stiffly, and walked off down the corridor, glancing sternly at the nurse who tried to divert him back to his room. He walked out through the door and into the sunshine.

Robert put the old cigar box on the table and raised the lid. Here it all was—the artifacts that had survived the years, all that was left of the war other than the memories. He hadn't kept much. The medals, the papers, all worn and discolored now, shut away in a box. One by one he lifted them out and laid them on the table.

Each one dragged a train of memory with it, a disjointed spool of images and half-remembered emotions that came to life in his old, trembling fingers. Near the bottom, still astonishingly bright after all these years, was the scarlet-and-green ribbon of the Croix de Guerre. Its silver star was tarnished almost black, but the ribbon was vivid and the cross still had a sheen. What a wonderful, warm surprise it had been to receive it. The memories that came with it were unalloyed, as fresh as ever.

It was in the middle of that troubled summer of 1945. He was down at San Antonio, waiting for his discharge. Peace had come; Spaatz's men had dropped the big one on Japan, and the war was finally over. Robert's time in the Army Air Forces was coming full circle, bringing him back to the very place where he'd begun his flying training. One afternoon, a voice barked over the camp PA, telling him to report to the adjutant's office. An order had come through for him to proceed to Wright Field, Ohio. The French government was going to give him a medal.

He was mystified. Why would the French want to give him a medal? And why now? And then he remembered that afternoon meeting in the eatery on the outskirts of Lwów, and the ring of pretty faces looking at him like he was some kind of unearthly hero.

Even now, holding the aged medal in his hands, touching the tarnished star, he could see their faces still, past all the intervening years, still feel the kisses on his cheeks. He couldn't recall their names (if he'd ever known them) except for one—Isabelle. She must have remembered his name, and told her story. The result had been this, the only official thank-you he ever received.

When he arrived at Wright Field, it was like a state fair on the first sunny Sunday. Teeming with GIs, WACs, trucks, jeeps, and planes, it was starting to gear up for the big Air Fair, scheduled for the fall, in which the USAAF would show off its latest technology and put on a public display of the amazing planes captured from the Nazis. Robert and two other American airmen were receiving the Croix de Guerre that day.[1] They'd been told that the presentation would be made by President Charles de Gaulle himself, who was visiting President Truman in Washington, but there had been some kind of spat between him and the United States, and the event had been removed from his itinerary.[2] Instead the French ambassador, M. Henri Bonnet, came and pinned the beautiful bronze cross on Captain Trimble's breast.

It looked such a small thing now, but it meant a lot. All those suffering people, sent on their way to home and freedom. When you came down to it, that was all the acknowledgment that mattered—the hugs and handshakes of those men and women long ago as they boarded the trains, his rubles and dollars in their pockets, along with a precious hope that the war and the NKVD between them had almost obliterated but which Robert had revived. He prayed they had all reached their homes, and rebuilt their lives, and been blessed with wonderful children and grandchildren as he had.

Maybe the time had come to talk about it. Several months had passed since his fall in the community garden. Lee had been asking about his war service, wanting to hear all over again the stories that had enthralled him as a boy. His sister Carol was encouraging him.[3] Until now she'd never seemed very interested in those distant events on the far side of the world when she was an infant. But her own kids were grown up now and had children too; that's when a person can grow conscious of the past and the way it pulls at the generations who follow after.

Robert's children knew nothing about their father's war service beyond his adventures as a bomber pilot. The Russian episode had been kept locked up. Maybe it was time now to unlock the box and let it all out.

In World War I there was a well-known recruitment poster designed to shame reluctant men into enlisting. It depicted an embarrassed-looking father being asked by his little kids, "Daddy, what did *you* do in the Great War?"

Every boy of my generation liked to believe that his dad was a war hero; when we got older, most of us were satisfied just to know that our fathers had given their best, that they had played a part in the great human machine that went overseas to defeat tyranny and end suffering. When I listened to Dad's tales of danger and excitement in the air war, it never occurred to me that there was a whole other half of his war story that he never spoke about.

I don't know for sure how much his silence was due to the secrecy of what he'd been involved in, and how much was due to the pain that went with the memories. As the years went by, I guess it just got easier for him to keep the lid shut down on it.

When it did come out, it took a long time. There was so much to tell, so many memories to untangle, and such complex emotions mixed up with them. I recorded what I could during my visits with Dad, but there were hours and days of talk that went unrecorded, mostly over games of pool. He rediscovered a few forgotten delights (the warmth of his bed at the hotel in Lwów was a particular joy, and the delight of those French girls at the prospect of freedom), and anything to do with airplanes was always a fond recollection. But as each memory was disinterred, the recurring themes were sadness and anger. His voice, gruff with age, still rasped with indignation when he talked about the fate of Poland. And when he spoke about the atrocities, about the abused and murdered prisoners of war, it was with a bleakness in his voice, so evocative you could almost feel the cold desolation of the railroads and the camps.

There was just a trace of sadness for himself, because he felt he hadn't done as well as he should, and that other people—from Colonel Hampton, relieved of his command, to the people he hadn't been able to bring out of Poland—had suffered because of him, either due to his actions or his failure to act. Like most of the men and women who undertook covert work—such as the two OSS agents who helped and advised him but whose names he never knew—he was given no token of appreciation by his own superiors, little indication of how valued, important, and successful his work had really been. That final interview in Washington withered his sense of self-worth. He was told that he would, at best, be given a "Satisfactory" rating, and not be eligible for any promotion. It's heartbreaking that he never knew exactly what his immediate superiors, Generals Hill and Deane, had said about him to General Spaatz—that he'd been commended for "the exceptional nature of his duties and performance" as well as for his outstanding service as commanding officer.

By the time I learned the full truth, buried in the archives, it was too late to tell him. But in his lifetime, we, his children, Carol, Robert, and I, believed in him.

My last memory of Dad is clear in my mind. I was at his bedside in his last few hours. He could no longer speak, and drifted in and out of consciousness. I took his hand and said, "Dad, if you can hear me, squeeze my hand." I was startled by his sudden, fierce grip. He was still with us. My heart swelling, I continued, "You can go to Mom now; go to Eleanor. You've done everything you can—for your family, for your country, and for the world. We all love you and thank you more than you could ever know."

Those were, as best I can remember, my exact last words to him.

Robert Trimble never wanted to be a hero. He just wanted to fly, and taste a little of what he believed would be the adventure of war. But when the time came to go beyond the call of duty, he went, and he did his best, laying his life on the line in order to bring his fellow Americans safely home.

BIBLIOGRAPHY

Abbreviations

AFHRA: Air Force Historical Research Agency, Maxwell Air Force Base
NARA: National Archives and Records Administration, Washington, DC

317 Squadron, RAF, *Chronicle of the 317th Polish Fighter Squadron, part I*, Polish Institute and Sikorski Museum, London, LOT.A.V.55/47 I.

Afkhami, Gholam Reza, *The Life and Times of the Shah*, Berkeley: University of California Press, 2008.

Association pour la Mémoire de la Déportation du Travail Forcé, online historical archive, www.requis deportes sto.com (retrieved January 24, 2014).

Bartov, Omer, "White Spaces and Black Holes: Eastern Galicia's Past and Present" in *The Shoah in Ukraine: History, Testimony, Memorialization*, ed. Ray Brandon and Wendy Lower, Bloomington: Indiana University Press, 2008.

Beadle, Sergeant R. J., "Joint Statement of Sgt R. J. Beadle and Ronald Gould" (statement regarding exfiltration from Lwów by Captain Trimble and party, March 1945), two copies, one signed by Beadle, one by Gould, NARA, RG 334, Box 22.

Beyer, John C., and Stephen A. Schneider, "Forced Labor Under the Third Reich," 2 vols, report published by Nathan Associates Inc., Washington, DC, 1999. Available online www.nathaninc.com/resources/forced-labor-under-third-reich (retrieved January 24, 2014).

Booth, Brigadier General Donald P., Cable PX 27223 to Deane and Eastern Command, March 19, 1945, "Arrival of POWs," NARA, RG 334, Box 24, POW Folder, File 3/13-3/26.

Borch, Fred L., "Two Americans and the Angry Russian Bear: Army Air Force Pilots Court-Martialed for Offending the Soviet Union during World War II," *Prologue*

Magazine 43/1 (Spring 2011). Available online at www.archives.gov/publications /prologue/2011/spring/court-martials.html (retrieved February 22, 2014).

Bories-Sawala, Helga Elisabeth, *Dans la gueule du loup: les Français requis du travail en Allemagne*, Villeneuve: Presses Universitaires du Sepentrion, 2010.

Bowman, Martin W., *The Bedford Triangle: U.S. Undercover Operations from England in World War 2*, Somerset: Patrick Stephens, 1988.

Bowman, Martin W., *B-17 Combat Missions*, London: Greenhill, 2007.

Bowman, Martin W., *The US Eighth Air Force in Europe: Black Thursday Blood and Oil, vol 2*, ebook edition, Barnsley: Pen & Sword, 2012.

Bowman, Martin W., and Truett Lee Woodall, *Helton's Hellcats: A Pictorial History of the 493rd Bomb Group*, Paducah, KY: Turner Publishing, 1998.

Bowyer, Michael J. F., *Action Stations 1: Wartime Military Airfields of East Anglia 1939–1945*, London: Patrick Stephens Ltd, 1979.

Brackman, Roman, *The Secret File of Joseph Stalin: A Hidden Life*, London: Frank Cass, 2001.

Buhite, Russell D., *Decisions at Yalta: An Appraisal of Summit Diplomacy*, Lanham, MD: SR Books, 1986.

Caldwell, Donald, and Richard Muller, *The Luftwaffe Over Germany: Defence of the Reich*, London: Greenhill, 2007.

Cannon, Lieutenant General John K., Cables MX-50976 and M-51026 to Gen. Deane concerning transport of Captain Shenderoff from Italy to Moscow, April 11, 1945, NARA, RG334, Box 67.

CIA, "Memoranda for the President: OSS/NKVD Liaison," *Studies in Intelligence* 7(3): 63–74 (declassified 1993). Available online at www.cia.gov/library/center-for-the -study-of-intelligence/kent-csi/vol7no3/pdf/v07i3a07p.pdf (retrieved February 11, 2014).

Conversino, Mark J., *At War with the Soviets: A Historical Perspective of Joint Soviet-American Air Operations*, Maxwell AFB, AL: Air University Press, 1991.

Conversino, Mark J., *Fighting with the Soviets*, Lawrence, KS: University Press of Kansas, 1997.

Correll, John T., "The Poltava Debacle," *Air Force Magazine* 94/3 (March 2011). Available online at www.airforcemag.com/MagazineArchive/Pages/2011/March%202011/0311 Poltava.aspx (retrieved December 14, 2013).

Cynk, Jerzy B., *The Polish Air Force at War: The Official History, vol.1: 1939–1943*, Atglen, PA: Schiffer, 2004.

David-Fox, Michael, *Showcasing the Great Experiment: Cultural Diplomacy and Western Visitors to the Soviet Union*, Oxford: Oxford University Press, 2012.

Deane, Major General John R., Cable M-22725 to Gen. Richards, Budget Division, War Department, on emergency evacuation of prisoners of war and appointment of an agent officer, February 15, 1945, NARA, RG 334, Box 22.

Deane, Major General John R., Cables M-23583 and MX-23677 to Gen. Marshall, Army Chief of Staff, concerning Soviet complaints about Lt King, Capt. Bridge, and Capt. Shenderoff, April 2 and April 5, 1945, NARA, RG 334, Box 67.

Deane, Major General John R., Cable M-24441 to Gen. Spaatz concerning promotion of Captain Trimble, May 24, 1945, NARA, RG334, Box 63, Adjutant General file.

Deane, Major General John R., Letter to Lt Col James D. Wilmeth, March 10, 1945, NARA, RG 334, Box 23, POW Folder March 1–March 12.

Deane, Major General John R., Letter to Lt Gen. Slavin concerning transport of Captain Shenderoff, April 11, 1945, NARA, RG334, Box 67.

Deane, Major General John R., *The Strange Alliance: The Story of American Efforts at Wartime Co-operation with Russia*, London: John Murray, 1947.

Dobbs, Michael, *Six Months in 1945: FDR, Stalin, Churchill, and Truman*, London: Arrow, 2013.

Doherty, Robert E., and Geoffrey D. Ward, *Snetterton Falcons: The 96th Bomb Group in World War II*, Dallas: Taylor, 1989.

Fisher, John C., and Carol Fisher, *Food in the American Military: A History*, Jefferson, NC: McFarland, 2010.

Fitchen, Captain William, Mission interrogation of Lt Beam crew, December 10, 1944, Eastern Command, NARA, RG 334, Box 67, Interrogation Reports Folder.

Fitchen, Captain William, Mission interrogation of Lt King crew, March 19, 1945, Eastern Command, NARA, RG 334, Box 67, Interrogation Reports Folder.

Fitchen, Captain William, Mission interrogation of 2nd Lt Moore crew, March 31, 1945, Eastern Command, NARA, RG 334, Box 67, Interrogation Reports Folder.

Foregger, Richard, "Soviet Rails to Odessa, British Ships to Freedom," *Journal of Slavic Military Studies* 8/1 (1995), pp. 811 60.

Freeman, Roger A., *The B-17 Flying Fortress Story: Design—Production—History*, London: Arms and Armour, 1998.

Freeman, Roger A., Alan Crouchman, and Vic Maslen, *The Mighty Eighth War Diary*, revised edition, London: Arms and Armour, 1990.

Golubev, Lieutenant General K. D., Letter to Maj. Gen. J. R. Deane, March 16, 1945, passing telephone message from Lt Col J. D. Wilmeth, NARA, RG 334, Box 24, POW Folder Mar 13–March 26.

Gross, Jan Tomasz, *Revolution from Abroad: the Soviet Conquest of Poland's Western Ukraine and Western Belorussia*, Princeton: Princeton University Press, 2002.

Hall, Major Paul S., "Supplement No. 4 to Interim Report on Odessa Transit Camp," March 8, 1945, NARA, RG 334, Box 22, POW Folder.

Hampton, Colonel Thomas K., Cables T-2668 and T-2756 to USSTAF concerning assignment of Capt. Trimble, February 8 and 20, 1945, AFHRA, Reel B5124, Eascom Cables, Sept 1944–May 1945.

Hampton, Colonel Thomas K., Cable T-3103 to USSTAF and 384th BG concerning crash-landed B-17, March 17, 1945, NARA, Box 24, POW Folder, File 3/13-3/26.

Hampton, Colonel Thomas K., Cable T-3457 to Gen. Deane concerning members of court for Lt King court martial, April 4, 1945, NARA, Box, RG 334, Box 67.

Hampton, Colonel Thomas K., Cable T-3550 to Gen. Hill concerning B-17 on Soviet mission, April 11, 1945, NARA, RG 334, Box 67.

Herbert, Ulrich, "Forced Laborers in the 'Third Reich'—an Overview," *International Labor and Working-Class History* 58 (Fall 2000) S: 192–218. Available online at herbert .geschichte.uni-freiburg.de/herbert/beitraege/vor_2003/24.pdf (retrieved January 24, 2014).

Herbert, Ulrich, *Hitler's Foreign Workers*, Cambridge: Cambridge University Press, 1997.

Higham, Robin D. S., and Abigail T. Siddall, *Flying Combat Aircraft of the USAAF-USAF*, vol. 2, Ames: Iowa State University Press, 1978.

Hill, Major General Edmund W., Cable M21977 to Colonel Hampton, Eastern Command, on assumption of command, December 8, 1944, NARA, RG 334, Box 63, Adjutant General File.

Hill, Major General Edmund W., Cable MX-22201 to Adjutant General, War Department, on Soviet non-cooperation with aircraft salvage clearances, December 29, 1944, NARA, RG 334, Box 16.

Hill, Major General Edmund W., Cable M23371 to USSTAF and War Department on Soviet dismantling and theft of US aircraft in Poland, March 22, 1945, NARA, RG 334, Box 16.

Hill, Major General Edmund W., Cable M-23827 to Gen. Spaatz, USSTAF, requesting experienced commander for Eastern Command, April 12, 1945, NARA, RG 334, Box 63, Adjutant General File.

Hill, Major General Edmund W., Letter to Gen. Spaatz, USSTAF, on promotion of officer (Capt. Robert M. Trimble), May 16, 1945, NARA, RG 334, Box 63, Adjutant General File.

Infield, Glenn B., *The Poltava Affair: The Secret World War II Operation That Foreshadowed the Cold War*, London: Robert Hale, 1973.

Kaluta, Lieutenant William R., Official history of Eastern Command, 3 vols: *Eascom History: 1 October 1944–1 April 1945, Eascom History, 1 April 1945–23 June 1945, Photographic History Eastern Command, 1 October 1944–23 June 1945*, NARA, RG 334, Box 66, and the AFHRA, reel 7216.

Langbein, Hermann, *People in Auschwitz*, Chapel Hill: University of North Carolina Press, 2004.

Leavell, Byrd Stuart, *The 8th Evac: A History of the University of Virginia Hospital Unit in World War II*, Richmond, VA: Dietz Press, 1970.

Lefèvre, Pierre, "La Fin Tragique de Trois STO," published online by Association pour la Mémoire de la Déportation du Travail Forcé, www.requis-deportes-sto.com /index.php/temoignages/autres/la-fin-tragique-de-trois-sto (retrieved January 24, 2014).

Lepawsky, Major Albert, *History of Eastern Command, USSTAF, 1941–1945* (official history of Eastern Command), AFHRA, reel 7216.

Marr, David G., *Vietnam: State, War, and Revolution (1945–1946)*, Berkeley: University of California Press, 2013.

Matloff, Maurice, *US Army in WW2: War Department, Strategic Planning for Coalition Warfare*, Washington, DC: Government Printing Office, 1959.

McAllister, James, *No Exit: America and the German Problem, 1943–1954*, New York: Cornell University Press, 2002.

McDonough, James L., *The Wars of Myron King: A B-17 Pilot Faces WWII and U.S.-Soviet Intrigue*, Knoxville: University of Tennessee Press, 2009.

Metz, David, *Master of Airpower: General Carl A. Spaatz*, ebook edition, Novato CA: Presidio, 1988.

Miller, Donald L., *Eighth Air Force: The American Bomber Crews in Britain*, London: Aurum, 2008.

Moore, Gale, "California to Combat in Eighty-One Days" in *Briefing Notes*, journal of the 493rd Bombardment Group (H) Memorial Association, 2007.

Nicholson, Major Donald S., Actual and necessary expenses of Ex-POWs and Casual Combat Personnel at Lwów, Poland, February 21, 1945, NARA, RG 334, Box 67.

Nicholson, Major Donald S., Mission interrogation of Lt Barnett crew, March 17, 1945, Eastern Command, NARA, RG 334, Box 67, Interrogation Reports Folder.

OSS/London, *Special Operations Branch and Secret Intelligence Branch War Diaries*, 12 vols (8 reels microfilm), Frederick, MD: University Publications of America, 1985.

Parrish, Michael, *The Lesser Terror: Soviet State Security, 1939–1953*, Westport, CT: Praeger, 1996.

Persico, Joseph E., *Piercing the Reich: the Penetration of Nazi Germany by OSS Agents During World War II*, London: Michael Joseph, 1979.

Plokhy, S. M., *Yalta: The Price of Peace*, New York: Viking, 2010.

Ratkin, Vladimir (transl. Zaur Eylanbekov), "Russia's US Bomber Force," *Combat Aircraft* 4/1 (January 2002): 87–89.

Rees, Laurence, *Auschwitz: The Nazis and the "Final Solution"*, London: BBC Books, 2005.

Rees, Laurence, *World War Two Behind Closed Doors: Stalin, the Nazis and the West*, London: BBC Books, 2008.

Roberts, Geoffrey, *Victory at Stalingrad: The Battle That Changed History*, Abingdon: Routledge, 2002.

Samuel, Wolfgang W. E., *American Raiders: The Race to Capture the Luftwaffe's Secrets*, Jackson MS: University of Mississippi Press, 2004.

Schoenberner, Gerhard, *The Yellow Star: The Persecution of the Jews in Europe, 1933–1945*, New York: Fordham University Press.

Sella, Amnon, *The Value of Human Life in Soviet Warfare*, New York: Routledge, 1992.

Task Force Russia, "TFR1 Repatriation of WWII POWs; German-held POWs transiting Odessa; Robert Reynolds Article; Americans in GULAG." Available online at Library of Congress, lcweb2.loc.gov/frd/tfrussia/tfrhtml/tfr001-1.html (retrieved December 27, 2013).

"Time sure flies!" (obituary recollection of John Matles), *Voice of the Valley*, December 4, 2012. Available online at www.voiceofthevalley.com/community_news/one_mans _opinion/article_9821fcb0-3e35-11e2-ab25-0019bb30f31a.html (retrieved January 16, 2014).

Trimble, Captain Robert M., Cable T 3706 to Gen. Deane concerning report of Capt. J. Pogue's salvage team, April 22, 1945, NARA, RG 334, Box 67.

Trimble, Captain Robert M., "Report on Flight to Rzeszow, Staszow, Lwów, Poland," signed by Capt. Trimble, Lt Jessee, Sergeant Matles, March 17,1945, NARA, RG 334, Box 67.

USAAF 493rd Bombardment Group mission reports, transcribed and compiled by David Schmitt.

USAAF interrogation report, 493rd Bombardment Group Mission #55, September 12, 1944.

USAAF interrogation report, 493rd Bombardment Group Mission #100, December 30, 1944.

USAAF 863rd Bombardment Squadron, 493rd Bombardment Group Record of Sorties, crew of R. M. Trimble.

US Department of State, *Foreign Relations of the United States: Diplomatic Papers, 1945, Europe*, vol. V, Washington, DC: US Government Printing Office, 1945.

USMA, West Point, *The Howitzer* yearbook, Class of 1934, West Point, New York: United States Military Academy.

Vergolina, Rudy, *Reflections of a Prisoner of War*, unpublished memoir in possession of Vergolina family.

Vinson, Ben, *Flight: The Story of Virgil Richardson, A Tuskegee Airman in Mexico*, New York: Palgrave Macmillan, 2004.

Wadley, Patricia L., *Even One Is Too Many: An Examination of the Soviet Refusal to Repatriate Liberated American World War II Prisoners of War*, unpublished PhD dissertation, Texas Christian University, 1993.

Wall, Irwin M., "Harry S. Truman and Charles de Gaulle" in *De Gaulle and the United States*, eds R. O. Paxton & N. Wahl, Oxford: Berg, 1994, pp. 117–129.

Watson, George M., *Secretaries and Chiefs of Staff of the United States Air Force*, Washington, DC: United States Air Force, 2001.

Weeks, Albert L. *Russia's Life-Saver: Lend-Lease Aid to the U.S.S.R. in World War II*, Lanham, MD: Lexington Books, 2004.

Weir, Gordon, "Navigating Through World War II: A Memoir of the War Years." Available online at www.arizonahandbook.com/8thAF.htm (retrieved October 6, 2013).

Whitlock, Flint, *The Rock of Anzio: From Sicily To Dachau, A History of the U.S. 45th Infantry Division*, Boulder, CO: Westview, 1998.

Wilmeth, Lieutenant Colonel James D., "Memorandum to General Deane reference Lublin Trip," April 13, 1945, NARA, RG 334, Box 22, POW Folder.

Wilmeth, Lieutenant Colonel James D., "Report of interview with three Prisoners of War," February 21, 1945, NARA, RG 334, Box 23, POW Folder, Mar 1–Mar 12.

Wilmeth, Lieutenant Colonel James D., "Report on a Visit to Lublin, Poland, February 27–March 28 1945," NARA, RG 334, Box 22.

Wilmeth, Lieutenant Colonel James D., "Russians Are Not Forty Feet Tall," *Military Review* 34/7 (1954): 3–8.

World War 2 POW Archive, "POW Record for Richard J Beadle." Available online at www.ww2pow.info/index.php?page=directory&rec=43215 (retrieved January 9, 2014).

Yones, Eliyahu, *Smoke in the Sand: The Jews of Lvov in the War Years 1939–1944*, Jerusalem/New York: Gefen, 2004.

NOTES

Prologue

1 By the end of 1944, more than 5 million forced foreign laborers, male and female, were working in German agriculture and industry, of whom about 1.3 million were French (see Herbert, *Hitler's Foreign Workers*, as well as Beyer and Schneider, "Forced Labor," for summaries).

2 The Soviet military and security police sometimes put abandoned Nazi prison camps to their own uses. For instance, the Janowska concentration camp in Lwów was taken over by the NKVD and used as a prison camp (Bartov, "White Spaces and Black Holes," p. 324). Likewise, the Majdanek death camp was briefly used to hold liberated British and American POWs (Wilmeth, "Report," pp. 2–3).

Chapter 1: One Lucky Bastard

1 Five members of the combat crew bailed out over the North Sea, while the remaining flight crew went on to make a forced landing at RAF Woodbridge, some five miles short of Debach (Freeman et al., *Mighty Eighth*, p. 410). Woodbridge, being near the coast, received thousands of emergency landings during the course of the war.

2 The 493rd did indeed move to the former fighter station at Little Walden in March 1945, while repairs were effected. They returned to Debach in April 1945 and flew their last combat mission on April 20. In August 1945 the 493rd returned to the United States (Bowyer, *Action Stations*, p. 92; Bowman and Woodall, *Helton's Hellcats*, p. 9).

3 This crew was fairly unusual in that all but three of them stayed together and completed their tour simultaneously (USAAF 863rd Bombardment Squadron, Record of Sorties). Crews were often split up, and their members finished their tours individually (or not at all, in many cases).

4 Mission #76 to Merseberg on October 30, 1944, was recalled when already over Germany, due to low cirrus cloud over the target and very heavy contrails from the bombers, obscuring one another's view (USAAF 493rd Bombardment Group mission reports). As they had experienced some light flak en route, the crews were credited with a combat mission (see Weir, "Navigating Through World War II").

5 USAAF interrogation report, Mission #100.

6 Elbert Helton was born in Clifton, Texas, in 1915, and joined the Army Air Corps (as it was then called) in 1936. By the time he took command of the newly created 493rd Bombardment Group in November 1943, at the age of twenty-eight, he was already a veteran squadron commander and combat pilot (Bowman and Woodall, *Helton's Hellcats*, p. 26).

7 Casualties from the mission of December 30, 1944, (mission #100 for the 493rd BG) were relatively light. Altogether the 3rd Air Division, of which the 493rd Bomb Group was a part, dispatched 526 bombers to various targets. Three aircraft were lost, 37 damaged, and 24 men were MIA (Freeman et al., *The Mighty Eighth*, p. 409).

8 The notorious Magdeburg mission took place on September 12, 1944. Due to slack formation flying, the bombers were insufficiently protected by the arcs of fire from their guns. The 493rd was attacked front and rear by Fw 190s from JG 53 and JG 300. Seven bombers were shot down and many more were damaged, two so badly that they had to make forced landings in Belgium. According to the official mission report, of the B-17s shot down, four "went down in flames and exploded." Of the seven planes lost over the target, just "five or six chutes were seen" (Freeman et al., *The Mighty Eighth*, p. 345; Caldwell and Muller, *Luftwaffe over Germany*, p. 235; USAAF interrogation report, Mission #55).

9 At this time, 8th Air Force bomb groups each comprised four squadrons of twelve aircraft each (for a total of forty-eight; in 1945 squadron size increased to eighteen, for a total of seventy-two). Normal mission procedure was for three squadrons to fly while the fourth stood down. Squadrons took turns to stand down.

10 Including dead, wounded, and missing, the Eighth Air Force lost 34 percent of its aircrew personnel in combat, "the highest casualty rate in the American armed forces in World War II"; Eighth Air Force aircrew accounted for about one-tenth of all America's war dead (Miller, *Eighth Air Force*, p. 471).

11 On the mission of December 31, 1944, the 3rd Air Division again dispatched 526 bombers to various targets, including Misburg. Twenty-seven bombers were lost and 288 were damaged; 5 men were killed, 29 wounded, and 248 missing (Freeman et al., *The Mighty Eighth*, pp. 410–11). The 493rd Bomb Group lost one aircraft from the 862nd Squadron (Bowman and Woodall, *Helton's Hellcats*, p. 14).

12 Thirteen days later, on January 13, 1945, B-17 43-38271, *Big Buster*, in which Robert Trimble had flown his last mission, was shot down by flak near Bauschheim during a mission to Mainz, Germany. It was being piloted by Lieutenant Norman S. Lamoreaux, who had flown alongside Captain Trimble on the Kassel mission on December 30. Six of the crew were killed and three taken prisoner (Bowman and Woodall, *Helton's Hellcats*, p. 21; Freeman, *The B-17 Flying Fortress Story*, p. 244).

Chapter 2: An American in London

1 Grosvenor Square still has a strong American presence, with statues of Roosevelt and Eisenhower in the central garden, along with a memorial to 9/11. The building at the southeast corner of the square, which in 1945 was the US Embassy, now houses the Canadian High Commission. The US Embassy moved to new premises at the other end of the square in 1960. In 2017 the embassy will move again, to a new site on the far side of central London. Once it goes, all that will be left of "Little America" will be the statues.

2 As described by Dorothy Brannan, former WAAF barrage balloon operator, in BBC WW2 People's War archive, available online at www.bbc.co.uk/history/ww2peopleswar/stories /83/a4551383.shtml (retrieved February 23, 2014).

3 "Whitewash" was the call sign of the 493rd Bomb Group control tower, "Pillar" was the call sign of the 863rd Bomb Squadron, and 366 was the individual ID number of the aircraft Captain Trimble's crew was flying that day (Bowman and Woodall, *Helton's Hellcats*, p. 9; USAAF 493rd Bombardment Group mission reports).

4 OSS/London, War Diaries, vol. 7, Apr.–Jun. 1944, p. 3; vol. 8, passim.

5 Ibid.

6 Bowman, *Bedford Triangle*, pp. 60–64.

7 For example: "5. Do not ask Joes personal questions. (For example: Questions concerning name, job or background.) ... 15. Neither you, nor any member of your crew, will give the Joes any information concerning past, present, or future operations. This includes flight plan, routes, and altitudes, etc., of the operation tonight." From "Hints for Dispatchers" in OSS/London, *War Diaries*, vol. 6, Jan. to Mar. 1944, pp. 43–44.

8 Bowman, *Bedford Triangle*, p. 45.

9 Persico, *Piercing the Reich*, pp. 41–42; 169–70.

Chapter 3: The Long Way Round

1 Originally a B-17 crew numbered ten men. By this stage in the war, the threat from enemy fighters had reduced, and the crew complement had been reduced to nine by the deletion of one of the waist gunners (a single gunner was thus responsible for both guns).

2 US Consular Service passport issued to Captain Robert M. Trimble, January 22, 1945.

3 Most military aircraft of this period did not have the range to make the crossing from the United States to the UK in one leg.

4 The stop at Fortaleza and the journey to Africa were described in a short memoir written by the crew's radio operator, Sergeant Gale D. Moore (Moore, "California to Combat").

5 Sulfonamide (or "sulfa") is an antimicrobial drug that was the standard treatment for infection at this time. Antimicrobials preceded antibiotics and work differently.

6 The North American B-25 Mitchell, despite having only two Wright Cyclone engines (the same type used in the B-17), was notoriously loud due to the design of the engine cowlings and exhaust system (Higham and Siddall, *Flying Combat Aircraft*, p. 8).

7 "Way the hell out over northern New Mexico someplace [Trimble] let his hair down a little.... We dropped down so we were just buzzing the coyotes and cacti and Johnson, the co-pilot played 'I'll Walk Alone' on his trumpet over the command radio." (Moore, "California to Combat.")

8 Leavell, *The 8th Evac*, pp. 50ff.

9 The description of the consulate here is based partly on the recollections of Tuskegee airman Virgil Richardson, who stayed there a couple of months after the Trimble crew (Vinson, *Flight*, pp. 65–66).

10 It's unclear why the crew was sent here, as it was a training base for fighter pilots, and a transshipment stop for troops and cargo going to the Pacific.

11 Both songs were hits during World War II. The former was a hit twice in 1942—for the Glenn Miller Orchestra and for the Andrews Sisters. "Till Then" was a hit in September 1944 (toward the end of Eleanor's pregnancy) for the the Mills Brothers. Both songs are about the parting of young couples in wartime. Whereas "Apple Tree" is humorous, "Till Then" is a much more moving song and was the one Eleanor remembered being particularly affected by.

12 A *ghalyan* is the Persian equivalent of the Arab hookah pipe.

13 Huge quantities of British aid and American Lend-Lease supplies were shipped into the USSR during the war. The Persian Corridor was one of the key routes, the others being the northern sea route into Murmansk and the Alaska-Siberia route. See Weeks, *Russia's Life-Saver*, pp. 27, 112–16; Matloff, *US Army in WW2*, pp. 283–84.

14 Mohammed Reza Shah was particularly deeply involved in American diplomacy in Iran (Afkhami, *Life and Times of the Shah*, pp. 161–66 ff).

15 Ibid, p. 311 ff.

16 The Tehran-Poltava route was served by three Poltava-based Soviet-crewed C-46 Commandos, flying twice a week (Kaluta, vol. I, ch. II, pp. 12–13). The C-46 model was older, much less reliable, and less numerous than the C-47, which may be why the USAAF allowed the Russians to have them.

17 Robert didn't recall who these were. Most likely they were officers returning from leave in Cairo, which was the regular leave destination for Poltava personnel.

18 A reference to this incident is given in Kaluta, vol. I, ch. II, p. 14.

Chapter 4: Behind the Curtain

1 Lepawsky, *History of Eastern Command*, chapter IV, p. 90.

2 Ibid, p. 101ff.

3 Eastern Command report on investigation into June 21/22 raid, copy included with Lepawsky, *History of Eastern Command*.

4 Ibid; also Infield, *Poltava Affair*, pp. 147–51.

5 Brigadier General Alfred A. Kessler, CO Eastern Command, interviewed July 5, 1944, transcript included in Lepawsky, *History of Eastern Command*.

6 Kaluta, vol. I, ch. I, p. 2.

7 Infield, *Poltava Affair*, pp. 162–63. At Mirgorod, most of the planes had been removed, but massive quantities of fuel and munitions were destroyed.

8 Rees, *World War Two Behind Closed Doors*, p. 54.

9 Ibid, p. 182ff. The atrocities became known as the Katyn Massacre because of the original discovery, but the majority of the killings were done elsewhere.

10 Deane, *Strange Alliance*, pp. 55–56.

11 CIA, "Memoranda for the President," pp. 66–67.

12 Ibid, pp. 73–74.

13 Deane, *Strange Alliance*, pp. 55–63.

14 Hill, Cable M21977 to Hampton.

15 Bowman, *Bedford Triangle*, p. 45.

16 Ibid, pp. 40–46.

17 If it is true that Hill was inserted as a deniable conduit for the OSS, it is extremely unlikely that it was done expressly for the purpose of POW exfiltration. More likely he was intended as a general OSS contact who could be used if and when required. The Soviets were deeply suspicious of him and at the end of the war tried to prevent his departure from the USSR (Infield, *Poltava Affair*, pp. 218–20).

18 Captain Trimble's arrival at Poltava was either February 14, based on the date given by Kaluta (vol. I, ch. II, p. 14) for the stopover at Armavir, or February 15, the date recorded for Trimble's appointment as assistant operations officer (Hill, letter to Spaatz on promotion of officer, May 16, 1945). Since it is possible that the stopovers in Armavir and Rostov lasted more than one night each (due to the continuing bad weather), February 15 is accepted here as the correct arrival date.

19 One such person was planning officer Major Albert Lepawsky, who became one of Eastern Command's official historians (see Lepawsky, *History of Eastern Command*, ch. VIII, p. 90ff, for his summary of Hampton's character).

20 Lepawsky, *History of Eastern Command*, ch. VIII, p. 91.

21 On February 8, Hampton cabled USSTAF asking for "info on nature of Capt Trimble's assignment to Eastern Command." Hampton received clarification from General Spaatz on February 11, and on February 20 he requested that Trimble's thirty-day temporary duty status be replaced with a permanent assignment (Hampton, cables to USSTAF concerning assignment of Captain Trimble, February 1945). We only have Hampton's side of this exchange; Spaatz's reply is missing. The query appears, however, to be concerned with the temporary/permanent nature of Trimble's appointment rather than any covert duties.

22 An eyewitness description of Majdanek was published in the *New York Times* of August 30, 1944 (quoted in Schoenberner, *Yellow Star*, p. 229).

23 Sella, *Value of Human Life in Soviet Warfare*, pp. 100–110. The full text of Order No. 270, including Stalin's preamble, is given in Roberts, *Victory at Stalingrad*, pp. 197–202; see also Plokhy, *Yalta*, p. 294ff.

24 Brackman, *Secret File of Joseph Stalin*, p. 297.

25 Sella, *Value of Human Life in Soviet Warfare*, p. 103.

26 Deane, *Strange Alliance*, p. 184; Wadley, *Even One Is Too Many*, ch. II.

27 Buhite, *Decisions at Yalta*, pp. 60–61.

Chapter 5: A Brutal Awakening

1 Lepawsky, *History of Eastern Command*, ch. VII, p. 98.

2 Kaluta, *Eascom History*, vol. I, ch. IV, p. 16. Even General Deane, head of the Military Mission, was not immune, remarking (*Strange Alliance*, p. 5) that "all [Russian] employees of foreigners" were used as informers by the NKVD.

3 Cable from US State Department to US Embassy in Moscow, February 14, 1945, quoted in Wadley, *Even One Is Too Many*, p. 111.

4 Wadley, *Even One Is Too Many*, p. 113. Colonel Jerry Sage had been captured in North Africa in 1943 while working for the OSS behind enemy lines. Sage was imprisoned in Stalag Luft III and is said to have been the model for the character played by Steve McQueen in *The Great Escape*. Colonel Charles Kouns was from the 82nd Airborne Division and had been captured during a behind-the-lines operation in Italy.

5 Kaluta, vol. I, ch. III, p. 36.

6 Deane, *Strange Alliance*, p. 195.

7 Kaluta, vol. I, ch. III, p. 36.

8 There is some doubt about this. Deane (*Strange Alliance*, p. 195) gives the date as the 14th, but Kaluta (vol. I, ch. III, p. 36) gives the 15th. On the other hand, Wadley (*Even One Is Too Many*, p. 118, citing Wilmeth's diary) gives the 16th. February 15 is taken here as an average.

9 Deane (*Strange Alliance*, ch. XI) consistently describes his feelings throughout this time as frustratation and/or disappointed optimism. Ever the diplomat, he gives little indication of the fact that he (and most of the American parties involved) privately expected the Russians to default on their obligations. In fact he had little faith in the official contact-team idea and had argued against it to General Marshall, the chief of staff (Marshall, cable to Deane, March 3, 1945, in US State Department, *Foreign Relations*, pp. 1072–73).

10 Wadley, *Even One Is Too Many*, p. 114.

11 Lieutenant John G. Winant Jr. was a B-17 pilot, shot down on a raid against Münster in October 1943 (Buhite, *Decisions at Yalta*, p. 60; *New York Times* obituary of John G. Winant Jr., November 2, 1993). Lieutenant Winant escaped Nazi captivity in May 1945 and was helped by the Red Cross to reach American lines.

12 They were still exchanging Christmas cards in the early 1950s, but apparently lost touch after that.

13 Bowman, *US Eighth Air Force in Europe*, ch. 4.

14 Michael Kowal, quoted in Parisi, "New Jersey Journal," *New York Times*, November 24, 1985. After the war, Kowal expressed his feelings about his wartime service by naming his eldest daughter after his B-17, *Carolee*.

15 Michael Kowal, quoted in Bowman, *US Eighth Air Force in Europe*, ch. 4. Kowal describes performing a sideslip in a Piper Cub that would bring the tail in front of the nose, and claims that he attempted (unsuccessfully) to do something similar in a B-17 under attack by fighters.

16 Lepawsky, *History of Eastern Command*, ch. VIII, pp. 108–9. As with Hampton, Lepawsky is critical of Kowal, describing him as "truculent" toward the Russians. However, a top secret cable from General Hill to the War Department on December 29 suggests that the barring of Kowal resulted from the "desire to preclude observation by foreign observers of activities at or near their front lines" (Hill, Cable MX-22201).

17 Lepawsky, *History of Eastern Command*, ch. VIII, p. 96.

18 Persico, *Piercing the Reich*, pp. 41–2; 169–70.

19 Given Soviet security at the base, the most likely way would have been on a diplomatic flight via Moscow. These were fairly frequent, as Poltava was a staging point for US diplomatic staff traveling between Moscow and the United States, as well as the Tehran route. No information is available on how long the two agents had been at Poltava prior to Captain Trimble's arrival.

20 Information about the identities and backgrounds of OSS intelligence agents was never shared. Even in the mission reports contained in the OSS/London *War Diaries*, declassified in 1985, the identities of agents were redacted.

21 OSS/London, *War Diaries*, vol. 7, to Dec. 1944, pp. 34–47; vol. 12, pp. 289–93. The Eagle project was still in the training phase in February 1945, scheduled for commencement in the spring. The agent personnel were former Polish soldiers who had been forced into service with the German Army and captured in Normandy. Eagle was expedited when the end of the war seemed imminent, but it is unlikely that fully trained agents would have been available by early February.

22 OSS/London, *War Diaries*, vol. 7, Apr.–Jun. 1944, pp. 3–4; Jan.–Jun. 1945, pp. 38–50. The operation had been initiated early in 1944, and by February 1945 Tissue agents were entering Germany via Sweden. The details of training come from the *War Diaries*' account of the Eagle project (vol. 7, to Dec. 1944, pp. 42–44), which was similar. Agents did 624 hours of paramilitary training over the course of five months.

23 Rees, *Auschwitz*, p. 329

24 Langbein, *People in Auschwitz*, pp. 57–58.

25 Described by Primo Levi (quoted in Langbein, *People in Auschwitz*, pp. 473–74). Levi was in the Buna-Monowitz camp ("Auschwitz III"), three miles from Birkenau, at the time of liberation.

26 Langbein, *People in Auschwitz*, p. 473.

27 Rees, *Auschwitz*, p. 329.

28 Deane, *Strange Alliance*, pp. 191–94.

Chapter 6: Running with the Bird Dogs

1 Stalag III-C was liberated on January 31 and Stalag XX-A on February 1. An officers' camp, Oflag 64, had been liberated earlier, on January 21. However, in all the various accounts of POWs in Poland, it is vanishingly rare to find cases of officers and enlisted men grouping together. It seems that the emotional criteria for POWs to bond with one another included similarity of combat experiences prior to captivity.

2 Vergolina, *Reflections of a Prisoner of War*.

3 Beadle, "Joint Statement."

4 Beadle, "Joint Statement"; Wilmeth, "Report on a Visit to Lublin," p. 4.

5 Wilmeth, "Report of Interview," p. 2.

6 "Intourist" is an abbreviation of *inostrannyy turist* ("foreign tourist"). Intourist was originally founded in 1929 as a commercial company, but was co-opted by Stalin in the 1930s for propaganda and security purposes, and filled with NKVD personnel (David-Fox, *Showcasing the Great Experiment*, p. 58 and passim). Intourist still exists, but is now an independent commercial entity.

7 In his recollections, Robert did not describe the coding method in detail, remarking merely that it revolved around messages dictated by phone, and that the coding system was simple. OSS agents were intensively trained in covert communication and had several secure encryption methods for use in the field. It is unlikely that these methods were used in this case, because of the likelihood of messages being intercepted by the NKVD; if Captain Trimble were known to be receiving encrypted messages, regardless of their content, he would certainly have been expelled by the Soviets from Poland (as had been Hampton and Kowal due to suspicions that they were spying). Since Robert was in Poland ostensibly as an aircrew rescue and salvage officer, the messages were presumably designed to resemble intelligence pertaining to that. A good deal of information about locations could be conveyed openly in that way, with secret information embedded inconspicuously.

8 The terms "class A agent" and "class B agent" were hardly ever used outside bureaucratic circles and weren't known to most military personnel. Because of this, and the hectic, disorientating nature of his briefing, when Captain Trimble was told that he was going to be a class B agent, he assumed it was in reference to his attachment to the OSS, and guessed that the two field agents he had met must be class A agents.

9 This was Major Donald S. Nicholson, Eastern Command's meteorologist (Wilmeth, "Report of Interview"; Nicholson report on "Actual and necessary expenses"). Don Nicholson (personal communication to Lee Trimble, February 6, 2014) does not now recall being made a "class B agent"—an indication of how rarely used and little-known the term was.

10 On February 15, the day of Robert's appointment, General Deane sent a cable to General Richards at the War Department, requesting retrospective approval for his appointment of an agent officer for the purpose of POW contact and relief (Deane, Cable M-22725 to Gen. Richards). Deane doesn't name the officer appointed. It is possible that it was Colonel Wilmeth, who was being briefed to enter Poland at this time to inspect POW facilities. In that case it is strange that (a) Deane doesn't name him, since his mission was official;

(b) Wadley (*Even One Is Too Many*, ch. III–IV) doesn't mention Wilmeth having such a status; and (c) Wilmeth himself doesn't appear to have had direct access to funds from a finance officer and had to ask Deane to send money (Wilmeth, "Report on a Visit to Lublin"; Wadley, *Even One Is Too Many*, p. 129). Another Moscow officer, Major Paul S. Hall, was appointed an agent officer and sent to inspect POW facilities at Odessa, but that was somewhat later in February (Deane, *Strange Alliance*, p. 197; Kaluta, vol. I, ch. V, p. 12), so Hall is also unlikely to be the officer referred to in Deane's February 15 letter.

11 Kaluta, vol. I, ch. V, pp. 13–14.

12 The information that all POWs must go to Odessa was passed to Eastern Command by Moscow on February 18 (Kaluta, vol. I, ch. III, p. 37).

13 Kaluta, vol. I, ch. III, pp. 37–38.

14 Ibid, p. 38.

15 "I am an American."

16 "Are they Krauts?"

Chapter 7: *Fighting Bastard of the Ukraine*

1 Narrative based on recollections by Sergeant Don MacLeod (ball-turret gunner) and Lieutenant Cornelius Daly (navigator), as told to William MacLeod (personal communication to Lee Trimble, February 12, 2014). Further details come from recollections by Sergeant Arnold Echola (Doherty and Ward, *Snetterton Falcons*; Geoff Ward, personal communication to Lee Trimble, February 14, 2014). Circumstances of landing supplemented by salvage report by Captain Robert M. Trimble (Trimble, "Report on Flight to Rzeszów," pp. 1–2).

2 Photo of Captain I. I. Kamynin, Lieutenant Tillman Collection, Texas Military Forces Museum.

3 Recollection by Sergeant Don MacLeod, as told to William MacLeod (personal communication to Lee Trimble, February 12, 2014).

4 Kaluta, vol. I, ch. III, p. 13.

5 Tadeusz Kratke served briefly with the French Air Force and, after the fall of France, joined the RAF, in which he flew Spitfires in No. 317 (Polish) Squadron (Cynk, *Polish Air Force*, pp. 136, 202, 216). A photo of Pilot Officer Kratke with his Spitfire can be seen at www.polishairforce.pl/dyw317zdj.html (retrieved February 14, 2014).

6 Letter to Tadeusz Kratke written at Staszów, February 17, 1945 (with translation) and photo of Lieutenant Kratke, Lieutenant Tillman Collection, Texas Military Forces Museum.

7 Shortened form of Tadeusz.

8 317 Squadron, *Chronicle*, p. 46.

9 The officer was Major Donald S. Nicholson, Eastern Command's meteorologist. The Tillman crew flew out of Lwów after three days and reached Poltava on February 21 (Kaluta, vol. I, ch. III, p. 13).

10 According to Lepawsky (*History of Eastern Command*, ch. V, pp. 64–65), the sobriquet was originally bestowed on Eastern Command by people from Persian Gulf Command.

Chapter 8: Kasia

1 The D-ration candy bars produced in the early war years were notoriously unpleasant compared to commercial ones. They had been deliberately designed to taste "just a little better than a boiled potato" in order to prevent troops gorging on them. But by 1945 the original "Logan bars" had been replaced by the much more pleasant chocolate made by Hershey (Fisher and Fisher, *Food in the American Military*, p. 148). The Russian soldiers were immensely fond of these chocolate bars, and thousands of them were stolen from Poltava during the final weeks of Eastern Command.

2 Now Łambinowice, Poland.

3 In his recollections, Robert was unable to remember (if he ever knew) the name of this camp. There were more than forty sub-camps attached to the Auschwitz complex, of which about a dozen were in the specific local area in which this encounter took place; it could have been almost any one of them.

4 Kaluta (vol. I, ch. IV, p. 16) remarks that this was a general pattern for American personnel on salvage missions; Red Army officers were happy to cooperate with Americans, and did so generously, until the NKVD put pressure on them to stop.

5 Wadley, *Even One Is Too Many*, pp. 121–23.

6 Captain Trimble's forebodings about Russian bad faith were shared by Colonel Wilmeth himself (quoted in Kaluta, vol. I, ch. III, pp. 39–40).

7 There are various theories about the origin of the term "short snorter." It is probably some long-forgotten association with alcohol, a "snorter" being a measure of spirits.

8 In 1941 the United States Army Air Corps had been changed to the United States Army Air Forces, but the name of the branch on personnel records and in colloquial use continued to be "Air Corps."

9 It is inferred that Robert added this slogan, as it appears to have been written with the same pen as his signature, and although the style differs from his regular handwriting, it matches a style known to have been used by him when trying to write clearly (as in the next-of-kin fields in his passport).

10 Lieutenant Tillman was remembered by crewmember Sergeant Don MacLeod as an aloof character, who didn't mix much with his crew. This wasn't unusual between officers and enlisted men. The signatures that subsequently accumulated on the snorter were (as far as can be discerned) from either officers or civilians.

11 It is still not known who kept the snorter. But it surfaced in El Paso, Texas, in 1969, when it was sold to a dealer in WWII memorabilia. He hung on to it for decades, and eventually sold it on eBay. It was bought by collector Mike Allard, who believed he recognized the name R. M. Trimble, and contacted his acquaintance Lee Trimble, who confirmed the identification.

Chapter 9: Night of the Cossacks

1 Fitchen, Mission interrogation of Lt Beam crew.

2 Matles's rank is given in different sources as both master sergeant and first sergeant. The latter is believed to be correct at this time.

3 Kaluta, vol I, ch. II, pp. 17–18.

4 Colonel Hampton used this incident, and another near-fatal flying error that occurred a few days later on the return journey, in another attempt to have Lieutenant Roklikov removed from flying duties. General Kovalev, the Soviet commander at Poltava, again rebuffed the request, insisting that Lieutenant Roklikov had shown "unique skill and initiative" in both incidents (Kaluta, vol. I, ch. II, pp. 16–17).

5 The woman's identity isn't given in Captain Trimble's report, so it isn't known whether she was from the Kratke family who accommodated Lieutenant Tillman and his crew.

Chapter 10: Russian Roulette

1 Many downed US aircraft were repaired by Soviet teams before Americans could get to them. The Soviets claimed that they were intending to fly these planes out to USAAF units in Italy. On March 8, Colonel Hampton cabled Lieutenant General Ira C. Eaker, commander of the Twelfth and Fifteenth Air Forces in Italy, to inquire about the truth of this claim. By the middle of April, Eaker was able to report that, of several B-17s, B-24s, and P-51 Mustangs reported by the Soviets as repaired and returned, only two B-24s had actually arrived. The rest disappeared (Hill, Cable M23371 to USSTAF, March 22, 1945; Kaluta, vol. I, ch. II, p. 29). Many of the American bombers ended up with the 890 BAP (Bomber Aviation Regiment), one of the Soviet rear units. Its rear pilots evaluated stolen B-17s and B-24s, using them as part of a research program to develop the USSR's own heavy bomber, the Tupolev Tu 4, which was mainly reverse engineered from the Boeing B-29 (Ratkin, "Russia's US Bomber Force").

2 Lepawsky, *History of Eastern Command*, ch. IV, pp. 35–40.

3 The same month, a P-51 was reported crash-landed at Kirovograd in the Ukraine, but when an investigator was sent from Poltava, there was nothing there (Kaluta, vol. I, ch. II, pp. 27–29).

4 Lepawsky, *History of Eastern Command*, ch. III, pp.46–47. In February 1945, Colonel Hampton gave instructions to USSTAF HQ advising aircrews on how to identify themselves to Soviet troops, as well as how to avoid antagonizing them. The advice included carrying a passport and a card with the word "American" in Polish, Ukrainian, and Russian, and presenting a smart appearance with all US Army insignia displayed clearly on the uniform (Kaluta, vol. I, ch. II, p. 28). Some of these measures were easier said than done.

5 It didn't go well (Kaluta, vol. I, ch. II, pp. 16–17). Roklikov's takeoff was even worse than his landing. Despite the delicate condition of the repaired C-47, he buzzed the town of Staszów several times and nearly collided with a church spire. Taking violent evasive action, he almost stalled the plane, and dived it to prevent the stall. The passengers and loose cargo were thrown around, and one of the American mechanics was injured. Rok-

likov himself had failed to secure his own safety belt and was thrown out of his seat, almost losing control of the aircraft completely. The Soviet authorities still insisted that he was a skilled pilot and refused to remove him from duty.

6 Ellis B. Woodward, pilot, 493rd Bomb Group, quoted in Bowman, *B-17 Combat Missions*, p. 29.

Chapter 11: *Suffer the Lost Prisoners*

1 Beadle, "Joint Statement." Beadle's rank was actually technician fourth grade, or T/4; however, T/4s were informally accorded the title Sergeant, and wore a three-stripe rank insignia.

2 Vergolina, *Reflections of a Prisoner of War*, pp. 18–19.

3 Beadle, "Joint Statement"; Wilmeth, "Report on a Visit to Lublin," pp. 9, 12.

4 Formerly part of Germany, now Gorzów Wielkopolski, Poland.

5 Formerly part of Germany, now Chwarszczany, Poland.

6 World War 2 POW Archive, "POW Record for Richard J Beadle."

7 Whitlock, *Rock of Anzio*, pp. 242–45.

8 Quoted in Whitlock, *Rock of Anzio*, p. 244. Richard Beadle earned the Silver Star for his conduct at Anzio; citation 45th Infantry Division, General Order No. 168 (1944).

9 Wadley, *Even One Is Too Many*, pp. 119–20.

10 Kisil was a technician fifth grade, or T/5. Just as T/4s were given the courtesy title Sergeant, T/5s were commonly addressed as Corporal.

11 Deane, *Strange Alliance*, p. 195.

12 Wadley, *Even One Is Too Many*, p. 123.

13 Wilmeth, "Report on a Visit to Lublin," pp. 1–2.

14 USMA, *Howitzer Yearbook*, p. 230.

15 Wadley, *Even One Is Too Many*, pp. 128–29; Wilmeth, "Report on a Visit to Lublin," pp. 2–3.

16 Wilmeth, "Report on a Visit to Lublin," p. 15.

17 Wilmeth, "Memorandum to General Deane," pp. 6–7.

18 Foregger ("Soviet Rails to Odessa," p. 844) puts the total figure for Americans evacuated by ship from Odessa from March to June 1945 at 2,858. In addition, there were 4,310 British and nearly 30,000 other nationalities.

19 Conversation summarized in Wilmeth, "Report on a Visit to Lublin," pp. 4–5.

20 Deane wrote to him: "We have had a few messages from you but they have been badly garbled." (Deane, Letter to Wilmeth, March 10).

21 The official exchange rate through Russian banks was 5 rubles or zlotys to 1 US dollar (Wadley, *Even One Is Too Many*, pp. 131–32). On the black market, rates of up to 200 rubles or zlotys to the dollar could be obtained, but at Soviet insistence, the Military Mission had barred US personnel from taking advantage of this exchange rate (Lepawsky, *History of Eastern Command*, ch. V, pp. 91–93).

22 Wadley, *Even One Is Too Many*, pp. 144–45.

23 Wadley, *Even One Is Too Many*, p. 146; Wilmeth, "Memorandum to General Deane," pp. 3–4.

24 Beadle in his statement estimates forty, but the figure given by Wilmeth ("Report on a Visit to Lublin," p. 6) is fifty-four.

25 Gould was from Croydon, Surrey, and served in the 5th Battalion of the Buffs (Rudy Vergolina address book; Beadle, "Joint Statement," Gould copy). He is not listed in contemporary British POW records compiled by the Red Cross; however, these records are not always complete or accurate.

26 Beadle ("Joint Statement") calls it the Russian border, but that is impossible; it must have been Ukraine (which was generally referred to by Americans as "Russia" at this time).

27 Beadle, "Joint Statement"; the names are given in Wadley, *Even One Is Too Many*, p. 144.

Chapter 12: American Gentlemen

1 The cliff or bluff at Lwów-Sknilow was an eccentric and dangerous feature. It was used as a takeoff point by glider pilots who used the airfield before the war. The cliff is now gone, erased by the construction of a modern airport.

2 Nicholson, Mission interrogation of Lt Barnett.

3 Hampton, Cable T-3103 to USSTAF, March 17.

4 Esa Lowry is the name as given in Captain Trimble's report ("Report on Flight to Rzeszow," p. 3); whether it is exact or a phonetic spelling of a more Slavonic name (e.g., Larysz) is not known.

5 When writing his report on the events in Lwów, Robert quoted his statement to Miss Lowry, still not noticing the accidental allusion. The fact that it was allowed to stand in the archived official report suggests that nobody else noticed the slip either. The probable reason is that he did in fact take some Americans home on this mission, despite the fact that it was not the mission's primary, let alone "only," interest.

6 Trimble ("Report on Flight to Rzeszow," p. 3) seems to imply that two POWs were found at the hotel upon arrival, along with the Barnett crew, but this appears to be a false impression caused by chronological compression in that part of the report; the POWs arrived later.

7 Beadle's description (in his "Joint Statement") and Matles's (given in Trimble's "Report on Flight to Rzeszow") differ. Beadle describes the rehabilitation center and the commandant's office being in the same place; Matles's version, used here, seems more accurate.

8 This is the term used by Beadle ("Joint Statement") and in many other contemporary sources referring to similar facilities. It was only after the war that the term "concentration camp" began to be exclusively associated with the extermination camps of the Holocaust. In this case it may have been apt; although it is impossible to be certain, the "rehabilitation center" was probably the former Nazi camp of Janowska in Lwów, which was reused by the NKVD for detention of political prisoners (Bartov, "White Spaces and Black Holes," p. 324).

9 Despite his rank, First Sergeant John Matles was a man of considerable authority in the military/diplomatic service. He went on to hold a number of highly responsible postings in US missions in various countries. According to a former Air Force colleague, Matles was offered a commission many times during his career but turned it down, believing that it would undermine his effectiveness ("Time sure flies!" in *Voice of the Valley*).

Chapter 13: Rising Tide

1 Rudy Vergolina (*Reflections*, p. 26) recalled that Captain Trimble "commanded some respect among the Russians." Vergolina misunderstood the circumstances of the Americans' presence in Lwów and mistakenly believed that "the Captain" (as he called him, having apparently forgotten his name in the intervening forty years), the Barnett crew, and the other POWs were all a single fourteen-man bomber crew. It was an understandable mistake for an infantryman to make in the circumstances.

2 Like Richard Beadle, Vergolina was actually a T/4 and accorded the courtesy title Sergeant.

3 Vergolina, *Reflections*, p. 27.

4 Rudy Vergolina's regiment landed on D + 1, but Rudy landed on D-Day itself, on temporary detachment with a unit in either the 1st or 29th Division (Joseph Vergolina, personal communication to Lee Trimble, March 3, 2014).

5 Vergolina, *Reflections*, p. 19.

6 This is the name given by Rudy Vergolina (*Reflections*, p. 21, although he misspells it "McNiesch"). He gives no further details, and no definite identification has been made. It is possible that the man was Gunner J. McNeish 2979918 of the Royal Artillery, who was a POW in Stalag XX-A at Torun, Poland ("Prisoners of War of British Army, WWII," unpublished data held by the Naval and Military Press, Ltd., available online through ancestry.com). Stalag XX-A was in the area where Vergolina says he met McNeish and had been liberated on February 1.

7 Wadley, *Even One Is Too Many*, p. 166.

8 B-17G 43-37687 eventually returned to England and rejoined the 96th Bomb Group. She was at last given a name—*Cash Crew's Pride*—and flew more missions before the war ended (William MacLeod, personal communication to Lee Trimble, February 12, 2014; and contemporary photo, Tillman collection, Texas Military Forces Museum). She survived the war, and returned to the USA, where her story ended in the great postwar aircraft graveyard at Kingman, Arizona (Freeman, *B-17 Flying Fortress Story*, p. 233).

9 According to Rudy Vergolina (*Reflections*, pp. 27–28), Jim McNeish was "sent on to a British embassy" before the rest of the group left Lwów. This must be a mistake, as Lepawsky (*History of Eastern Command*, ch. VI, p. 21) records that Captain Trimble brought two British POWs disguised as aircrew to Poltava on March 17.

10 Lepawsky, *History of Eastern Command*, ch. VI, p. 21.

11 See McDonald and Dronfield, *A Very Dangerous Woman: The Lives, Loves and Lies of Russia's Most Seductive Spy* (London: Oneworld, 2015).

12 Lepawsky, *History of Eastern Command*, ch. IV, p. 66.

13 Lepawsky, *History of Eastern Command*, ch. VI, p. 21.

14 Booth, Cable PX 27223 to Deane and Eastern Command.

Chapter 14: Far from Home

1 Wilmeth ("Report on a Visit to Lublin," p. 9) gives the number as seven, but official communications at the time (e.g., the cable from Stalin to Roosevelt cited below) give a figure of seventeen. Seventeen seems to include these seven plus other sick Americans who were later evacuated with them.

2 Wilmeth, "Report on a Visit to Lublin," p. 9.

3 Beadle, "Joint Statement"; Wilmeth, "Report on a Visit to Lublin," p. 12.

4 Wilmeth, unpublished memoir, cited in Wadley, *Even One Is Too Many*, pp. 163–64.

5 The meeting occurred on March 12 (Wilmeth, unpublished memoir, cited in Wadley, *Even One Is Too Many*, pp. 148–9, and Wilmeth, "Report on a Visit to Lublin," pp. 6–8).

6 Wilmeth, "Memorandum to General Deane," p. 8.

7 Wilmeth, unpublished memoir, cited in Wadley, *Even One Is Too Many*, p. 149.

8 Ibid.

9 Wilmeth, "Report on a Visit to Lublin," p. 10.

10 For example, the version of a telephone message from Wilmeth to Moscow on March 16, stating that there were no more ex-prisoners in Lublin or expected there (Golubev, Letter to Maj. Gen J. R. Deane).

11 Wadley (*Even One Is Too Many*, p. 114) infers from Deane's actions and sequence of decisions that his intelligence concerning ex-POWs was more extensive and detailed than he acknowledged in his memoir, and that he must have had covert sources.

12 Deane, *Strange Alliance*, pp. 198–99 (dates of telegrams given by Deane differ from those in official archives; his dates are one day later; official dates are given here).

13 Deane, *Strange Alliance*, p. 198; Roosevelt, telegram to Stalin, March 17, 1945, in US Department of State, *Foreign Relations*, p. 1082.

14 Deane, *Strange Alliance*, p. 198–99; Stalin, telegram to Roosevelt, March 22, in US Department of State, *Foreign Relations*, pp. 1082–83.

15 Harriman, cable to President Roosevelt, March 24, 1945, in US Department of State, *Foreign Relations*, pp. 1084–86.

16 Wadley, *Even One Is Too Many*, p. 158.

17 Ibid., p. 165.

18 Ibid.

19 Foregger, "Soviet Rails to Odessa," pp. 852–53.

20 Hall, "Supplement No. 4 to Interim Report on Odessa Transit Camp."

21 Foregger, "Soviet Rails to Odessa," p. 855; Harriman, cable to US secretary of state, June 11, in US Department of State, *Foreign Relations*, pp. 1097–98.

22 Rees, *World War Two Behind Closed Doors*, p. 393; Plokhy, *Yalta*, pp. 304–5. The Russian POWs knew what to expect, and there were many suicides in Western holding camps and aboard the troopships among prisoners faced with repatriation.

23 Wadley, *Even One Is Too Many*, p. 161.

24 Decades later, Robert was unable to recall exactly where this episode took place, other than that it was near Lublin. The description of the setting and the circumstances indicate that it was probably in the vicinity of the small town of Pulawy, twenty-five miles north-west of Lublin.

25 By 1944 the total number of subsidiary camps involved in the Holocaust had grown to 660, and most served as accommodations for slave laborers taken from the main extermination camps (Herbert, "Forced Laborers").

26 Sella, *Value of Human Life*, pp. 105–10.

27 Russian ex-POWs who fought with Polish partisans against the Germans "were tormented by the thought: will they, former POWs, be accepted in their own country. Unfortunately, very often their apprehensions were found to be justified" (R. Nazarevich, quoted in Sella, *Value of Human Life*, p. 109).

28 The murder of German prisoners was quite commonplace on the Eastern Front, just as the murder of Soviet POWs by Germans had been. What was unusual here was the mode of killing.

Chapter 15: Isabelle

1 Bartov, "White Spaces and Black Holes," p. 324.

2 Gross, *Revolution from Abroad*, pp. 179–82; Parrish, *Lesser Terror*, p. 48; Yones, *Smoke in the Sand*, p. 79. The number of prisoners said to have been killed by the NKVD varies from source to source. Twelve thousand is the figure given by Parrish, and probably includes Ukrainians murdered throughout the city during the panic. Three thousand is a more widely cited figure. Because of the city's history, there had long been ethnic tensions between its German, Polish, Ukrainian, and Jewish populations, which were ripe for exploitation by powers such as the SS and the NKVD.

3 Yones, *Smoke in the Sand*, pp. 79–81.

4 ". . . all labor which the government shall judge useful in the best interests of the nation." Wording of the law of September 4, 1942.

5 Bories-Sawala, *Dans la gueule du loup*, p. 56.

6 Figure from Ministère de la Production industrielle, February 18, 1943, quoted in Association pour la Mémoire de la Déportation du Travail Forcé, online archive.

7 Herbert, "Forced Laborers." Beyer and Schneider (*Forced Labor*, part 1, p. 3) put the proportion of forced labor at one-fifth of the labor force.

8 Herbert, *Hitler's Foreign Workers*, p. 219.

9 Ibid, p. 130.

10 Ibid, pp. 369–73.

11 Formerly part of Germany, now Opole, Poland.

12 Lefévre, "La Fin Tragique de Trois STO."

13 Colonel Wilmeth ("Memorandum to General Deane," p. 4) believed that the warnings about the curfew and German spies were given mainly to intimidate American visitors, but Captain Trimble's experiences suggest otherwise; there really was a paranoia.

14 The crew of AAF pilot Second Lieutenant L. E. Moore, who passed through Lwów en route to Poltava, found a body on the street outside their hotel; they were told by Russians that the man had been a spy (Fitchen, Mission interrogation of 2nd Lt Moore crew, p. 2).

15 The ships that took liberated prisoners from Odessa were British troopships. Nineteen such vessels departed from the port between March 7 and June 22, 1945 (Foregger, "Soviet Rails to Odessa," pp. 855–57).

Chapter 16: Bait and Switch

1 The official exchange rate through Russian banks was 5 rubles to 1 US dollar (Wadley, *Even One Is Too Many*, pp. 131–32). This rate was designed to be favorable to the Soviets, and a fairer rate would have been between 12 and 17 rubles to the dollar. On the black market, rates of up to 175 or even 200 rubles to the dollar could be obtained, and at Soviet insistence the Military Mission had barred US personnel from taking advantage of this exchange rate (Lepawsky, *History of Eastern Command*, ch. V, pp. 89–93).

Chapter 17: Blood Sacrifice

1 Kaluta, vol. I, ch. II, pp. 26–27; vol. II, ch. I, p. 1.

2 Trimble, cable T 3706 to Gen. Deane.

3 Antonov, letter to General Deane, March 30, 1945, reproduced in Borch, "Two Americans."

4 Harriman, memo on meeting with Stalin, April 15, 1945, quoted in Dobbs, *Six Months in 1945*, p. 195.

5 Detailed narratives are given in Borch, "Two Americans," and McDonough, *Wars of Myron King*.

6 The name is usually given as "Kuflevo" (e.g., Borch, "Two Americans"; McDonough, *Wars of Myron King*, p. 103). There is no place in Poland with that name. It might have been Kuflew or Huta Kuflewska, which are in about the right location. There was a Nazi concentration camp at Kuflew, but no record of an airfield has been found. The actual location might have been Mińsk Mazowiecki, where there is a modern air base. Alternatively, the crew interrogation report (Fitchen, Mission interrogation of Lt King crew, pp. 1–2) implies that the "airfield" might have been just a farm field.

7   In the version of events told by the Russians to General Deane, it was claimed that Jack
    Smith was a known "terrorist and saboteur" and that Lieutenant King had knowingly helped
    him disguise himself as an American airman (Deane, Cable M-23583 to Gen. Marshall).

8   Detailed narrative given in Borch, "Two Americans." Borch gives Bridge's rank as first
    lieutenant; Deane (Cable M-23583 to Gen. Marshall) gives it as captain, apparently mis-
    takenly.

9   Detailed narrative given in Borch, "Two Americans."

10 Slavin, letter to Deane, quoted in Deane, cable MX-23677 to Gen. Marshall. (Slavin gave
    the pilot's name as Roli; according to Borch it was Raleigh.)

11 Antonov, letter to General Deane, March 30, 1945, reproduced in Borch, "Two Amer-
    icans."

12 SMERSH report to Stalin, April 2, 1945, quoted in Dobbs, *Six Months in 1945*, p. 195.

13 Kaluta, vol. I, ch. I, pp. 8–9.

14 Harriman, cable to secretary of state, April 2, in US Department of State, *Foreign Relations*,
    pp. 1086–88.

15 Halifax, letter to US secretary of state, in US Department of State, *Foreign Relations*,
    pp. 1088–90.

16 Hill, cable M-23792 to Hampton, April 10, 1945, quoted in Kaluta, vol. II, ch. I, p. 7.

17 Hill, cable M-23828 to Hampton, April 12, 1945, quoted in Kaluta, vol. II, ch. I, p. 7.

18 Hill, Cable M-23827 to Gen. Spaatz, April 12, 1945.

19 Hampton, cable T-3550 to Gen. Hill, Apr. 11, 1945. Adding to the confusion, Hampton had
    been informed that the "B-17" would be arriving that day, Apr. 11.

20 Foregger, "Soviet Rails to Odessa," pp. 852–55.

21 Kaluta, vol. II, ch. I, p. 4.

22 The aircraft photographed at Poltava on April 12 matches the serial number and descrip-
    tion given to General Deane by General Cannon (Cannon, Cable M-51026 to Gen. Deane,
    April 11, 1945).

23 Kaluta, vol. III, photo 19–21.

24 In response to the SMERSH report on actions at Poltava in early April, Stalin ordered,
    "Calm Comrade Kovalev down. . . . Prevent him from taking independent actions" (Dobbs,
    Six Months in 1945, p. 196).

25 License discovered by Tom Lingerfelter. Described online at www.heritagecs.com/1928
    _Balloon_Pilot_license.htm (retrieved February 26, 2014).

26 General Deane had been informed in detail about the flight. He passed the full details on
    to the Soviets, but not to Eastern Command. It was a high-ranking crew that took Morris
    Shenderoff to Moscow, hand-picked on behalf of Lieutenant General John K. Cannon,
    commander of Allied Air Forces in the Mediterranean: pilot Major Walter C. Cannon
    (possibly a relative); copilot Captain James R. Mayer; navigator Captain Arthur F. Butler;
    engineer Second Lieutenant Melton E. Bloom; and radioman Staff Sergeant James W.

Wells. Shenderoff was escorted by Captains Harold W. Crowell and Beverley H. Tripp of the Corps of Military Police, and by Major Orfutt and Lieutenant Colonel Stepanovich, American officers who spoke Russian. Lieutenant Colonel Stepanovich was responsible for delivering Shenderoff into Soviet hands (Cannon, Cables MX-50976 and M-51026 to Gen. Deane, April 11, 1945; Deane, Letter to Lt Gen Slavin, April 11, 1945).

27 The photo of the Shenderoff plane in the USAF archive is erroneously captioned, "American and Russian personnel wave their greetings as the Consolidated B-24 'JUDITH ANN,' carrying Major General Deane and Major General Edmund W. Hill, comes to a halt on the steel mat runway at Poltava Airbase, a shuttle mission base in Russia. 12 April 1945." In the official history of Eastern Command, the same photo is captioned, "Secret arrival at Poltava of B-24 from Italy" (Kaluta, vol. III, photo 71–11).

28 Borch, "Two Americans."

29 Kaluta, vol. I, ch. I, p. 4. Apparently the rumor originated with Lieutenant Myron King, who heard the story when he was in Moscow for his court-martial (Borch, "Two Americans").

Chapter 18: Spare the Conquered, Confront the Proud

1 Kaluta, vol. II, ch. II, p. 1. Eastern Command had opted not to fly their flag permanently in case it irritated the Russians.

2 Roosevelt died at 3:35 P.M. on April 12, which was the middle of the night in Russia. The Americans there woke to the news on April 13.

3 Kaluta, vol. II, ch. II, p. 1.

4 Kaluta, vol. II, ch. II, p. 1; Lepawsky, *History of Eastern Command*, ch. VIII, pp. 38–39.

5 The artist was Senior Sergeant Sapokar. The theater was shared between American and Russian personnel and, until the rise of tensions in March 1945, had been a focus of good relations between the two sides (Kaluta, vol. I, ch. V, pp. 21–22).

6 Quoted in Kaluta, vol. II, ch. I, p. 10.

7 The similarity was noted at the time by Eastern Command (Kaluta, vol. II, ch. I, p. 10).

8 Captain Trimble made this plain at the commencement of the conference (report by adjutant Captain Fischer, quoted in Kaluta, vol. II, ch. I, p. 10).

9 Kaluta, vol. II, ch. I, p. 13.

10 Trimble, cable to Hill, April 21, 1945, quoted in Kaluta, vol. II, ch. I, pp. 13–14.

11 Hill, cable to Trimble, quoted in Lepawsky, *History of Eastern Command*, ch. 6, p. 83.

12 Trimble, cable to Hill, April 21, 1945, quoted in Kaluta, vol. II, ch. I, pp. 13–14.

13 Narratives in Borch, "Two Americans."

14 Dolin had met Wilmeth and Kingsbury in Lublin. Strangely, Dolin believed that the POW contact mission was a front and that the two colonels were actually spying on the Soviets (Dolin, quoted by McDonough, *Wars of Myron King*, p. 174). The allegation is fairly preposterous. It rests on the claim that Dolin saw documents containing intelligence

about Soviet forces on Wilmeth's desk. The claim assumes that Wilmeth, as a spy, had recorded his data in plain text and left it lying about where anybody entering his office could see and read it. Given that he was constantly being spied on by the NKVD, this would make him the most incompetent (and the luckiest) spy who ever lived. The "intelligence" documents were probably details of Red Army POW collection points, Odessa transports, and prison camps, as well as information about the dispersal of POWs obtained from Wilmeth's POW agents.

15 Trimble, letter to Kovalev, April 18, 1945, quoted in Kaluta, vol. II, ch. I, p. 11.

16 Kaluta, vol. II, ch. I, pp. 11–12.

17 Wilmeth, cable to Deane, April 9, 1945, quoted in Kaluta, vol. II, ch. II, p. 6.

18 In 1952, after a review of his case by the US Air Force, King's guilty verdict was overturned. His fine was refunded and his military record cleared (Borch, "Two Americans").

19 Trimble, cable to Hill, quoted in Kaluta, vol. II, ch. I, p. 4.

20 Hampton, Cable T-3457 to Gen. Deane, April 4, 1945.

21 McDonough, *Wars of Myron King*, pp. 192–93.

22 Except for tail gunner Sergeant George Atkinson, who had been involved in a road accident in Poltava on April 19, in which a local woman was killed. Atkinson bumped his truck into a Russian truck, which, not properly braked, rolled onto the sidewalk and crushed the woman. Despite attempts by Captain Trimble, General Deane, and Deane's chief of staff to settle the case quietly with the Soviets and get Atkinson flown out to Tehran, the Soviets insisted that he be subject to their jurisdiction. He was fined heavily, and the Military Mission paid compensation to the woman's family (Kaluta, vol. II, ch. II, pp. 7–8).

23 According to Kaluta (vol. II, ch. II, p. 7), Kovalev had preapproved King's departure. However, Robert Trimble recalled that Kovalev complained about it after the event. Knowing the Soviet habit of giving and then rescinding permissions, this isn't surprising (permission to fly injured combat men to Tehran had been given and rescinded several times during the flying ban). Recalling the fate of Morris Shenderoff, Robert said later, "I'd be damned if we were going to let that happen to King."

24 Kaluta, vol. II, ch. II, p. 2.

25 The old building is still part of the US Embassy, now serving as the US Citizen Center.

26 These complaints are reviewed throughout all three volumes of the official history; some were true (such as the black market dealing, detailed in Lepawsky, *History of Eastern Command*, ch. V, pp. 86–92), whereas others were exaggerated or dubious.

27 Plokhy, *Yalta*, pp. 155–56, 168–69.

28 Winston Churchill, address to the House of Commons, December 14, 1950, *Hansard* vol. 482, col. 1368.

29 In his memoir, *The Strange Alliance*, written shortly after the war, John R. Deane's diplomatic tone often gives way to anger over the POW issue. Likewise, Averell Harriman was sufficiently angry about the issue to suggest retaliation against Soviet POW contact teams

in American-occupied territory (Harriman, cable to secretary of state, March 14, 1945, in US Department of State, *Foreign Relations*, pp. 1079–81).

30 Deane, *Strange Alliance*, p. 197.

31 Winston Churchill, address to the House of Commons, December 14, 1950, *Hansard* vol. 482, col. 1367.

Chapter 19: The Long Way Home

1 Kaluta, vol. II, ch. III, pp. 2–5.

2 Lieutenant William R. Kaluta, Corps of Engineers, became one of Eastern Command's official historians.

3 Infield, *Poltava Affair*, pp. 223–24. Unfortunately, Infield cites no source for the story, and there are problems with it. First, Infield is under the impression that Ritchie was CO at Poltava (he was just visiting to finalize the evacuation), and he is said to have dumped the material in the lake "through a hole in the ice" (in June). However, it is plausible that OSS equipment could have been stored at Poltava, given the planned cooperation program (Deane, *Strange Alliance*, pp. 50–59). It is unlikely (although not impossible) that the cache had any direct connection to Robert Trimble's mission.

4 Hill, Letter to Gen. Spaatz, May 16, 1945. What is significant is that the only exceptional thing Robert had officially done was take command at Poltava, and at the time the letter was written he had only been in that post one month. His officially recorded work as assistant operations officer was (for Eastern Command) fairly standard. It is clear that Hill was alluding to Captain Trimble's truly exceptional off-the-record mission.

5 Deane, Cable M 24441 to Gen. Spaatz, May 24, 1945.

6 Many biographical accounts of Spaatz at this period have him moving to USAAF HQ in Washington, DC, in early June, prior to taking up command in the Pacific in late July (e.g., Watson, *Secretaries and Chiefs of Staff*, p. 109). However, in late June he was still in Europe, having resumed command of USSTAF from June 13 to June 30. On the 27th he visited Melun Airfield in France, where American test pilots were evaluating captured German Me-262 jet fighters (Samuel, *American Raiders*, pp. 271–77).

7 Metz, *Master of Airpower*, ch. I.

8 American Legion Baseball was (and still is) a baseball league for teenage boys, founded by the American Legion veterans' organization in 1926.

9 In practice, it is almost certain that Robert Trimble would not have been one of those pilots, even had he accepted Spaatz's offer. The 509th Composite Group was a specialized unit that had trained intensively for the atomic bomb missions. Robert probably could not have completed conversion training on the B-29 in time to join the 509th, let alone take part in any missions. But that wasn't known at the time—it was anticipated that there would be more than just the Hiroshima and Nagasaki missions, and that the war might go on much longer.

10 There seem to have been two contradictory views of Robert Trimble's (officially recorded) service with Eastern Command. Major Albert Lepawsky, the command's first historian, is dismissive of him as commander. Lepawsky was sympathetic to the Russians and writes disparagingly about both Colonel Hampton and Major Kowal. While acknowledging that Trimble was a congenial character and inexperienced in command, he claims that he was antagonistic toward the Russians (Lepawsky, *History of Eastern Command*, ch. VIII, pp. 101–11). However, Lepawsky was not at Poltava during Trimble's time, and his version is flatly contradicted by the volumes of the official history written by Lieutenant William Kaluta (who was there) and by the testimonials of General Hill and General Deane cited above. It is probable that the unnamed general who called Robert to Washington had heard a version of events propagated by Lepawsky, since the latter had been producing negative reports on Eastern Command personnel for the War Department since at least December 1944 (Lepawsky, *History of Eastern Command*, ch. VIII, pp. 49–51).

11 Captain Trimble initially declined to take part, because his personnel were busy with urgent administrative duties, having been told a few days earlier by General Deane that Eastern Command was about to be shut down and evacuated—an order that was later rescinded (Kaluta, vol. II, ch. III, p. 2). Captain Trimble immediately apologized to General Kovalev for the confusion and authorized American participation in the celebration (Lepawsky, *History of Eastern Command*, ch. VIII, p. 111).

Epilogue: Not Without Honor

1 The Croix de Guerre citation for Robert Trimble is listed in French government records under "decision no 1029, division level [with silver star]" dated August 20, 1945. The actual citation document has unfortunately been lost in the French archives.

2 De Gaulle visited Washington for talks with President Truman from August 22 to 24. The meetings were generally civil, but there were ongoing disagreements between de Gaulle and the United States that year over the postwar plan for Germany and French plans to reestablish a hold on Indochina (Wall, "Harry S. Truman and Charles de Gaulle," pp. 123–29; McAllister, *No Exit*, pp. 99–103; Marr, *Vietnam*, pp. 183–84).

3 At some time between infancy and later childhood, the second part of Carol Ann's name fell out of use. She has no memory of when or why, only the knowledge that "Carol Ann" was what her father called her when she was a baby.

INDEX

Page numbers in *italics* indicate maps.